A
STEADY
TRADE

"A steady trade"

Other Published Works by Tristan Jones

Autobiographical
The Incredible Voyage
Ice!
Saga of a Wayward Sailor
Seagulls in My Soup
Adrift

Commentarial
*One Hand for Yourself, One for the Ship: The Essentials of
  Single-Handed Sailing*

Translation and Interpretation
Echoes of Distant Thunder (from the Welsh *Mabinogion*)

Novels
Dutch Treat: A Novel of World War II
Aka

Short Stories
"Breakdown"
"Sherlock Holmes and the Mystery of the *Marie Celeste*"
"The Old Hundredth"
"The Signal Lamp"
"Rewards and Remembrances"

Lectures
"The Reasons Why: The Psychology of Adventure"
"The Incredible Voyage"
"The Bravest of the Brave: Sir Ernest Shackleton"
"The Most Remarkable Small-Boat Voyage Ever Made—
  Captain William Bligh of *Bounty*"

A STEADY TRADE

A Boyhood at Sea

Tristan Jones

Drawings by John Cayea

St. Martin's Press   New York

014523 ✓

15.95

A STEADY TRADE: A BOYHOOD AT SEA. Copyright © 1982 by Tristan Jones. Illustrations copyright © 1982 by John Cayea. All rights reserved. Printed in the United States of America. No part of this book may be used or reproduced in any manner whatsoever without written permission except in the case of brief quotations embodied in critical articles or reviews. For information, address St. Martin's Press, 175 Fifth Avenue, New York, N.Y. 10010.

Design by Kingsley Parker

Library of Congress Cataloging in Publication Data
Jones, Tristan, 1924–
    A steady trade.
    1. Jones, Tristan, 1924–   . 2. Voyages
and travels—1951–   . 3. Seamen—Wales—
Biography.   I. Title.
G465.J68   910.4'5   82-5803
ISBN 0-312-76138-4   AACR2

10 9 8 7 6 5 4 3 2

Dedicated to the Welsh and their descendants the world over, including the many in the Falkland Islands; and to my good friends Wally and Marie Herbert, Allan Gill, and Bernard Moitessier, explorers.

Contents

Acknowledgments

Many thanks to Joe Gribbins, editor of *Nautical Quarterly*, in which this tale first appeared in a much shorter form; to the members of the Atlantis Society, who gave me peace while I wrote this book; and to my agent, Richard Curtis, for his enthusiastic activities on my behalf.

August 1981–March 1982

New Orleans, St. Louis, Santa Barbara, San Francisco, London, Stratford-upon-Avon, Llandudno, Abermo, Aberytswyth, and New York

Foreword

During anyone's life there are many experiences, emotions, and discoveries that are the common lot of many other people; there are others that, by the very nature of one's birth, upbringing, times, and circumstances, are shared with only a few others. Some events and encounters, strung together in a certain order, are one person's alone; they are what makes that person unique; they are what makes a *life.*

This book is the earliest in a series of five—someday to be eight—volumes about my life. Enjoy them all; if you can learn from them or laugh and cry with me, then my life shall have been made worth more. This added worth I shall accept gratefully.

Circumstances, too complex to go into here, drove me to write these books about my life out of their chronological order. The four volumes about the years from 1952 to 1977 were published between 1977 and 1981. They are about the deeds and misdeeds, the adventures and misadventures of my middle years. This book is about my boyhood and youth, about the forces that coiled my spring.

In offering these accounts of my life, I affirm my belief in everyone's uniqueness. Without the recognition of each other's individuality there can be no dignity. Without dignity there can be neither honor nor justice, and without honor and justice mankind will surely descend into the abyss.

Note: Some of the names of people, places, and ships in this story have been changed, to avoid embarrassment to people who may still live, or to their relatives and friends.

"Cas gŵr ni char y wlad a'i maco."

("Cursed is the man who loves
not the land that raised him.")

—DAFYDD AP GWILYM, fourteenth-century Welsh poet

1

Boyhood

The force that through the green fuse drives the flower
Drives my green age; that blasts the roots of trees
Is my destroyer.
And I am dumb to tell the crooked rose
My youth is bent by the same wintry fever.

The force that drives the water through the rocks
Drives my red blood; that drives the mouthing streams
Turns mine to wax.
And I am dumb to mouth unto my veins
How at the mountain spring the same mouth sucks.

The hand that whirls the water in the pool
Stirs the quicksand; that ropes the blowing wind
Hauls my shroud sail.
And I am dumb to tell the hanging man
How of my clay is made the hangman's lime.

The lips of time leech to the fountain head;
Love drips and gathers, but the fallen blood
Shall calm her sores.
And I am dumb to tell a weather's wind
How time has ticked a heaven round the stars.

And I am dumb to tell the lover's tomb
How at my sheet goes the same crooked worm.

—DYLAN THOMAS
"The Force That Through the
Green Fuse Drives the Flower"

1

Llangareth

There's almost always a westerly wind over Merioneth. On winter days it's a wet west wind, whistling under clouds black and funereal, like a hundred hearses bringing back home the ghosts of the drowned sailors of Wales to weep over their mountains. The west wind sighs in from the Celtic Sea, driving before it a billion charging white hor- ses, sending them smashing to their deaths on the shores of Gwynned. The escaped seas scoot frothing, eventually subsiding on the long sands of Tywyn. The west wind, insistent, tenacious, tendentious, scores the black, lonely peak of Cader Idris. Fat wool sheep bleat under the shelter of low walls built before Rome, old when the Norsemen were beaten back from them, well-mossed when the Normans flung up their grim, gray castles on the shores of Wales.

In the patched sunlit summer, though, with the wind tame and temperate, almost kind, the tiny hamlet of Llangareth—a chapel, three cottages, and our house—nestled, chimneys smoking, hidden in a little valley so green that the golden rocky outcrops of the Ffestiniog mountains looked from the heights to us children like the claws of an eagle outsplayed on well-brushed green baize.

Three miles up and down this valley my sister, Angharad, and I rode our pony, Caradoc. He was now so old that he needed no guidance but frequent rest as he clambered down to and from the brew, or hill, to the Barmouth-Harlech road, a narrow ribbon of sandy tar threading the ocher and emerald hollows along the coastal hinterland.

In 1935 I was almost eleven, Angharad was seven. She was attending the elementary school a few miles away. One of my jobs, now that I was grown, was to see that she met the rickety little bus that took her to and from the school. In the mornings, with Angharad safely onboard the bus, I waited for Rhys-the-Post, who, in his blue serge cape and double-peaked, flat-topped helmet with its great brass-horn badge, rode his pony, Powis, on the rural mail round winter and summer. On joyful occasions there would be a letter from my dad, far away in England, where God directed the railway lines and telegraph poles from Dolgellau. There, it was said, the folk were strange and many and did not know each other's names. England, the homeland of *Mister* Jeffreys-Geography, our thin, bald-headed, bespectacled teacher, who spoke English so lispingly and strangely that only Educated Evans, the fat boy from Aran Fawddwy, could understand more than three words he said in any one sentence. England was *Lloegr*, "the Land of the Moonrise," in our language, the tongue of the Cymry. "A language ancient when Homer was a lad," my dad used to observe.

Dad was a master mariner, a Trinity House (British Port Authority) relief pilot in the slump of the twenties. He guided great liners and cargo steamers into and out of the ports of Britain. Now he was the first mate in a tug. He was the son, the grandson, and the great- and great-great-grandson of master mariners going back, so family legend had it, through Christopher Jones, master of the *Mayflower* on her epic voyage from Plymouth, England, to Massachusetts in 1620. Certainly he could trace his line back to William Jones, born in 1749 at Beddgelert, who was master of *Harlech Castle*, a brig of eighty-five tons, which was at St. Petersburg, Russia, in 1795. The next year, *Harlech Castle* was captured by a French frigate. Captain William and two of his crew were taken to France and lodged in Arras prison. They escaped the following year, 1797, and crossed the stormy English Channel in a rowboat. When they eventually landed at Hythe, Kent, they were greeted—to their delight and surprise—in Welsh by men of the Flintshire Militia, stationed there against an expected Napoleonic invasion.

William's son, Emrys, born in 1800, was lost off the coast of Madagascar in 1844, sunk by pirates, it was said.

Emrys's son, Cadwaladr, born in 1843, went down off Brazil in a great storm in 1896. He was one of the few men ever to have a ship named after him while he was still alive. She was the 103-ton schooner *Cadwaladr Jones,* built in Borthygest in 1878. She sailed the hard North Atlantic passage to and from Newfoundland and the Mediterranean for more than four decades; then she was sold to someone in Argentina and was finally lost off the Scilly Isles in 1933, while under the command of a retired Royal Navy officer.

Cadwaladr's son, John Jones (my grandfather), was known as "Johnny Star" and gained the reputation of being *the* crackerjack skipper of the Western Ocean Yachts, as the Welsh tops'l schooners were known. He made the fastest run ever from Portmadoc to Harburg, Germany, where Welsh slate was unloaded. That was in five days. Almost seven hundred miles of some of the most difficult seas in the world for a sail-craft, what with the shifting winds, strong tides, and hidden hazards of the Celtic Sea, the English Channel, and the North Sea. That was around 1902.

Johnny Star went down in the schooner *Alpha* in the Irish Sea, bound from Dublin to Amlwch in 1906. Not as well known as Johnny Star, perhaps because he was a less colorful character, was his brother (my uncle) Evan Lewis Jones of Barmouth. Evan Lewis was the master of one of the Lister vessels, *Cariad,* and in about 1896 he made the fastest-ever transatlantic passage for a small merchant sailing vessel. That was from Eurges, Newfoundland, to Oporto, Portugal. The voyage lasted just under ten days; the cargo was salted codfish.

My dad had been at sea since 1909, and, like most of the Welsh master mariners, he had worked his way up from cook/deckboy to master, under sail until 1916, in voyages as far as Seattle and Calcutta. Then, when the German U-boats found small, defenseless sailing craft to be easy pickings and sank one-third of the British sail tonnage in the first eighteen months of World War I, he went into steam. From 1920 to

1924 my mam accompanied him the world over in the eight-thousand-ton tramp steamer *Western Star.* The tramp ships were so called because they sailed no particular or regular route, but picked up their cargoes where and when they could.

It was onboard the S.S. *Western Star,* on one of these tramping voyages, from Perth, Australia, to Halifax, Nova Scotia, that I was born on May 8, 1924. The ship was approximately 150 miles northeast of the remote island of Tristan Da Cunha, in the southern South Atlantic Ocean. The cargo was a strange one by any standard. It consisted of about a thousand tons of sheep bones and the first roller-skating rink exported from Australia, where that pastime was, I understand, invented.

My mother, in later years, often told me the story of my birth, although my dad was almost always silent, and shook his head and pursed his lips whenever the episode was mentioned. I was a breech birth; in other words, I was upside down in my mother. It was ten hours of pure hell for her, in a ship bucking crazily in a full storm, with her hanging onto the deckhead (ceiling) of the master's cabin, one foot on Dad's desk and the other on the sofa, which the mate, Ebenezar Roberts, had ripped away from the ship's side. The wireless operator, Owen Thomas of Nevin, tried to contact the resident doctor on the island of Tristan Da Cunha, but the weather conditions were such that very little of what that gentleman instructed could be understood. My dad told me that it was exactly at sunrise that he and the mate finally got my shoulders away from my poor mam, then my head last. It was covered with a caul—a membrane. Ebenezar ripped it off and slapped me on the back. I squawled, and Ebenezar said to my dad: "By God, this one will always land on his feet! He may be a candidate for a hanging one day, but he'll never drown!" Dad grinned when he told me that.

Now, almost sixty years later, the resident doctor of Tristan Da Cunha, Jones by name, has named his son, born in England, after me. So goes the wheel.

The ship was ostensibly bound for Halifax, Canada. In those days, when the British Empire was still far-flung, the law was that if a person was born onboard a British-registered vessel at sea, he or she became a citizen of the country of the parents and of the first British Empire land the ship touched. If the ship had gone to Canada, then I would have been a Canadian citizen as well as British. But a week after my birth a radio signal was received onboard from the owners in Liverpool, changing the ship's destination to that port. Later, it turned out that the reason for this was that the proprietors of the New Brighton Palace, a dance hall near Liverpool, had agreed to try out the roller-skating rink, with an option to buy it if it was a success. I am probably the only British subject ever made so by a telegram and a roller-skating rink. It was rather a pity in a way. If I'd been in the Royal Canadian Navy instead of the Royal Navy, my invaliding pension would have been about ten times the amount it is today. But then, I might not have been propelled into sailing and writing, and my life in the past thirty years would most likely not have been anywhere near as rewarding, and surely not as much fun.

My mother never moaned about my birth, nor did she ever resent it. She seemed to treat it as an exercise in affection—and of that she had more than her share. She was a Roberts, and her grandfather, Hugh, master of the 216-ton brig *Evelyn*, son of Hugh, master of the 142-ton *Constance*, had been one of the most renowned Welsh seafarers of the nineteenth century. In *Evelyn* great-grandpa Hugh Roberts made voyages to every port on the east coast of South America, and he took many hundreds of emigrants from Wales to the Falkland Islands and Porto Madryn, in Patagonia, Argentina. After sailing *Evelyn* for thirty-six years, without ever once having a serious illness or accident onboard, Hugh Roberts finally lost her in a tremendous mid-Atlantic hurricane in May 1914. He and the crew of three were saved by a steamer minutes before the *Evelyn* surrendered to the ocean. Hugh said afterward that they would have died anyway, as they had fresh water left for only one more day. For thirty-six years *Evelyn* had plied the oceans from St. Petersburg to the Horn and had carried hundreds of thousands of tons of freight—fertilizer, slate, phosphate, fish, salt, coal—over the whole Atlantic. Bear in mind that *Evelyn* was only 109 feet long, had no engine, and was manned by only three men and a boy; she paid for herself hundreds of times over, and did it gracefully.

After we reached Liverpool, Mam took me to Llangareth while Dad continued plying his craft on the oceans. That lasted until 1926, when hundreds of cargo ships were laid up because of a shipping slump. Dad went to work as an assistant supervisor on the Liverpool docks for two years. Then he landed the relief pilot's post. That meant that he traveled from port to port in the British Isles, filling in for men sick or dead, and for pilots on vacation—which in those days meant about the same thing. Then, in 1931, he was laid off and was lucky to find the job on the tugs. He came home for a few days every six months or so to Llangareth and an excited family, in his bowler hat, pea jacket, corduroy trousers, and black boots, and always with some money, toys, books, and wonderful tales told in gusts of laughter.

The only clear memories I have of between 1924 and 1930 are of being chased by a hen, gigantic to me at three, across a farmyard; and of staring through the front window through the drizzle in the valley at the sea, gray and beckoning, a half mile away; and of cold and wet rides on the pony, Caradoc, to the one-room church school two miles away. There, Jeffreys-Geography tried to ram into us what was, as he put it, "entirely for your own benefit."

Another early memory is of being in chapel. I must have been six or seven at the time. My parents were liberals in the old British tradition of self-sufficiency and hard work. Mam packed my sister Angharad and me off to chapel every Sunday. Angharad was three years younger than I was and a lot more romantic, so she took much more notice of the preacher, while I tended to daydream and itch to get out into the fresh air, even in winter. I don't recall who the preacher was on this particular occasion; I vaguely remember the fire and brimstone bit coming out, and I clearly recollect suddenly asking myself, "Who gave him the right to tell us what we should do or not do?" I've been asking myself that question ever since, every time I encounter anyone who exercises, or tries to exercise, power over anyone else. But then I kept my thoughts to myself. I was, with my family, on to far too good a thing. There was no point in upsetting the status quo. I became a secret rebel. With my mother and sister, and Dad too when he was home, there was very little imposition. It was more a case of their helping me to grow from the inside out than of pushing their thoughts and beliefs onto me. "He will be what he will be," Mam used to say. Whether it would be right for other parents to have that attitude is not for me to say. I know that for me it was exactly right. I was never pushed toward classical music or literature, for example. Hints were given, examples were made, but I was never led by the nose, and for that I have always been grateful to my family. If I had been forced into those things, I am sure I would have rebelled and lost interest in them, and my life would have been much the poorer for having missed a great deal of the wonderful human heritage that has been passed on to us.

The world that I first knew as a child was vastly different from the one we know now, fifty-odd years later. West Wales, particularly the rural areas, was—apart from the odd bus, steam engine, and motorcar—still, in effect, in the mid-nineteenth century. It had been touched very little by the Industrial Revolution. For the majority of people, communications were difficult. For example, our mail was delivered by a pony rider. He had collected it from a horse-drawn coach which, complete with horn blower perched atop, had delivered it from a steam-engined train in Dolgellau. I do not recall seeing any airplanes. The first man-made thing I ever saw in the sky was, I think, the German Graf Zeppelin, with the great Nazi swastikas on its rudders. That must have been in 1937.

Practically everything we had in Llangareth had been made in the area, by hand. The furniture was highly polished, with gracefully carved chairs for the drawing room and sturdy, solid ones for the kitchen, where we usually lived. The drawing room was used only when there were special guests visiting us. There were also a sofa and intricately carved china dressers in the drawing room. The only things in that room, and probably in the whole house, that had not been made in Merioneth were the carpet, brought back from India by Grandfather Johnny Star; the grandfather clock, brought from France by Grandfather Roberts; and the piano (every Welsh dwelling in those days had a piano—and people who could play it and accompany it superbly). The piano had been brought from Germany by Grandfather Hugh Roberts. The tale was that as his ship *Evelyn* bounced and bucketed her way through a full gale in the

North Sea, the piano was heard playing itself down in the hold
—"Guide Me, O Thou Great Jehovah" ("Ciom Rhondda") was
the tune, according to some accounts. Grandpa Roberts is supposed to have told the scared helmsman, Hugh Parry of Talsar-
nau, "That's all very well, but I'd rather get a sight of the North
Foreland light!" For a deeply religious man he had a great sense
of humor.

The wooden-handled knives and forks, the china plates and
tea service (they are great tea-drinkers in West Wales), even
the brass-bound wooden water buckets hanging on their iron
hooks on the whitewashed kitchen wall—everything had been
made locally. The materials we lived with were wood of all
kinds (some brought from as far away as California and
Burma), brass, iron (beautifully worked by Velog Hammer, the
local blacksmith), steel, copper, bronze, tin, stone, lace, linen,
wool, and cotton.

Next to the drawing room, which was a holy of holies, the
most important room in our cottage was the kitchen. The insides of the two-foot-thick outside walls of the cottage were
whitewashed in the kitchen. The outside door was of massive
oak and divided into two parts, so that the upper part could be
opened while the lower part was kept closed to keep cold drafts
and farm animals out of the house, and to keep small children
in.

On one side of the flagstoned kitchen was a massive fireplace, so big that two adults could sit inside it close to the fire
in wintertime. Chains and hooks hung down the chimney for
hanging hams to smoke and suspending a stewpot over the fire.
Since the patent stove had been brought into the house, back
in the 1860s, the fireplace was not used much for cooking or
water-heating. The patent stove was of black iron, with brass
and steel trimmings kept brightly burnished. One of my chores
was to blacken the stove every Saturday morning, and to bur-
nish the brass and steel. The stove had an oven on either side
of the grate that burned coal, coke, or wood, and on each side
of the ovens were hot-water heating tanks, which contained
about five gallons of water each. The water was brought into
the house by a hand pump from a spring only a few feet away
from the outside wall. It was pumped into a bucket and poured
into the heaters through a lid-opening in the top of each

heater. There were brass taps in front of both heaters. The stove stood on ornate iron legs about two feet off the hearth, so the ashes fell into a sort of iron box. I remember that the stove fire was never allowed to die out, even in summer.

In the corner of the kitchen was a large pot-boiler. This was a triangular brick furnace with a large, hemispherical iron water pot that held about ten gallons of water set inside it. This was used for doing the laundry and for heating up bathwater, and it was drained through another brass tap. Baths were taken in a zinc hip bath which, when not in use, hung on the outside wall of the kitchen. The only time we children were ever alone in the holy drawing room was on Friday and Monday nights for an hour, when Mam took her bath.

By the pot-boiler was the mangle. This was a contraption set in an iron frame, standing about four feet tall and three feet wide, in which two wooden rollers could be turned by means of a handled wheel. Wet clothes from the pot-boiler were inserted into the rollers, the handle was turned (usually by me), and the water was squeezed out of the clothes. The ironing board and three different-size irons, heated on the stove; the outside clothesline; and a drying rack on the kitchen ceiling that could be raised and lowered by means of a rope reeved through pulleys completed the laundry arrangements. The inside clothesrack was used in wintertime, of course.

The kitchen was almost always busy. It was someone's bath night every night, except Sundays, and Mam baked all of her own bread and made all the cakes and biscuits we ever saw as children. Afternoons were for pastry-making, and the large, heavy, wooden kitchen table was rarely not in use for something or other. Mam made all of her own jam and bottled all of her own fruit. There was no refrigeration, of course, but there was—at one end of the kitchen, under the stairs—a deep, stone-built larder, and there anything that might "go off" was kept in cool darkness: cheeses, hams, milk, cream, and preserves.

Practically all of the victuals we ate and drank in Llangareth were home-grown, with the exception of tea, sugar, salt, pepper, and the like. Our garden was about an acre and a half, and much of my childhood not spent in school, in bed, or reading was spent working there. This had to be so, as my dad was rarely home. We grew all of our own potatoes, beans, cabbages, broccoli, Brussels sprouts, peas, strawberries, gooseberries, onions, lettuce, and a score of other things, and we had about two dozen hens, which gave a regular supply of eggs. There were half a dozen pigs. Lamb could be obtained very cheaply from the neighboring farmers. Even though there was very little money in the house at any time, we never were short of food, and there was always roast lamb on Sunday. It was hard work looking after the garden and the stock, and from the age of six onward all of my days were fully occupied from the time the family rose at sunrise until about nine o'clock, when everyone turned in.

There was no electricity in Llangareth in those days, and so most of my reading was done in bed by the light of a small oil lamp. I started reading very early, and I clearly recall ploughing through Gibbon's *Rise and Fall of the Roman Empire* when I was about eight or nine. Of course there were *Treasure Island, Tom Sawyer,* and *Black Beauty,* among many others of that kind, but my favorites were a vast heap of very old *Illustrated London News* magazines from the 1880s onward, right through the Boer War and the Great War, as we called World War I. Now, fifty years later, I often wonder what those old magazines would be worth. Most of the books I read were fetched by Mam from the public library in Dolgellau, and gradually I discovered the Welsh writers of the thirties, who were creating some exciting new forms in literature: Glyn Jones, John Pritchard, Nigel Heseltine, Idris Davies, and, later on, Dylan Thomas and Vernon Watkins. It was necessary for a boy to know the works of those writers in order to be able to understand what some of the people who visited Mam and Dad (when he was home) were talking about.

It wasn't all work, though. There were rides among the hills on Caradoc with Angharad perched in front of me, hanging on but ladylike, and there were fishing trips out into Tremadoc Bay in the summer with local fishermen, as we shall see.

There was only one kind of plastic in existence in those days. It was called Bakelite, and it came in only one color—brown. I think I saw my first piece of it in 1935, when I was eleven.

It was when Dad proudly brought home to us our first radio set, only it was called a "wireless" then. It was an ungainly box shaped like a nonconformist chapel with its embroidered, silken, round speaker looking like a Bethel window. It was powered by two glass batteries filled with acid and distilled water. One of my jobs was to take the spare battery into town to get it recharged with electricity at Evans-the-Garage. That was a chore, because over rough country I could not ride Caradoc. His jogging caused the batteries to jerk and the acid to spill, so I was forced to walk about half the distance—six miles or so. Then I found that by blocking up the ventilation holes in the Bakelite battery compartment stoppers with Plasticine —a sort of elastic clay popular with children for making toys—I could stop the spillage and so could ride all the way to Dolgellau and back with the batteries slung onto Caradoc's saddle. The look of absolute astonishment and delight on the faces of Angharad and me when Dad first switched on the wireless and we heard the voice of a singer far away in London must have been something to behold. Time had been miraculously compressed. Two or three days had been cut down to a split second. That is how the Age of Communications, and with it an inkling of the twentieth century, first came to Llangareth. That sudden leap is taking place still, all over the world. I have seen it happen from New Guinea to Greenland, for good or ill.

Our neighbors were simple folk. There was the widow Carregen, who was rumored to be a witch, but a kindly one, and who could cure any ailment with the herbs and berries she collected in her meanderings along the walls and hedgerows of the fields. She must have been in her eighties, with a face like a relief map of Gwynned. Her English was nonexistent, but her Welsh was pure music, and she made lace that would have been the envy of any Belgian lass. She was the widow of a mate who had gone down off Para, Brazil, in the brig *Wild Rose,* lost with all hands in 1889. She was tiny, frail, and always dressed completely in black, from her straw bonnet to her button-up calf boots. She had two cows and about six sheep, and she did all her own gardening. Her income was mainly from midwifery and fortune-telling. She invited Angharad and me into her cottage on rare occasions and told us tales of her girlhood in

Pwllheli, across Tremadoc Bay, where she had been born in the 1840s. Her cottage was sparsely furnished but spotlessly clean, apart from about a hundred fading photographs in silver and brass frames and lace clothes everywhere, even on the mantelpiece. I sometimes saw her on her hands and knees scrubbing the stone kitchen floor with a pumice stone. Once, when I was about seven and very ill with bronchial pneumonia, she cured me with goose grease and vinegar. It made me sweat like a Caerphilly cheese on a hot July day.

The third cottage in the hamlet was the home of the Powell family. There were Davy, the father, a farm laborer, dark and morose; his wife Catrin, a big woman with wide hips, red hair, and beauty enough for the whole of Wales; and their four children, two lads and two lasses. Catrin was a literary woman, well read in both English and Welsh, and she had named her children well: Cei, the eldest boy, named after Sir Kay, the senior of King Arthur's knights; Gwrtheyrn (Vortigern), after the British king who first invited the Saxons over to England to fight his enemies, the Picts and the Scots; Branwen, the oldest daughter, after the princess in the *Mabinogion,* whose burial on the cliffs of Gwynned is one of the most moving tales in literature, and Lisbeth, named after Queen Elizabeth I of England, "a Welshwoman through and through if there ever was one," as Catrin explained, with no sign of a blush on the fair, milky skin of her face.

The other building in the hamlet, apart from two barns and a few hen houses, was the chapel. This brought people in from the more remote farms and cottages every Sunday. There the news and gossip from six miles around was exchanged. Business was initiated and concluded, marriages were arranged, and the Celtic longing to touch and see the dark Secret of the Universe was partly fulfilled, for some at least. The singing was . . . angelic. I suspect that for many members of the congregation the singing was the main reason for attendance. I cannot imagine a Welsh congregation in a church or a chapel where there is no singing. The hills all around seemed to shake when the choral "Oh Hear My Plea" was raised. The hills shook and the light over the sea trembled and the Archangel Gabriel must have wished that he was himself in the chapel at Llangareth, horn and all. They sang in four parts—the men, the women, the lads, and the lasses—and the parts went so well, each with the others, that it was as if they had been mitered together by Johann Sebastian Bach himself.

We were simple. We believed, for example, that if money was washed in rainwater it would never be stolen, and that if a newborn child was washed in rainwater it would speak perfect Welsh by the age of two. We were not well off. To one side of us we had the frowning, dark mountains and to the other side the fickle sea. We knew full well that in the south, in Dyfed, the coal pits were closed and the miners hungry for bread and work, and that in the rest of Wales stark poverty stalked through the land and near-despair was the order of the day; but in Llangareth we were safe. No one had ever done anything for us in the past, and it was natural for us to shift for ourselves. But we had the singing, and as long as we had that we were safe and strong; we were ourselves and Wales was our land.

2

Blind Johnny

Angharad cried only twice on her seventh birthday. In West Wales that was all right; if she had cried three times bad luck would have been hers for the rest of the year, or so it was said.

As a birthday treat, and because it was a Saturday afternoon in June, Mam allowed her to go with me—I should say that I had been persuaded to take her—on Caradoc to the penny cinema in Barmouth, the seaport eight miles from Llangareth. Visits to the cinema were very rare events for us. Mam gave us threepence apiece: a penny for the show and twopence to spend on candy or chocolate. It was a beautiful summer day, with hardly any rain about at all, and we set off for Barmouth in high spirits. The film soundtrack was always in English, and usually in the very strange-sounding English of America. It was a bit difficult for a ten-year-old Welsh lad like me to follow everything perfectly, but on that occasion I managed to interpret most of what was said for Angharad. At that time her English was practically nil, as she had been at school for only a month or so.

The road traffic in Merioneth in 1934 was sparse, mainly horse-drawn farm carts and pony-traps. Most of the country people, though, walked. Now and again the local doctor drove past in his new, open-backed motorcar, which seemed to us children like the chariot of the heralding angel of birth and death. On the Saturdays of summer the road saw quite a few charabancs. These were gaudily colored tourist buses that plied mainly between the railway station at Barmouth and the rural coastal boarding houses, with the few English people who could afford to vacation then.

On our way back home, after four or five of the charabancs had noisily roared past, Caradoc was becoming nervous and distraught. Sensing his distress, I steered him off the highway onto a narrow path that wound up onto the ridge of hills that front the coast. The path, which I had never traveled before, led up over the short grass of the open sheep meadows, then through low brush and gorse. Soon it was closed in between high blackberry and bramble bushes, over which it was difficult, and often impossible, for me to see. After a while, the path reached the crest of the ridge. There we found that the way ahead along the ridge was so thickly overgrown that it was impossible for Caradoc to go on. Instead of sensibly returning to the highway, I decided to push on along the narrow trail down the far slope of the ridge. I didn't want to look like a fool before either the pony or Angharad.

Down we went, over the stony, broken ground, weaving this way and that between the thorny bushes, until we were down in a narrow, deep valley, more like a gulley; an arroyo, I suppose the Americans would call it. There, in a dense copse of thickets and brambles, not knowing whether to go forward or back, I lost my sense of direction. The sky was overcast with dark clouds, and dusk was falling. That was when Angharad started to cry, and no wonder; by that time we were both badly scratched on our bare arms and legs by the thorns, which seemed to reach out for us malignantly as Caradoc pushed his way through the almost solid wall of spiky vegetation around us.

As Caradoc struggled bravely along through the dense brambles, I saw in my head Mam's strong, dark features as they would be when we arrived home two or three hours late, or perhaps even more. I hoped that she might have visitors—perhaps Cadell Rum, an old sailor friend of Dad's. Mam was always good-tempered when Cadell was around—he made her laugh. I imagined his devilish face, dark, sharp-featured, with his black eyes gleaming in the firelight; but that brought to me visions of shadowy things and demons of the night, or the *Tylwyth Teg,* the little folk, who might be lurking down there in that death-quiet, tangled grove. We might even be at the entrance to *Annwfn,* the Other World, the Welsh Hades; we might be held there for a hundred years by Arawn the Mighty

King, and return home to find everyone we knew dead and gone.

Anxiously now, I drove Caradoc on with my heels, kicking his belly and the grasping branches that impeded us, and shouting at him, not so much to press him on as to somehow cast away from us the somber, demoniacal forces that I thought I could see all around.

Caradoc pushed on, his head jerking this way and that to avoid the clutching thorns. Then, with my insistence that he follow as straight a line as possible, he had scrambled his way right through the miniature jungle. By that time he was bleeding from a score of deep scratches. Both Angharad's clothes and mine were torn in a dozen places, and our arms and legs were a mass of cuts and nicks. Dusk was upon us and I was completely lost.

We came across the road just as complete darkness fell. It was a narrow, macadamized track only about twelve feet wide that wound its way along the bottom of the valley. When we reached it, I hesitated for a few moments, puzzling out which way to head. I decided to turn left along the road, calculating that that would be a northerly direction, toward the neighborhood of Llangareth.

Angharad, even though she had many scratches from the thorns, was very brave until we followed the lane around a bend and saw in the deepening gloom yet another bend ahead; and the night was upon us. Then, even though I gave her my last toffee, she sniffled quietly, sobbed, and finally gave way to tears. I too felt like crying, but I couldn't do that in front of Caradoc and my sister. I was the man of the house while Dad was away from home, and men didn't cry. I decided to push on into the darkness.

Now we were in wooded country, and on both sides of the lane the elm and ash trees rustled in the light breeze overhead. Behind the high roadside hedge things whispered and stirred in the undergrowth, but the sky was clearing and the moon shone fitfully between the high branches. Angharad and I kept silent, afraid to attract the attention of the *Tylwyth Teg,* who must surely be busy planning the night's mischief in the darkness under the trees, or perhaps watching us with their little brown eyes from behind the hedgerow, waiting for Caradoc to stop so that they could overcome us and take us to the Other World, there to make us tend the magic caldron for ever and a day, as they were said to have done with other children who had disappeared.

Then, as we passed from under the shadows of the trees, we saw a figure walking ahead of us under the moon. I urged Caradoc on. He too had seen the dark shape along the road and loped off at an easy trot toward it. As we drew near to the figure, it stopped and turned to face us. When we drew closer yet, I saw that it was the form of a big man. His hair was gray under a flat, peaked cap, and he had about a week's growth of whiskers. He was smoking a short clay pipe, upside down, and above it his eyes smiled as he stood and waited for us to pass him. He wore a red neckerchief around his neck, and his jacket was grubby gray in the moonlight. Below the jacket he wore black moleskin trousers tied with thick string below the knees, and we knew that he was either a farm laborer or a roadman, for that was how they dressed. As we approached him Angharad sobbed even louder as she clung to my back.

"Syr!" I hailed him. Welsh is usually an informal language among the country folk, and normally I would have called *"Cyfaill!"*—"Friend!"—but this was something of an urgent occasion. For all I knew we could have strayed into some strange country, even China or England, or someplace where there were black-armored giants and dragons.

The man smiled broadly at me as Caradoc stopped a yard from him. Then he said in a high-pitched yet strong voice, in Welsh, "Is that a little wench I can hear crying?"

"It is." I tried to deepen my voice. Then, despite my wish to appear manly before the man, I blurted out: "We're lost! We've been to the pictures in Abermo. Our way has taken its own road, and it won't let us know it!"

"Where do you live, *bach?*" He almost coughed the end of the word, so I knew he was from Gwynedd. Angharad still sniffled as the man addressed me.

"Llangareth, sir."

The man leaned closer to me. He had a strange way of looking slightly to one side of me, as though he were avoiding my eyes, yet his eyes were open and clear, and he stared straight ahead, unblinking. "Llangareth, is it? Well, come on, lass," he said to Angharad. She was straightening her auburn hair silently now. "Llangareth isn't far—it's on my way home; come, I'll take you."

As the man took hold of Caradoc's bridle, Angharad burst out, "Our mam will be angry with us and send us to bed early every night for a week!"

The man leaned toward Angharad. "Hush now, *cariadbach-gen*"—"little sweetheart"—"Llangareth's only two miles away over the next hill. I'll tell you what I'll do; as we brave the road it's a story you will hear from me; one told to me when I was your age. . . ." The man stroked Caradoc's nose, then took the pony's bridle and led him and us along the road between the shadows of the scudding clouds under the moon.

We reached home at our bedtime, but by the time our guide knocked on the cottage door I cared little how late it was, and so, I think, did Angharad. The story that the old man told us, as he steadily plodded on leading Caradoc, had enchanted and delighted us. He had brought to our minds picture after picture of a world full of magic and wonder, mystery and brave doings. The story he told us, I found later, was a tale from the *Mabino-gion,* the ancient collection of Welsh legends. It was about a Roman emperor, Magnus Maximus, who had a dream that he was to rule Britain first, with a British wife, and then to rule Rome. In the *Mabinogion* the tale is called "Macsen." The way the man described the emperor's dream—the castles, the meadows, the rivers, the ships "all silver and gold and precious stones"—was spellbinding to us, so that we completely forgot the film we had seen that afternoon, it seemed such a tawdry thing.

Mam greeted the man—she obviously knew him. She was somewhat short with him because she was both angry at me yet relieved at our return, late as it was. The man went off into the night. Mam walloped me on the ear and sent me straight to bed with no supper.

Later, Angharad brought me some buttered bread and jam, so I didn't suffer too much. We whispered in the night, as the druid moon cast silver beams through the open windows and a soft breeze fluttered the lace curtains. We whispered about the story that the man had recounted to us, and I retold to Angharad what I could remember of it, until she closed her eyes and fell asleep. Then I told the rest of what I could remember to myself.

Our mam depended upon me too much to be angry with me for long, so next day, when I woke her with a mug of tea to make up for what I'd done the previous day, she was affable enough.

"How was Sioni last night when he brought you home?" she asked me. I told her how we had met him in the dark, frightening lane, and of the marvelous tale he had told us as he led Caradoc by the bridle in the darkness and moonlight.

"Aye," said Mam, "he is a good storyteller, that's for sure. The old people still call him round for birthdays and burials and such, to tell his tales."

I stood for a moment at Mam's bedside. I stared at the blue ribbon on her nightgown, where it was tied at the neck. It was forever strange for me to see Mam with her hair down. She was always more tender toward me then. I asked her: "What does he do? I mean, where do the stories come from? Does he read them and learn them off by heart?"

Mam smiled at me. Then she took a sip of tea and replied: "Bless you lad, no. Sioni ap Rhisiart has been as blind as a bat since he was six years old. His brother Dilwyn shot him with an arrow. It was accidental, of course. They were shooting quail up on the marshes below Dolgellau. That's all of seventy years ago. Sioni's never read a word in his life! He breaks up the stones for the road-mending gangs. Well, after all, bach, it's better than being a charge on the parish, isn't it?"

I met Sioni many times after that, in the next four years. Now that I knew him I could go and find him, where he sat at the roadside breaking stones with his hammer. Summer and winter, on days when I had time off, I looked for Sioni, and listened to him as he cracked away at the stones and told me his tales. Some of them, like the legends of Peredur, and Gereint and Math, were so long that they took several days in the telling.

Forty-seven years after I first met Sioni I wrote down an

English translation of all the *Mabinogion* tales as he had re-counted them to me in Welsh—only to find that publishers thought the public would not be interested. They felt that readers would prefer the translations by Lady Charlotte Guest, an English aristocrat, or George Borrow, English; or A. P. Graves, Irish; or T. M. Chotzen, Dutch; or the Anglo-Welsh brothers Gwyn and Thomas Jones, with all their *thees* and *thous* and *forsooths*; or works by Italians and Germans—anything but the real thing, anything but the direct translation from the old Welsh oral legends, pure, raw, and uninhibited.

But Sioni ap Rhisiart taught me the best lesson of my life; to appreciate our inheritance of the past. That drew me even more to literature, then in turn to music, painting, sculpture, and architecture, and in those arts I retained my interest all through an otherwise hard existence at sea. Life would have been much tougher without those solaces.

Mam was a strong-willed woman with a deep belief in independence and self-reliance. As far back as I remember, I was left to fend for myself in practically everything except clothes and food. If I had a problem of any kind, she told me to try to sort it out for myself. If I failed, and went back to her for advice, only then would she give it, and she was usually right about whatever it was. Her days were always full; she was at the household chores from dawn to dusk, but I don't recall her ever resenting it, not before us children, at any rate; nor do I recall her treating any man as more than an equal. She wasn't "liberated" in the modern, specious, sense of the word. There was no electricity, nor washing machine, nor dryer, nor unending hours of inane television soap operas to impel her into dissatisfaction with her lot as a woman and a mother. She was certainly not unschooled, nor was she ignorant of what was going on outside the cottage door in the world outside. That she loved Dad, Angharad, and me there was never any doubt; but for us children, at least, it was a practical love, with little sentimentality. In the mid-thirties, every day that went by with food on the table and a fire in the hearth was a victory to her. She was rarely idle. She knitted all of our underwear, jerseys, socks, and scarves, and she made most of her own clothes, too. She had little patience with gossip, which made her an exception in that part of Wales, and yet she seemed to know everything that was happening, and to whom, for miles around. She had a good sense of humor, and she was a brilliant mimic, yet she could be acerbic in the extreme if she wanted to be.

She missed Dad while he was away, and after four or five months of his absence she became edgy and morose. But all that changed as soon as Dad showed up; then she blossomed. Both she and Dad had been born in the last decade of the nineteenth century, but in retrospect they were surprisingly modern in their outlooks and beliefs.

I doubt that there is very much in the general discourse now that Mam and Dad would not sympathize with, except for the loosening of sexual morality. In that matter they were truly Victorian. I never once heard sex discussed at home, and rarely outside, apart from a few jokes heard at school, which these days would be considered innocuous. If an unmarried girl became pregnant she was "in trouble," and it was *always* the man's fault. Mam said "Only good girls get into trouble, the really bad ones know how to avoid it." If the girl's family could afford it, she went "on holiday" to Dublin. Years later I discovered that before abortion became legal in Great Britain, Dublin provided that service, as there was a surplus of doctors there and the job could be done much more cheaply. If the girl's family could not afford an abortion, the offspring was usually put in a home or farmed out to a foster parent, until it was of age to go into the navy or the army, into "service," or on the dole.

Wales was not all hills and valleys and violets and sweet innocence, as some would have us believe. Nor was it all doom and despair. It was arduous work making something out of nothing each and every day, and I had to force myself, at times, to love the bleak land. At other times, as I watched the clouds fly over the hills, and the changing greens and purples of the heights, the majesty of it all came home to me. Then the love in me for our perplexing land gushed forth so strongly that it was a physical thing, almost beyond my restraining. It was as though my heart flew with the clouds over the mountains, as if my blood ran down the streams into the sea.

On my eleventh birthday I was to have received the first significant material gift I had ever had. Mam hid it with the Powell family just down the valley, but I knew it was there days before the great day. My best friend, Cei, the oldest of the Powell boys, had told me, and he took me to their toolshed to see it. It wasn't new—Mam could never have afforded that—but to me it was magnificent.

Dusk was approaching when Cei took me to the shed. He opened the door quietly so as not to be heard by his parents, and there it was, a bicycle leaning against the workbench. It was one of the old-fashioned sit-up-and-beg models, and in its new black paint it looked stately indeed. Silently I felt the bike's frame and the pneumatic tires. There was even a pump to blow up the tires, and an acetylene lamp on the handlebars, just as Williams-the-Police had on his bicycle.

"Look," whispered Cei, "even a tool bag, there is, hanging on the back of the saddle." He opened the small leather bag. "Spanners and all inside it . . ."

"It's a beauty, Cei, but it's a shame I can't ride it until my birthday. It's only the fifth—three days to go."

There was silence in the shed for a moment or two, as Cei knit his brows in thought. He was already eleven, and so wiser than I was. Then he said: "Well, if we're quiet there'd be no harm in having a little go on the bike now, would there? As long as you don't make any noise getting out of the gate. Once you're out there my mam and dad won't hear you. . . ."

I started. "Do you think I could?" I asked.

In reply Cei grasped hold of the bike's handlebars and quietly, slowly, started to wheel it out of the open shed door, into the deepening gloaming. We wheeled the bike, me holding on to the saddle, along the grass verge by the path, so as not to make a noise scrunching the gravel. Soon we were at the gate and out onto the rough trail that served as a roadway down to the pond at the bottom of the valley.

"Come on, hop on," whispered Cei. "I'll hold the bike for you."

I perched my leg over the frame and hunched myself up onto the saddle. The distance from the saddle to the pedals was a bit too much for my legs. "It's too bloody big, Cei," I said in English.

"Perch your bottom over the crossbar," he whispered. "You'll be able to manage then."

I did as I was bid. Cei was right. I could reach the pedals. "What about lighting the lamp? It's a bit dark in the hollow," I said.

"Don't be daft, man. If Dad comes out and sees the light he'll know what's up and flay me alive," replied Cei. "Go on, you don't need to go far. Just try it out. You've to be home shortly, anyway."

"Right. Here we go," I murmured, and started to pedal down the rocky hill. As the bike gathered speed I stopped pedaling. It was as much as I could do to avoid the big rocks that burst out of the trail. The night wind was on my face, and I was afraid, but determined not to show it in front of Cei. On down the hill the bike flew, with bushes and sheep on each side flashing by faster and faster. I remembered the brakes. I grabbed at them and slowly squeezed them—neither one worked. There was evidently no rubber in the brake pads. Headlong down the steep hill I clattered, sparks flying from both wheels. I was only yards from the pond. To either side of the path were big boulders. If I crashed into one of them I would surely break something. In a flash of fear and terror I decided, and . . . went splash into the pond.

There was black, cold water all around me. The bike had disappeared. I was struggling on the surface of the pond, spluttering green slime and reaching for the overgrowing plants on the edge of the pool. Then I had a willow branch in my hand and dragged myself, dripping wet and freezing, onto the grass. Cei was at my side.

"That's done it," he said.

I climbed to my feet, struggling to hold back tears and shivering violently. "Wha . . . what . . . what about the bike, Cei?"

"It's too deep. We'll never get it out tonight. We'll have to get a hook and a line and drag for it. We'll have to make a raft. . . . Thank Jesus it's Saturday tomorrow."

"What about Mam?" I asked him. "She'll kill me for this."

"Don't tell her about the bike. Tell her you fell into the pond walking by it," he replied.

"What about your dad, Cei?"

"Oh, he won't go into the shed tonight, and he's off very early tomorrow, repairing a wall up in Ty-Glyn. His day tools are in his bag in the kitchen, see." Cei took my arm. "You'd better get home and out of those wet clothes, Tristan. You'll catch pneumonia."

Silently, with me quaking like a leaf in a gale, we walked back up the treacherous rock trail. Cei, with a whispered *"Nos dda,"* disappeared into his cottage. I continued on home, trembling with cold and trepidation.

As I neared our house, I had a bright idea. The front door was never locked unless Mam went out. I crept around to the front of the cottage, opened the door quietly, and gingerly made my way up the stairs. They were old stairs, centuries old, but I knew every squeak and creak in them. Once in my room I quickly changed into dry trousers and a jersey and slippers. Then I silently made my way out again through the front door and so round to the kitchen door. I took some wood logs in with me, so as to appear more casual.

Mam looked up from her sewing. "When did you change your clothes, bach?" she asked me quietly.

"Er . . . just now. . . . I went through the front . . . didn't want to disturb you, Mam."

"You're late, bach."

"Yes, I was out repairing the fence over by the pigsty and tore my shirt on the wire."

"Well, your supper's in the oven. Wash up when you've done, and let me have your shirt in the morning so I can mend it."

I was able to dry my clothes by hanging them out of the bedroom window. I stayed awake most of the night, watching that it didn't rain. Making a tear in the shirt was simple. I ripped it on a nail before I took it down to the kitchen.

After doing my chores and eating breakfast, I was just about to set off down the valley to the Powells' cottage when Branwen Powell, Cei's oldest sister, about nine, appeared at our door, her face as gloomy as her dad's. "Mrs. Jones," said she sorrowfully to Mam, "it's gone!"

"What's gone, *bachgen?*" said Mam.

"The thing that you put in our shed . . . you know. . . ." Branwen had seen me glaring at her. Her face was almost as red as her hair.

Mam bustled out of the door, out into the yard. There they talked in low tones for a few minutes. Mam came steaming back into the kitchen. She stared at me sternly for a moment or two. Then she said, "Tristan, bach, what happened last night?"

My eyes dropped from Mam's, I shuffled my feet, and I kept silent.

"Were you riding a bike last night, by any chance?" Mam asked.

As I looked up at her I could feel the tears welling in my eyes, despite my trying manfully to hold them back. Suddenly there was a big dollop on one of my cheeks, then another, and another. I burst out crying. Then, in fitful sobs, I told Mam what had happened as she stood, her arms folded across her apron bib in front of me. When I'd finished the tale, I started to inform Mam how Cei and I were going to salvage the bike that very day. She grabbed me by my ear and twisted it as she dragged me toward the door. She flung me through the door. I went skittering out into the yard, still sobbing pitifully. "Now," she cried, "you go down to the pond and you get that bicycle out yourself. If I see anyone else with you it's early bed for you for a whole year! You put the thing in—now you get it out, and don't come back here until you've done it. You get that thing out of where you put it, or you're no son of mine!"

When I'd recovered my wits I started off down the valley. Cei and his brother Gwrtheyrn were both out in their garden when I passed by. They did not appear to look at me as I shambled down the hill. Branwen must have told them what Mam had said. She had witnessed the anger and humiliation.

Near the pond I had a bright idea. I flew all the way down the valley, right to the shed where Goodness Gracious Jenkins kept his fishing tackle. When I got to the beach he was just about to shove off in a dinghy out to his lugger. I hailed him at the top of my voice. He stopped pushing his boat down the beach and turned to me.

"Are you coming out with me?" asked Goodness Gracious.

"I can't. I'm in trouble. . . ." I told Jenkins the story of what had occurred. "I want to borrow a bit of line and one of your shark hooks, Mister Jenkins," I pleaded.

"What about a grapnel?" he suggested.

"Even better."

Jenkins disappeared into his shed and came out after a moment with a four-pronged grappling iron and a length of rope. "This should do the trick, bach. Now, it's off I must go, for I'm late already."

I ran back up the hill to the pond as fast as I could, and was soon casting the grappling iron into the water. It took a half hour for me to finally get a grip on the bike, but finally it surfaced and I dragged it onto the bank. There I found that the front wheel was buckled. I managed to wheel it back home on its back wheel only. I leaned the bike on the outside wall and quietly entered the kitchen. Mam was sewing my shirt. She looked up at me seriously. "Well?"

"I've got it, Mam . . . but the front wheel is bent."

She looked down at her sewing. "Then go and straighten it," she said, almost inaudibly.

Cei and I straightened the wheel as best we could, using the simple tools in the Powells' toolshed. It never was perfectly straight, but I managed to ride the bike a few times before Dad came home and did the job properly. I never did ride the bike much, though; I was too fond of Caradoc for that.

Of course Mam was right. She taught me self-reliance, and I honor her memory all the more for that.

3

Goodness Gracious

My closest friend, Cei Powell, was three months older than I was and slightly taller. Like his mam, he had red hair and light hazel eyes, but his face was a mass of freckles. He was always on the go, in complete contrast to his brother, Gwrtheyrn, who was two years younger. Gwrtheyrn was dark, quiet, and slow-moving, like his father, and preferred the company of his two sisters to that of Cei and me. Despite that, Cei was always protective toward him. Cei hated school lessons and was never happier than when he was out fishing with Goodness Gracious, birds-nesting, or making something in his dad's toolshed. Once or twice I tried to get him interested in reading, but it was no use; his eyes glazed over and he looked around for something to do with his hands.

At school Cei kept as quiet as could be in the classroom. He sat at the next desk to me, and practically every examination paper or composition he wrote was copied from mine, while Jeffreys-Geography gazed through the schoolroom window, dreaming of England, tea, crumpets, and cricket.

Outside, in the schoolyard, Cei became a dynamo, a whirling dervish of devilment. At soccer and rugby he was almost always center-forward. While he scored the goals I tagged along at his side, wondering about the logistics of the game. Naturally, in a tiny school like ours the teams were a very mixed bag, ranging in age from strapping lads of thirteen down to sprogs of eight or so. Cei was the hero of them all, but it was to me that they came for advice. I invented many an excuse for them when they in some way transgressed the school rules. No harm in that; they were Jeffreys-Geography's rules, not ours.

At home, Cei was generally in one kind of trouble or another. It was rare to see him without a bruise or two where his dad had belted him. That was not too unusual in those days; most fathers had the Bible in one hand and the belt in the other. "Spare the rod and spoil the child," they piously quoted the Old Testament at home, and the New Testament—"Suffer the little children to come unto me"—they reserved for best-dressed Sundays at chapel. In that respect I was most fortunate; never once did my father lay his hand on me. He didn't need to; a mere dark glance, a quiet word of warning or chastisement was enough to curb the most mischievous spirit. With Mam it was different. She cuffed my ear or spanked me a few times, but that was only when I really deserved it, when I had driven her beyond her tether.

When Cei and I were not at school, working in our gardens, or tending livestock, there was always something else to do. We went on the cliffs collecting sea gulls' eggs, or up on the hills gathering mushrooms or dandelion leaves, burdock and sorrel for greens, or wild watercress in the brooks nearby. We also set rabbit snares where there were no sheep. In the summer we collected many pounds of blackberries and wild strawberries, which our mothers used to make jam. If there was a surplus of jam it was bartered in Barmouth for other foodstuffs such as tea or sugar. In the wintertime we caught blackbirds; this was done using a net frame propped up with a stick at one end. On the stick was tied a long string that led through a crack in the kitchen window, and under the frame was set bread and other tidbits. In went the bird, jerk went the string, down went the frame, and there we had another bit of meat for the pie.

The only time Cei and I ever went hunting was for a wildcat that had gone on a rampage and was coming down from the mountains, killing our hens. It took us three nights of silent stalking, but eventually Cei got the cat with a steel arrow, and finished it off with a blow from a sawed-off broomstick. The wildcat was huge by domestic standards and as black as a preacher's hat. Dead, it had a sneer like the devil himself. Cei skinned the cat, intending to present the pelt to his mother for a rug. He nailed it to the toolshed door, but after two or three days it stank so much that he had to throw it into the cesspit at the end of the Powells' garden.

Generally, the girls of Llangareth helped their mothers in-doors. They started this at an early age, and by the time they were nine or ten, as our Angharad and Branwen Powell were, they had become quite expert at housewifery and cooking, and adept at sewing and knitting. This tended to make them lady-like at a tender age, compared to modern little girls, but I don't think that the girls I knew when I was a boy were any less happy than the ones I know now. I think that those I knew in my childhood were more content, somehow. Despite their being in the house much of the time, they also did many things we boys did. They went riding and walking the hills, fishing and swimming. I think the only reason they were not quite as active is that it was not usually considered to be the female nature.

Rock-climbing was a venture in which only boys took part. I don't recall hearing of it causing any deaths, although I expect it did, considering some of the hazardous climbs made with none of the usual mountaineering paraphernalia. It must have been in 1936 when the story got around that Germany, in connection with the Olympics, had sent a rock-climbing team to climb the highest cliff in Britain, somewhere in North Wales. The cliff was over a thousand feet high and overhung the sea. The Germans climbed it, using pitons and ropes and other fancy foreign impedimenta, and when they were close to the top, after many hours of climbing, they planted a big Nazi flag in the cliff face. They then retired to the local inn to swig beer and eat their fill, thinking, naturally, that they had well earned it.

The local lads, seeing the alien flag hanging there, deter-mined to remove it. They set out to climb the cliff using noth-ing but their hands and feet, and on the way up they removed every piton that the Germans had set into the face, as well as the flag, which they carried back triumphantly to the inn and returned to the Nazis just before pub-closing time.

Cei, a few other local boys, and I used to go climbing in the foothills a few miles off when the weather was fine. Even now I shudder when I think of some of the risks we took, our toes clinging to an inch-wide ledge in the rock, our numb fingers gripping another tiny nub or crack in the face of the rock. I did not dare tell Mam I was going rock-climbing, but instead lied, saying that I was going fishing or walking. The elation I felt when we had made it to the top of an almost sheer hundred-foot cliff still returns whenever I think of it. Then we used to throw ourselves on to the top of the rock and lay there, panting at the sky, silently grinning at the blue above and the green below, then at each other, until it was time to make our way back down again and tramp the long weary trudge back home as the light faded. We took very little with us; perhaps a jam or dripping (fat) sandwich and a bottle of water. If Educated Evans from Aran Fawddwy came along, though, he always had some candy, his uncle being well off. That was the only reason we let him come. He was too fat to climb, and used to wait for us at the bottom of the rock.

I think that rock-climbing was the only activity for us boys, apart from our schooling, that did not produce something toward the family larder. That was the way it was in West Wales in those days, for everyone except the lucky few who were rich.

There were several longshoremen on the coast near Llangareth. They were the local fishermen. Most of them did their work in small open boats close to shore, but a few others, like Goodness Gracious Jenkins, worked Tenby luggers, which they kept moored off the beach when they were not in use. The longshore-fishermen were in general the peasants of the West Wales seafaring community. While they could claim some kind of independence, being self-employed, they were also usually at the mercy of the middlemen in the towns, who bought their catch, and they prospered according to the whims of the weather and the sea that beat against their abodes. They were a very close-knit lot, as it was the custom for a longshoreman to marry another longshoreman's daughter. How else could it be? What other woman would know how to braid nets, bait long-lines, make lobster and crab pots, search for bait along the mud flats and rocks, or smoke fish?

Goodness Gracious was fortunate. He had a contract to supply a couple of small hotels and boardinghouses on the coast with fresh fish. Now and again he found an English gentleman who hired his boat and him to go out mackerel spinning.

Sometimes he picked up a group of tourists from the hotels or boardinghouses and took them out on Tremadoc Bay for a few shillings. But that was only in the summertime, in the high tourist season. In the mid-thirties that season was nowhere near high enough; tourists were rare creatures. Goodness Gracious (who was so called because that was the only expletive he had ever been heard to use) mostly scrabbled a living on his vegetable plot or by doing casual work, when that was needed, on a local farm.

Goodness Gracious was a thin, wiry man of medium height, about as old as the century, I guessed. He had jet-black hair and startlingly light-blue eyes, the color of Ffestiniog slate when it's dry. Unlike many of the longshoremen, he was clean-shaven, at least when he was ashore. He had a small, sparrow-like wife who, despite appearances, was as tough as a grave-stone and about as loquacious. He also had two sons, Tomas, nineteen in 1936, and Pedr, eighteen. They were, of course, part of the baby boom that immediately followed World War I—Goodness Gracious had spent the war on Royal Navy armed trawlers. Now Tomas was in the Royal Naval Reserve, and for a week in the summer he went off to Plymouth for bugle calls, shouted commands, and incessant drill, on what he thought was—compared to working with his dad—a good, relaxing vacation. Tomas, being an enterprising lad, also sometimes went crewing on yachts for fine English gentry down off the Isle of Wight. He had arranged this through his naval friends, and he thought that several days and nights of contin-uous labor, hauling sails up and down, repairing them, scrub-bing decks, sleeping in a crabbed yacht foc'sle, was a bit like heaven after a winter of hauling nets and long-lines onboard *Gwenhyfar,* his father's Tenby lugger fishing boat. While Tomas was away, it was a chance for us local lads to accompany Goodness Gracious and Pedr to sea. There was no pay, of course, except perhaps a few fish at the end of the trip, but it was interesting and adventurous, at least to Cei Powell and me.

Gwenhyfar was a typical Tenby lugger, launched at that small port on the western end of Carmarthen Bay. She was comfort-ably built, of massive timbers for her size, and about twenty-two feet overall. She was clinker-built; that is, her planks overlapped one another. The hull was decked from the bow to the mainmast, and below the deck forward there was a small, triangular cuddy about seven feet long. That was the only shelter in the boat. She had three rowing thwarts (seats) along the hull, and another thwart aft for the helmsman, who steered with a tiller. Stone ballast was carried in the bottom of the boat, under a floor supported by massive beams. The heavy wooden keel was about eighteen inches deep. The mainmast was stepped about one-third of the way back from the stempost. The mizzen was stepped on the transom (sternpiece) and followed its sharp rake. Forward, a bowsprit, about seven feet long, was carried through a gammon iron, while an outrigger for the mizzen was stepped through a hole in the transom. The mainsail was a dipping lug, with three rows of reef-points, but in winter this was replaced by a trysail that was secured to the mast by parrels (hoops). *Gwenhyfar* had three jibs of different sizes that were set according to the strength of the wind. She sailed surprisingly well on the wind, although to us youngsters it was at first a mite frightening to be in an almost open boat with a tremendous spread of sail for her size, heeled over so that on the lee side there were no more than three or four inches of freeboard (the amount of hull above water level).

Goodness Gracious usually fished offshore from the Merioneth coast, but now and again, if the weather signs looked fair (a licked thumb stuck up into the breeze), he took off for Pencilan Head, thirty miles away across Tremadoc Bay. He made the crossing overnight and arrived off the Head just as dawn was breaking. I made my first night sail in 1936. It was unforgettable: the sea gleaming in the moonlight, the soft breeze, and a field of stars overhead. I was a mere twelve years old, but I felt, as I drank in the scene and my heart quickened, as if I had been, would be, alive forever.

An hour before dawn, as we approached the Head about five miles off, the wind dropped and the sea flattened, so Cei, Pedr, and I set to pulling the oars. By the time *Gwenhyfar* lay off Pencilan we were exhausted. We grabbed the jam sandwiches and cold cocoa that Goodness Gracious handed us for breakfast. We were just about to wolf down the repast when he held up his calloused hand. There was a flat silence, except for the creaking of the boat's gear. "Boys," said Goodness Gracious in a sepulchral tone, "*Gwenhyfar* is a Christian vessel." A sea gull cried in the distance.

We knew what he meant, so we bent our heads while Goodness Gracious intoned the breakfast grace: "Lord, accept your servants' thanks for this day, for the work of the day, and for the food you have given us. Amen."

Cei and I scoffed down the sandwiches and cold cocoa, after which we helped Pedr set the nets. Then we set to rowing up and down off the headland. We pulled all morning but caught only a dozen fish. I think they were bream. Lunch was the same: grace, jam sandwiches, and cold cocoa, but it was welcomed. Then followed eight more hours of back-breaking oar-pulling, until dusk, when we hauled our nets again. This time there were about three dozen fish, which were all thrown into wooden barrels. Goodness Gracious grinned at us when everything had been squared away. "A special treat for you tonight, lads," he cried. He delved into the cuddy and brought out a clay pot and four pint-sized tea mugs. From the pot he ladled out a cold lamb-and-potato stew, and then he said grace. To us, the stew was delicious. In the years since, decades later, I have eaten in some of the world's finest restaurants, but that cold lamb-and-potato stew at dusk in an open boat reeking of fish, rocking away off the coast of Caernarvon, was one of the most memorable meals I have ever partaken of. There were no spoons in the boat. Goodness Gracious and Pedr merely lifted the pint mugs to their lips and let the stew slide down, and then they refilled their mugs. Seeing this, Cei and I did the same. With the stew finished and everything washed in salt water, we set off to row back the thirty miles to Merioneth, each of the four of us with half-hour spells on the tiller as a relief.

It was well into the morning when *Gwenhyfar* finally was pulled slowly up to her mooring. There had been not a capful of wind all the night. Even Goodness Gracious said, "It's as if God was resting."

Both Cei and I got three good-sized fish each for our labors. My mam's face, when I turned up at the cottage with my prizes, was a study in relief, surprise, and delight. One of the bream we had that night for supper, and the other two she smoke-dried in the chimney for use later on.

On a later trip in *Gwenhyfar* in that summer of thirty-six, there was a good breeze and the lugger was dancing along bravely with Pedr at the helm, while his dad and I (Cei was not with us) got the nets ready for shooting. We were heading up the coast off Harlech, when there appeared a sight any lad of twelve would recall until his dying day. It was a fine day, blue sky and sunshine in between fluffy white clouds, and we could clearly see all the coasts of Merioneth and Caernarvon to our north. The wind was in a rare quarter, northeast. Suddenly, from behind the headland at the mouth of the River Glaslyn we saw emerge a fully rigged Welsh Topsail Schooner, one of the last of the Western Ocean Yachts, as they used to be called. As she headed south, past us, we could clearly make out her squaresail under her foreyard, and a stunsail and boom hoisted to the upper yardarm. She carried three jibs, two squaresails, a staysail, a fisherman's staysail, a foresail (quite small), a mainsail, and a main spritsail as well. As the breeze freshened, the stunsail and boom were taken in even as she approached our beam. She had a figurehead on her stem-post, but she was too far away for me to see it clearly. The lines of her hull were fine and graceful, and she had a rounded stern. She was painted black with white trimming and was about ninety feet long overall, at a guess. Goodness Gracious said that he thought she was *M. A. James,* but we had no way of knowing for sure, as she was too far away for us to read her name on her stern. If she was *M. A. James,* then she was the very same ship in which my grandfather Johnny Star made the fastest run ever from Port Madoc to Harburg—and that had been about thirty-four years before I saw her. Whatever craft she was, she was beautiful, a proud cloud of shining canvas over an elegant, powerful hull and a sparkling sea.

"They had to be good and fast," remarked Goodness Gracious. "They were in the fish and fruit trade, see, boys? Fish from Newfoundland to the Mediterranean, and fruit from Italy and Greece to Britain. You had to know your stuff and have a good fast ship when most of what you carried was going to rot in the hold if you didn't get a move on, see?"

The next year, in the autumn of 1937, Cei and I were again invited to go out fishing in *Gwenhyfar.* Tomas, Goodness Gracious's oldest son, had gone to join the Merchant Service, and

Pedr had cut his thumb rather deeply with a fish-gutting knife and was able only to manage the tiller. It was to be another all-night trip, and Goodness Gracious said we would be back at Llangareth by noon the next day. That was a school day, but by this time Cei and I were both thirteen and *Mister* Jeffreys-Geography had long given up trying to make little Englishmen of us, so he willingly gave himself the day off.

As we gathered on the beach in the evening, Cei, Pedr, Goodness Gracious, and I, to push the Jenkins' battered old dinghy into the water, the sea was all crinkled silver. *"Gwenhyfar"* rode to her rusty old mooring chain like a swan. The breeze was from the southwest, not very strong, but steady. Goodness Gracious, standing in his oilskin jacket, heavy woollen jersey, moleskin trousers, and knee-length sea boots, sniffed the air and looked around him. Under his dark blue woollen bobble cap his blue eyes gleamed. "Fine night tonight, boys," he crowed, as we all piled into the dinghy. Cei and I had no sea boots. We had to take our boots and socks off, and roll our trousers up to the knees in order to board the bobbing boat. The water was freezing, so it seemed. Once onboard *"Gwenhyfar,"* we dried our legs and feet with the outsides of our jackets, and then we donned our boots and socks again.

Soon we had let go of *Gwenhyfar's* mooring chain, after securing the dinghy to it. Cei and I set to on the oars, pulling her out to sea, while Goodness Gracious hauled up the jib, main, and mizzen. *Gwenhyfar* felt the wind in her sails, raised her fine bow to a swell, and lowered her fat little stern in a trough; we were off. She was only a scruffy little fishing boat with discolored red sails, but to me she was an exotic ship taking an ambassador and his court to the golden halls of the emperor of China.

The night breeze remained surprisingly steady for the Irish Sea. All night *Gwenhyfar* slowly shoved the sea out of her path with a chubby sort of joy, until at false dawn we could discern Pencilan Head and Bardsey Island out to the west under the descending moon. We set the trawl over the stern just as the wind dropped. Cei, Jenkins, and I set to pulling the oars, while Pedr managed the tiller. Apart from the squeak of the oars in the rowlocks, there was only the thin, plaintive cry of the dry main halyard block jerking to and fro above us to pierce the quietness of the dawn. The sky had clouded over; above us was a gray, sloppy sky, all around us a gray, sloppy sea. The air was heavy with moisture, and the breeze had a faint iodine, kelp-like smell. Goodness Gracious stopped rowing, sniffed the air, and said, "Boys, we're in for a bit of fog." Then he lowered his head and gazed along the tops of the slight swells, like a pool player sighting a shot. He glanced up at Bardsey Island from under his brows the while; then murmured, "Just so's I'll know which way to go home if it gets too thick, see?" There was no compass in the boat. Goodness Gracious stood up in the boat and gazed around the horizon. "No other craft nearby—just a couple of rowboats way up to the north. They must be out from Criccieth." He doled out breakfast—jam sandwiches and cold tea—and said grace, and we boys had the lot scoffed down almost as fast as the fog came down around us like cold cotton wool. It was uncanny, not to be able to see anything in a fog so white, so full of light in itself. It was so thick that soon I could barely make out the dark shape of Cei, only three feet away from me on the next thwart.

The only sound we heard, apart from the squeaking block overhead, was the plaintive sound of Jenkins's voice. "Goodness gracious," he said quietly. I thought I heard Cei giggle ahead of me, but I wasn't sure; it could have been a wavelet lapping *Gwenhyfar's* side. Many of the other local fishermen would have made God's ears ring with their cursing.

There was almost dead silence for a minute or so, broken now and again by the deep, faraway moan of the Bardsey lighthouse foghorn. Then Jenkins repeated, "Goodness gracious!" We heard him cluck his tongue in annoyance, then sigh and say: "Well, boys, we'd better get the net up. This is going to last for hours. Be very slow and careful."

We slowly and carefully made our way aft to help with the net. Goodness Gracious changed places with Pedr and took the tiller. Cei and I started rowing through the thick fog. It was eerie; a bit, I imagine, like sleepwalking through an empty space. We kept pulling at the oars for six or seven hours, a steady stroke, stopping only now and then to listen in trepidation for other craft. When the fog lifted, toward 1:00 P.M., I saw to my amazement that *Gwenhyfar* was only a mile or so from her mooring off Llangareth.

How Jenkins did it, how he found his way without a compass or another type of navigational aid, I can only guess, but I'll never know for sure. All he said when Cei blurted out his surprise was, "Well, goodness gracious, you wouldn't want me to go to Barmouth now, would you?"

There was no fish for Mam, of course, but she was happy enough to see me back that it didn't seem to matter to her.

Another fisherman I went out with a couple of times was Morgan Whistle. He, too, had a Tenby lugger, *Lovely Lass*, but he was a difficult man to work with. In the Great War he'd been a deckhand on a trawler that was shelled and sunk by a German surface raider. The explosion had blown off his lower jaw. The German surface raider's crew had picked up some of the trawler crew from the water and had taken them back to Germany as prisoners. The German doctors did what they could for Morgan, but his face was still quite a mess. They replaced his lower jaw with a stainless steel one covered with a pink material of some kind. Morgan could eat in a fashion, by opening and closing the jaw by hand. Otherwise the jaw was kept closed by a strap that passed over his bald head. However, he couldn't speak. Instead, he used a police-type whistle, with which he blew signals, high-pitched and low. Despite his handicap, he was a lively man, and he could be very funny with his eyes rolling and the whistle playing. It was said that there was hardly a barmaid in any pub on the coast of North Wales who was not enamored of Morgan Whistle, though he must have been well into his late thirties and was as bald as an egg. It might have been because, apart from being cheerful and funny ashore, he was also reputed to be the best fisherman in West or North Wales. He used to teach us lads the Morse code, blowing on his whistle in dots and dashes and at the same time writing down what he was signaling. He wasn't married, which was just as well, as legend had it that he had a girl in every port. He was so successful with women and fish that jealous competitors said his catch was becharmed by the music of his whistle. He always carried a mouth organ, too, which he somehow could play quite well. With the whistle and the harmonica, Morgan was the life and soul of any

gathering, and soon had everyone dancing and jigging or singing to his pipe.

At sea in his lugger, though, he was a different man, always
edgy and nervous, frowning to himself and cursing in quiet
hoots, as if he hated the sea. But I never saw any fisherman,
anywhere in the world, braid a net faster or more neatly than
Morgan Whistle. His fingers flashed quickly as his shuttle flew,
and the net he was making seemed to grow on its own, as if
by magic.

Morgan slept in his boat shed, among all the fishing gear, but
he had started to build a cottage a few hundred yards up from
the beach. There, if he wasn't out trawling, we would find him
quietly whistling to himself as he lugged the heavy stones up
his ladder to the top of the wall.

The cottage was never finished. Morgan was wrecked on
Bardsey Island in early thirty-eight and was drowned trying to
get ashore on the steep rocks.

4

Cadell Rum

My father was not a big man physically, but neither were most of the sailing captains and mates that I met as a child. They were wiry but very tough. If they survived the hard life at sea, the tropical diseases and other misadventures common to sea rovers, they generally lived to a decent old age. Most of them were religious: Welsh ships were renowned the world over for hymn-singing at Sunday services onboard. They were also famous—back in the days before David Lloyd George introduced his parliamentary bill to ease the lot of deep-sea sailors—for the humane conduct of the skippers and the good, if plain, food doled out daily in the clean, spartan crews' quarters. Pay, before the demise of sail in the mid-twenties, had not been overgenerous, ranging from about five pounds—twenty dollars—a month for a master, to fifteen shillings—three dollars—a month for a deck-boy.

Most of the very old captains and mates I knew had started their sea careers at an early age, some of them as young as ten and eleven. A few of them, by the time they were ready to retire, could make their way with ease in a half-dozen languages and corresponded with old friends all over the world.

Three kinds of men were truly respected in West Wales: a learned man, a man who could tell a story well, and a master of his trade. My dad was all three, and so when he was at home in Llangareth we were visited by many of the leading maritime lights from Merioneth, Caernarvon, and Cardigan, and on rarer occasions from as far afield as Pembroke, Carmarthen, and Glamorgan, too. Then, with the fire blazing in the hearth and the Aladdin oil lamp at full blast, our kitchen was warm and crowded and full of the tales of the old sail-in-trade.

There might be Morgan Lewis, a robust man of saturnine appearance with a huge walrus mustache and a sharp memory despite his seventy-odd years. He was from the now-deserted harbor of Barmouth, but he was still a Power-to-Be-Reckoned-With. He could reel off the names of all the three-hundred-odd sailing ships known on the coast of Wales during the past sixty years. *Hope, Isallt, Jenny Jones, Linus, Maid of Meiron, Palestine, Oleander, Six Brothers, Wave of Life, Twelve Apostles, Summer Cloud, Pride of Wales* (What names they had!), *My Lady, Morning Star, New Blessing, Fleetwing, Excelsior, Confidence,* and *Cariad:* Captain Morgan Lewis described them in all the shifting glory of canvas, sea, and sky. He could also name practically every man-jack who had ever shipped onboard each craft on every trip of note that she had made. The tall ships were all gone now, at the bottom of the sea or skulking in some faraway backwater. Now Morgan Lewis was a lay preacher at his local chapel. When he rendered, for example, his account of how starving rats in the hold of *Palestine,* bound from Manchester to Capetown with coal in 1892, had gnawed holes through the ship's side and sunk her in the South Atlantic, and how her captain, Owen Parry of Criccieth, had navigated all his crew safely to the African shore in an eighteen-foot open boat, it was as if he had learned it from Saint Paul's Epistle to the Corinthians. His words rolled and thundered like a telling of the *Odyssey.*

There might also be Mereddyd Philips, a short, rotund man with hair and beard as white as sea foam, a large, red nose, and a wooden leg. Mereddyd talked little. He was in his late sixties and had rounded the Horn under sail fifteen times—he carried a big red star tattoo on his forehead to show it. There was, it was said, no waterfront pub in Hamburg or Liverpool that had charged Mereddyd for a drink in the past thirty years, nor in Bristol, Harburg, Copenhagen, or Amsterdam, either. As Dad commented out of Mereddyd's hearing: "By God, his nose shows it, too. Why, two foxes could hide in it!"

Angharad and I liked Mereddyd a great deal; he always brought some toffees for us, dredging them from the depths of his blue serge watch coat before he perched Angharad on his lap above his wooden leg. He was the only square-rig sailor-man I ever saw with more than one ring on his fingers, and one of those was mounted with a huge onyx. On his one foot he wore a red leather boot with beautiful chasing worked into it.

Two other memorable men were Rhodri Griffiths and his brother Iago, ancients from Neath in South Wales, but still merry for all that. They had sailed, always together, on Norwegian and American whalers in the mid- and late 1800s. Their hands were scored with deep scars from the fletching knives and freezing lines, their eyes were green and bright-shining, and they held themselves as upright as expectant lighthouses. Their whaling had been by hand-hurled harpoons from open boats, and many a tale of capsizing in the freezing waters of the southern ocean, many a story of dories and the Azores they had to tell in voices strong and quiet, like the hum of forebraces in a stiff breeze. Behind all their gentle words was suspense and a threat of impending calamity. "Rhodri's ninety-three next month," I remember Mam whispering in an awed voice as he and his brother sprang down from the pony-trap and rolled their wide shoulders up to the cottage door. Rhodri carried a walking stick, but that was, as he delighted in showing us wondering children, only to contain a two-foot-long glass phial of a sparkling golden liquid. "Hebridean sunshine" Rhodri called it, his eyes twinkling. Iago had only one eye. The other he had lost when a harpoon line snapped as a right whale sounded; the broken end had cracked him in the eye. He wore no patch, and the blinded eye stared, forever open and innocent, at the middle ground between him and the far horizon. The two brothers always wore bowler hats, pilot jackets (Rhodri's had brass buttons), and corduroy trousers, and Iago's black boots shone like sea slugs. Iago was the religious one of the two and carried a Bible with him wherever he went. Both had been widowers for some years and now lived with their sister, who was older than either of them. She was, they said, "too busy looking after the house to go gallivanting around the countryside." They were strong people on the Gower; it's still winter in summer there. The two brothers, when they spoke Welsh, did so in the funny accent of South Wales. Compared to the bubbling tones of Gwynned, they sounded a bit, to us children at any rate, like the outlet of the kitchen pump at full gush.

A great deal of the Welsh slate trade had been with Germany. When the First World War broke out it had been a cataclysmic disaster for North Wales, but the friendly ties with German mariners had been so strong that when the kaiser started his war the tug masters of Bremen, Hamburg, and Harburg actually towed many Welsh sailing ships out to sea after the British declaration. The few ships and crews remaining in Germany had been interned, but the German sailors made sure that the Welsh seamen in internment camps were fed and looked after right through the four years of purgatory.

Apart from sustaining the close bonds forged through the previous decades between Welsh and German mariners, though, the war did little good for West Wales. Sail was finished by 1918, shelled, torpedoed, sold into neutral countries, stranded, and abandoned. Early in the war the U-boat captains had been professional sailors, many of them trained in sail. They had allowed the ship's crews fair warning, and even let them take with them into the lifeboats personal effects and mementoes of the ship, but as the war ground on, younger, more ruthless men were promoted in the German Imperial Navy, and there were many tales of utter callousness and barbarity, especially toward the end of the war. The collapse of Wales's slate industry and the loss of most of her great sailing fleet during the First World War was the start of an economic decline that was to continue for the next two and a half decades. As I recall, the consensus in Llangareth was that although the Allies had defeated Germany, it had done Wales no good at all; we might even have been better off had Germany won the war (which God forbid, said everyone but Fychan Evans, who had married a German woman from Nordenham and so was silent on the matter). Ports such as Portmadoc and Barmouth, which before the war had been full of sailing ships mustered for their passages, were now deserted, except for a few small coastal schooners and bobbing fishing boats. The mountain brooks that once had filled the water barrels for voyages to Aruba and Newfoundland now cried directly into the sea. The great blue slate mountain of Blaenau Ffestiniog, where half a thousand men had wrested a fortune in the rain, was still and dead. But, as Meryddyd Philips pointed out, the quays in Portmadoc bore eternal testimony to the old hard passages. They were constructed of Welsh granite and filled with ballast from Chile, Newfoundland, Greece, and Germany, all mixed with the soil of Wales. On the roofs of Valdivia, the Falkland Islands, Buenos Aires, San Francisco, and Baltimore can still be seen the slate of Blaenau Ffestiniog, as gray and blue as the rains of Eryri, as unmistakable as the lines of a Borth-y-gest schooner.

In the late afternoon, when there were visitors, Mam set out high tea: a cold leg of lamb, a great China tureen of boiled potatoes, ham and beef sandwiches, a pudding and custard, tea cakes, and the biggest teapot we had, which held about half a gallon. Then the grand captains sat meekly around the table, Morgan Lewis with his napkin tucked up under his chin, beneath his walrus mustache. Angharad and I were placed at the far end of the table from Dad, staring at Morgan, waiting for him to sip his tea, wondering how he managed it with a half-pound of hair sprouting from his upper lip and never a drop of tea spilled on his napkin. When Iago was there, Dad always asked him to say the grace. When he wasn't, Dad usually said, "God save all here," and left it at that. When Dad wasn't there, Mam said, "Eat your greens, bach."

Once or twice a year Mam's sister, Lowri, came to visit us on holiday, bringing her English husband, John, a railway guard from Manchester, with her. He was a mild little man with sandy hair, fish eyes, and a pension due in fifteen years. On arrival, Aunt Lowri would hand us a largesse of lollipops, sweets, and comics, the only ones we ever saw. She wore powder and scent, so it took time for Angharad and me to get used to her; by the time we'd done that it was time for her to go back to England. So many rings and bracelets had she that it was like being visited by the empress of China, and there was only Uncle John to spoil the illusion. Uncle John rarely talked of anything but his work. Listening to him was like having a London and Northeastern Railway timetable read to us. He used to go down to the shore, roll his trousers up to the knee, and wade in the sea along the sand—some people thought he was an escaped lunatic. He did not drink at all, but he smoked foul-smelling tobacco in a huge curved pipe and wore suspenders as well as a belt. He had been gassed on the Somme battlefield in the war and had asthma, and he snored so loudly that we were always glad to see his back when the time came for him to leave. He was a very short man, and Dad said he had duck's disease: "His rear end is too near the deck."

But the most memorable of all our visitors, as his voice rose and fell with the firelight leaping on the whitewashed kitchen wall, was Cadell Rum, a tall, lanky, gaunt sailing skipper of a man of around sixty. His hair, eyes, and beard were gypsy-dark. He had the face of a weather-worn devil when he was worked up, and of a benign sea sprite when in repose. He was a magical man who carried with him to Llangareth the emerald palms of silver coral islands waving in the trade wind breeze. He brought them to moving life; he made them weave in the wind, like shaggy mountain bulls at the challenge.

As Mam poured the tea from the great cozied pot, her dark head bent, her eyes forever glancing and smiling at Dad, Cadell's voice sang and chanted, and he took us to where the bergs calve off the glaciers, or up some dark alleyway rife with skullduggery in Bombay or Madagascar, or to a storm-swept open anchorage on the bleak coast of Chile. When Cadell told a tale everyone, even *Mister* Jeffreys-Geography (although he understood little Welsh), stared, entranced by his gestures and expressions, as Cadell's voice, full of the rolling seas and the calls of the petrel, nailed us all to his eyes, lashed us to his memories, and carried us on his laughter. In those moments Cadell held Llangareth in his warm, gentle, callused hands.

I don't recall Cadell's real family name, if I ever knew it. It was probably Jones, Roberts, Williams, Hughes, Jenkins, Lewis, Evans, Griffiths, Lloyd, Morris, Powell, Parry, Pugh, Howard, Rhys, or Thomas. Family names in West Wales are few, mainly because of the want of imagination on the part of the English censors who first imposed surnames on the Welsh in the early seventeenth century. Before that, and still among the Welsh, a person was and is known by his calling, the locality of his home, or some personal idiosyncrasy. The nature of Cadell's tendency was quite clear. If rum and bottles had not been invented, they would have been for Cadell; yet I never once saw him falter or stagger, nor did I ever hear him swear or slur a word.

Once, a discussion was taking place between Dad, Morgan Lewis, and Cadell on the differences between sailing in the far north and the far south. "The arctic," expounded Cadell, "and the sky a hummingbird's wing, all the rainbows that had ever been lighting the ice with the gleams of Paradise; the sea slate blue and the hump of Cape Farewell away to the north, the only welcome farewell that ever a sailor had in a lively wind and a rising sea." He hesitated, took a swig of strong tea, frowned, and went on: "The antarctic, and the sky a lake of blood painting the ripples of the sea with snakes' forked tongues and scorpions' stings, and the sea green-deep over the skulls of the green navies shimmering below and above the light leaping. Our ship a poor intruder in the halls of the Mighty and the words of mere men nibbling at the moon's face under the Aurora Australis and the frosted Cross over the edge of a frozen universe, and shadows of priestlike clouds traipsing over the rimed beaches like mammoths tramping over stones, and a scavenger's wind, cold and vengeful over the world. In those seas' dark coming it is all a man can do to remember the presence of Jehovah . . . and the penguins (Welsh word that is, bach) debating over bleached bones of deep-diving right whales, like landlords arguing a rent raise on the day before the crack of doom. . . ."

"Hard winds in the north, hard men in the south," concluded Morgan Lewis.

Dad was home for Christmas only once between 1934 and 1937. That, of course, was a more joyful Christmas than the others, although Mam always did her best for us. We took no trees to the houses in West Wales, but we did hang holly and mistletoe around. No one wore their best clothes at Christmas or Easter; it was supposed to be an affront to God. There was a droll contrast between the drawing room, with a sparkling white tablecloth and the best china service out for Christmas dinner, and our family, the widow Carregen, and Blind Sioni, all in our oldest clothes. I don't know whether this was the custom in the rest of Wales, but in the west it was. The widow and Blind Sioni were invited not only because they were friends and poorer than we; Carregen played the piano well, and Sioni had a very good bass voice. In those days, when the wireless reception left much to be desired, that was important. The presents for Angharad and me were put before the fireplace on the day *after* Christmas. The ones from Santa Claus were unwrapped, so Angharad knew what he had brought, and, by the wrappings, what Mam and Dad had given her. They were not much, for we were not well off, but as we had no comparisons to make we were content enough.

Presents to outsiders were mainly food from the garden—eggs for the postman, a sack of potatoes for Carregen—and only Blind Sioni had a bought present, a half-pound of Dutch tobacco.

The winters were hard outside the cottage. The rain drove in almost continually from the Irish Sea, and the wind scrambled over the roof and howled up on the heights, but inside the house we were warm and cozy enough, and so was Caradoc in his stable. We had three big wooden barrels of fresh water inside the house by the end of October, in case the spring supply froze. When the hay was taken in during the late autumn, some of it was carried up into the attic of the house, to act as extra insulation under the slate roof. This worked, and it gave refuge to a host of mice, so our two cats were both well fed all winter, until the last of the hay was taken outside in the springtime.

Cesar, our dog, was a Welsh collie. He slept in a kennel outside the kitchen door, winter and summer, guarding everything around. He was so jealous of Llangareth that he would never leave the place willingly, and instead of running on the uplands, like the other dogs around, he ran barking and woofing around and around the house. Except, that is, when the widow Carregen's bulldog bitch was in heat; then Cesar haunted her gate, but he never, I believe, got anywhere with her—she was a fierce bitch and proud of her lineage. In some ways that was a pity; it would have been interesting to see the outcome of that union.

Throughout my schooling, the days were long and wearisome for much of the time. Although Mam was always up before me, I rose at dawn and was out of the house to feed Caradoc, the pigs, and the chickens. Then I got the day's coal into the kitchen and pumped water into the pot-boiler while Mam got the breakfast ready. It was usually oatmeal. By seven o'clock Angharad and I had eaten, and I had saddled Caradoc. By seven-thirty we were off to school, at Penybont, four miles away, where we arrived about eight-thirty. We always took our lunches with us, usually bread and drippings in the winter, bread and jam in the summer. We stayed in the one classroom all day, except for the hour lunch break, when we were forced out into the playground, regardless of the weather, to play and fight with the other children. I don't recall learning much at school: simple sums, and that a lot of the map of the world was colored red, and that we had a new king in London (the old one had died after his Jubilee mugs had been passed out to us in 1935). The new king was the old Prince of Wales, and we were told that he was going to usher in a new world of hope and joy for the Principality of Wales.

Our teacher, *Mister* Jeffreys-Geography, was a tall, ascetic Englishman, with gingery hair sparse above his ears and nothing on the crown of his head but skin and the light that shone through the classroom window. He always wore a jersey, a tweed jacket, and gray flannel slacks, and he pursed his lips as if he were sucking on a gooseberry. When he spoke fast, which was about 80 percent of the time, he immediately lost the attention of the twenty-nine Welsh-speakers out of his thirty pupils. The one exception was Iolo (Educated Evans), the fat boy from Aran Fawddwy, away up over the uplands. He was staying with his uncle a mile or two from Llangareth, his English mother having gone to London with her fancy man.

At school I enjoyed history, geography, art (which meant drawing on a slate in one chalk color—white), and composition. It was only in composition that we children of the singing land were ever allowed to let our imaginations roam freely—as long as it was not too freely. The lessons I disliked most were religious instruction (which bored me to silent tears), arithmetic, and algebra.

History generally commenced with an account of how the Greeks and Romans were the only fount of our culture, and how the rest of humanity (the Celts especially) had been savage barbarians. History generally stopped somewhere in the 1880s, with the English having civilized practically all of the world. Very little was ever taught of the American Revolution and the first loss of a British colony, but *Mister* Jeffreys-Geography went into minute detail about how the heathen Indian mutineers had imprisoned English women and children in the Black Hole of Calcutta, and how General Gordon had quelled whole armies of the fanatical enemy in China. Nothing was ever mentioned of the Chinese Opium Wars. The greatest heroes were Wolfe of Quebec, Clive of India, and David Livingstone. The heroines were Queen Elizabeth I, Florence Nightingale, Grace Darling, and Queen Victoria. I never knew, until I was much older, that, for example, the men who won the battle of Agincourt were Welsh archers. To *Mister* Jeffreys-Geography, Wales seemed to be a sort of appendix to England. In what little he taught us of literature, there was Chaucer and Shakespeare, of course, and Milton, Byron, Keats, and Tennyson, but I don't recall his once mentioning any of the Welsh poets or writers. No Daffyd ap Gwilyn, no Taliesin, no Caradoc Evans, no Rhys Davies, no Arthur Machen, no W. H. Davies; it was as if the mountains of Wales had always been deathly silent, and as if the echoing valleys and the chanting uplands had been the home of faceless, dumb illiterates, as cloddy as the bogs of Saxonia, as dim and silent as the fog-bound marshes of East Anglia.

But you can't make an Englishman out of a Welshman any more than you can a cat out of a canary, and so it was that toward the end of my school days *Mister* Jeffreys-Geography was beginning to show signs of discouragement. He even, in unthinking moments of frustration, descended into mocking mimicry of the English-speaking Welsh, of such worthies as the local tobacconists and post-office proprietors, with their "Indeed to goodness" and "Look you, man," and all that false balderdash.

Caradoc was left tied to a tree while we were in school. The ride to and from school in the spring and summer was always a pleasure, but in wintertime it could be a misery. At least we were so near to the sea that we rarely got more than a foot of snow at a time. Llangareth was snowbound only once; I think that was in the winter of thirty-six. Along the road there was very little traffic, perhaps a horse-pulled hay wain and one or two motorcars or a lorry (truck) but most of the time the road was deserted except for a few foot travelers, tramping gentlemen of the road and gypsys, whom we avoided as they were (falsely) supposed to steal children. In the summer I took short cuts on Caradoc across the uplands, among the gorse and heather in the patches of sunlight between the rolling shadows of the clouds.

In the evening, after tea, there was, except in the depths of winter, always an hour or two's stint for me in the garden or in the small greenhouse where we grew young plants for spring sowing. There was always something to do. Then it was supper at eight o'clock and bed at nine, but I was allowed to read with my little oil lamp until ten o'clock. So the days went, except for Sundays. No one worked then, of course, except for Mam and me—I fed the livestock.

Mine was not an easy childhood, but it had its compensations, and it was good training for the many harder years to follow. It was not an unusual childhood for that part of Wales. The land was harsh and not easily worked. Money was in short supply, and I doubt that, between 1934 and 1938, I ever saw more cash at any one time than a half-crown piece (fifty cents); I doubt that anyone in the neighborhood did. The average pay for a farm laborer then was rarely more than twenty-eight shillings a week (just under six dollars). Throughout the land, hundreds of thousands of unemployed men and their families subsisted on a dole of only about seventeen shillings (three and a half dollars) a week.

Sometimes, in the early autumn harvest time, we saw men, shabbily dressed and gaunt, who had tramped the eighty miles or so from the idle coalfields of the Rhondda Valley, in South Wales, looking for casual work. They were a piteous sight, with patched-up clothes and broken boots, but they were generally given food and drink and some kind of shelter by the country folk. Some of them were so poor that they split up wooden matches with a razor blade, in four slivers, to save spending a farthing (a cent) on a box of matches. But toward the time I left home, in late spring of 1938, the situation had eased a little and there were fewer men on the road. We didn't know why this was, of course. We didn't know that the country had started slowly, very slowly, to gear itself for another war.

5

Something for Wales

During the winter of 1937–38 Dad came home for about three weeks. The tug on which he worked was in dock for an engine replacement. I got to know him, and his ideas, more during that period than any other. Although he was very proud of being Welsh, he was far from being a Nationalist. His attitude was that the Welsh were the ancient British race, and we were therefore more British than anyone else. If any nation in the British Islands wanted to separate themselves, then it was from *us* they should separate, and not us from them.

We had a radio by then, and on the night of the Tommy Farr–Joe Louis boxing match in New York, all the neighbors from miles around crowded into our kitchen to hear the fight, which, I believe, was the first direct transatlantic public broadcast ever made. After a hard, punch-for-punch match, Joe Louis was declared the winner on points. When the results were declared, as millions listened in all over the English-speaking world, the American radio-commentator shoved his microphone under Tommy Farr's nose and asked him how he felt. Tommy, an ex-miner from the South of Wales, replied bloodily and breathlessly: "Well, as you can see, I've got plenty of guts. That's old Tommy Farr, you know. . . ." Then, as if it explained everything that made him stay the whole course hammering away at and being hammered by the "Brown Bomber," he said quietly, "I'm a Welshman, you know."

"There's a real Welshman for you!" cried Educated Evans, the fat boy from Aran Fawddwy, him with an English mother. All over the little, tight land of Wales two million people had been waiting for many years for someone to say that to the world.

Dad said: "If Tommy Farr had been Irish everyone in America would have known he was, long ago. The Irish make such a noise over there, what with songs and films, and here we are, the Irish the closest race to us physically and mentally (except for their religion), and no one knows the Welsh even exist. They look upon us as some kind of semi-English, and the land as a sort of English county. God knows we've been here twice as long as the English, probably twice as long as that, too."

"Arr, you're just jealous of the Irish," retorted Cadell Rum, "the Irish who've almost completely lost the Gaelic tongue and are so busy beating down the English with their own language; so busy proving that they are capable of doing anything the English can do, and do it better; so busy aping the English— especially in America. Why, I never met an Irish-American yet that wasn't so busy trying to clamber up the ladder of social success that he'd never had the time to even think about his own true culture. There's damned few of them I ever met that knew anything farther back than the potato famine, and none at all who ever knew that before the American Revolution a good third of emigrants to America were Welsh folk, starved out of their own land . . . but practically everyone in the States knows about how hard the Irish have had it, and the Irish, with their damned sentimentality, and penchant for self-pity, play on the tune to the hilt. Let's face it, we Welsh are just plain jealous of the Irish. We're jealous of the English, too, the Germans, the Russians, the Italians, even the Americans, God help us! But most of all we're jealous of the Irish in America. We can't see why everyone in America knows all about Ireland, takes Irish names—except most of the Negroes; they have Welsh names they got from the white plantation settlers in the South (there's a shame on us!) during their slavery. Why, the Americans like to sing Irish songs—what there are of them, for compared to our many songs, Irish songs are like palm trees in Wales—few, far between, and ragged. We can't understand why the Americans like to crack Irish jokes and visit Irish beauty spots (if there are any). We think that the English and the Americans should do all these things with us, for we're far more richly endowed with them, Lord knows."

"So we are, so we are," murmured Dad in agreement. Then he added: "Wales is one of the smallest countries in the world, right enough, but there's no earthly reason why it should be, and it certainly is one of the least efficiently publicized. Although we have, by every reasonable criterion, far better claims to be labeled a 'nation' [when Dad said this we could hear the quotation marks] than either Scotland or Ireland, it is, as you well know, practically impossible to find anyone in all of Europe, away from the docks, who knows that Wales even exists."

"True," said Cadell, "and most of those that do know it exists think that our land is part of England."

Dad warmed to his subject, "Right! *You* try to tell them about Wales. I've tried it, God knows I've tried it! Tell them about our language, one of the oldest in Europe, and probably the most beautiful and musical. Talk to them in Welsh. They listen dubiously, skeptically, not knowing what they are hearing, but they nod knowingly and say—and this is the ultimate insult—'No doubt it is an English dialect.' This they say of a language as different from English as is Greek, a language which has ten different words for one English word, which boasts art forms and poetic rhythms unknown in any other language, and which, God save us, has attracted scholars from all over Europe for centuries." Dad paused for a moment to let all this sink in.

"Right you are, Sion," agreed Catrin Powell, who, besides Dad and Cadell, was probably the best-read person in the room.

Dad was warming up even more now. He stood up and placed his thumb inside his jacket armpit, just like Morgan Morbid Preacher, who visited Llangareth Chapel from time to time, whenever the congregation was off guard. Dad went on: "We Welsh are not a popular race. That, we know, is true. The English don't like us much, but we don't allow that to worry us. The English have verbs—'to Scotch,' 'to Jew,' 'to Welsh.' There are subtle distinctions. 'To Scotch' is to get the better of someone, vigorously, even ruthlessly, but not exactly unfairly. 'To Jew' is to swindle, right enough, but there is the suggestion that the victim got all he deserved. 'To Welsh,' however, means to be just sheer mean, 'caddish,' as the English say. It's as if you took money out of a blind man's collection tin. When a bookie tries to clear off without settling his debts on winnings due, that's 'Welshing.' That meaning of the word, that obscenity, is used all over the English-speaking world."

Everyone was silent as Dad thought for a moment. Then he said quietly, "Perhaps it's us who've been *Englished?*"

There was muffled laughter in the kitchen for a moment, until Cadell raised his hand for silence. "The English, in their wisdom," he said, "are convinced that we are a dishonest race of people. A lot of Welsh lasses work as servants in London; the English, who don't at all mind having them because they work hard without grumbling, say they tell lies and steal silk stockings. The English, poetic souls that they are, have a rhyme —'Taffy was a Welshman, Taffy was a thief, Taffy came to my house and stole a side of beef. . . .' Of course, they don't know that they are referring to the frequent invasions of England in the Middle Ages by Welsh cattle rustlers—if you can call stealing stock on land which by rights should be yours 'rustling'— but we have our own subtle and secret notions about property and abstract truths, because we are odd, tortuous people. George Meredith, who was Welsh-descended, said, 'There are two natures—Human Nature and Welsh Nature!' Then again, my son in America sent me a cutting from a magazine which is published over there. In it, the Scottish Professor J. B. S. Haldane—a biologist, in case anyone here is unfamiliar with the name—wrote about the English for the Americans. He referred to the unpopularity of the Welsh among the English and said that for himself he found us quick-witted, emotional, and, if you please, delightful company. This is probably the first time that a Scotsman has ever called the Welsh delightful, and no doubt it will be the last, and I think it is a good job that the article was not printed in Wales. We've *hauled* a few *Danes* before, usually six feet off the ground with a rope."

Almost everyone in the room, with the exception of the youngest children, caught Cadell's pun and laughed uproariously. When the merriment ceased, Dad rejoined: "The English find us cocksure and offensive. This is curious, because we ourselves by this time, after four hundred and two years of English domination, are rather proud of boasting of our sense of racial inferiority. The national pastime in Wales is using this as an alibi for failure to make money or become famous. Our sense of racial inferiority is the handiest crutch most of us have at this time, and without it we'd be limping along. There are a lot of Welsh folk in England today, right enough—about one hundred thousand in Liverpool alone, and probably a quarter of a million in Greater London—and probably a million in Patagonia, God only knows how many in Australia, New Zealand, and the Falklands, and three million or so in America, if you count the ones with parents born in Wales—and if we have not the commercial insidiousness of the Armenian in Istanbul or the blatant acquisitiveness of the Corsican in Marseilles, at any rate, we are not doing too badly."

Dad paused for another moment, to let all this sink in, and to take a swig from the mug of hot tea that Mam had set before him. He went back to his declamation: "Welsh politicians are shrewd, flexible, telepathic fellows who, once they abjure principle, become extremely useful instruments of the vested interests [an American would have said 'big business']. David Lloyd George, J. H. Thomas, Frank Hodges, and others are Welshmen who have gained considerable rewards for their services to England, to John Bull, Limited, from time to time. Wales has specialized in helping the British Empire to turn nasty corners. A Welsh family, the Tudors, took over after the bloody gang warfare of the Wars of the Roses; Oliver and Richard Cromwell were Welshmen—their real name was Williams; Lloyd George took over as prime minister in 1917, when the war was going at its worst for the Allies. That was a job no Scot or Saxon was keen on at all."

Dad took another sip of tea and stared for a moment through the kitchen window. Outside, rain was falling, veiling the early-evening hills in a blue mist.

"Today," Dad's voice filled the room, "in the year of grace 1938, Welsh politics are . . . complex. Our tradition is Liberalism, which was Wales's way of showing she wasn't too enthusiastic about British jingoism and the Empire, but today the South is solidly Socialist, with strong Communist leanings, and no wonder, with an unemployment rate of twenty-eight percent, and even more among the miners! The tradition in recent

English politics suggests that if ever there is a revolution in Great Britain it will come about through a general strike. This strike will be forced by the miners, nearly a million of them, and it will be forced on the miners by the South Wales Miners' Federation, the most militant organization of its kind in Western Europe. That federation is in the charge of a man that very few people in Britain know anything about, and of whom practically nobody in Europe or America has heard. He is Arthur Horner, known to every industrial worker in South Wales as the president of the SWMF. He is a tiny, bespectacled Marxist who really means business, and his business is a Soviet Britian. The problem is that Horner is respected by even his bitterest opponents. That makes him the most important man in Wales in 1938. If socialism ever comes about in Britain, it will be through people whom Horner has sponsored, or at least sanctioned—men like Nye Bevan of Ebbw Vale."

"What about the Welsh in America?" asked Educated Evans, who had relatives in California.

"We made our mark mainly in New England, New York, and Pennsylvania, though there are Welsh-descended communities in many other states. Many of the earliest settlers in Maine, Massachusetts, and Connecticut were Welsh, great believers in tolerance and freedom—from one of them that keen egalitarian J. P. Morgan is descended. The iron and coal industries of Pennsylvania owe much to Welsh skill and labor. Thousands of Welsh families—many of them still speaking Welsh at home—live around Scranton and Pittsburgh. In American politics Welsh names are legion, from Thomas Jefferson and Governor Morgan of New York (who arranged the financing of Washington's army) onward. In all, we have given the United States fourteen presidents who were Welsh on at least one side of their families, fifteen if you count Jefferson Davis of the Confederacy. His adversary, Lincoln, was Welsh on his mother's side. There have been more presidents of the United States with Welsh blood than of any other race except the English. John L. Lewis, the president of the United Mineworker's Union, is Welsh on both sides. Justices Charles Evans Hughes and Owen Josephus Roberts of the United States Supreme Court are both the sons of Welsh fathers.

"What about the pictures? The films?" chirped Educated

Evans. Films were practically our only source of information on America.

"The father of American filming was a pure Welshman, D. W. Griffith. Among your so-called stars, Myrna Loy is Welsh. Her name, like Cromwell's, is really Williams. Cary Grant, too. There are many more, to be sure," replied Dad.

"Frank Lloyd Wright," said Catrin Powell. "I read that he was born in a Welsh settlement in Wisconsin."

There were puzzled looks all around, except on Dad and Cadell.

"He's a famous architect," Catrin explained, "and Frank Harris, the author, was born here."

"And Meredith Lewis, of the Lewis and Clark Expedition," added Dad.

"So was Stanley, the man who found Livingstone in Africa," said Cadell Rum, "and John Paul Jones was Welsh on both sides, although he was born in Scotland. Most Americans don't know about these things. All they know us for is some vague vision of miles and miles of coalfields. They don't know that Wales has more castles than any other country in Europe—and probably the world—and that most of the land is wild and beautiful . . . and that we once had more sailors and sailing vessels for the size of our population than any other country on earth. Few Welsh people go to America now; for the most part we are not rich, although we Welsh sailors, as we all know, get around the world energetically, only to pull silently at our pipes when we get back home. We never sent to America the five million that Ireland sent after the potato famine. The English didn't treat us quite as badly as that. Peaceful penetration is our method—not only over here, but in America, Canada, Argentina, Australia, and New Zealand, too. The other folk in those lands may not be aware of us Welsh, but we are everywhere, and at least we know each other." Cadell, as he said this, gestured toward each one of us in turn.

Heads were nodding in agreement as Cei stuck his head out of the door and announced that the rain had stopped. One by one our guests bade us good night, and soon Angharad and I crept up to bed, and left Mam and Dad alone in the kitchen, in the firelight and their own warmth for each other.

We were proud, after all, that Tommy Farr, a Welshman, one

of a nation of only two million, had stayed the course with the best boxer in a nation of one hundred seventy million souls. It wasn't a great deal, except for Tommy Farr, but it was something that someone, at long, long last, had done for Wales.

6

To England and to Sea

The widow Carregen died early in April 1938. Mam had visited the old woman two or three times a day for weeks, taking gruel and clean clothes down to her cottage and trying to find out whether she had any relatives. Finally, just before she died, the widow gave Mam the address of a grandson of hers in Monmouth named Davy Harris. Mam wrote to Davy right away, but by the time he arrived, chubby and prosperous-looking in his melton overcoat, brown shoes, and motorcar, Carregen was already in her coffin. That had been made by Goodness Gracious Jenkins, who served Llangareth as undertaker and gravedigger. Davy stayed for the wake, which was a lively affair. People came from miles around, because Carregen had delivered practically every child in the area for thirty-five years and more, and she'd cured just about anyone who either couldn't afford or did not trust the doctors.

Davy's car was a tiny Austin Seven with a dicky (or outside back) seat. It wasn't practical to carry the coffin on it, so the local men, Goodness Gracious and Pedr and Blind Sioni among them, all in their best Sunday suits, lugged it up the hill from Bwthyn Carregen to Llangareth Chapel. The choir and other folk had a fine time roaring out "Nearer My God to Thee" and other hymns. After the service they set to on the wake high-tea that Mam and Mrs. Powell had worked to put together all the previous night in the Cottage Carregen. It was a quite a spread. Beef and lamb sandwiches, biscuits and pastry, and a half-dozen bottles of ale that Davy had brought over in his Austin Seven for each of the men. Everyone seemed to have a good time, even Angharad, who had loved Carregen more than anyone else had. The wake ended about dusk, and then Davy was left alone in his grandmother's cottage. After a day or so he returned to his job as a traveling salesman, saying that on his rounds he would look for a new tenant for the cottage.

By this time I was almost fourteen. Both Cei and I were missing school now more and more, but *Mister* Jeffreys-Geography didn't seem to mind. He knew that we were working whenever we could find the opportunity to earn a few pennies or shillings for our families: planting potatoes, digging ditches, repairing stone walls—whatever odd jobs we could find on the local farms. It was not unusual in those days for boys still at school to do that. We were also going out fishing more, and on a few occasions Goodness Gracious's catch was good enough for him to give us both a shilling or two to take home.

As we were now earning a little money, Cei and I were allowed to go into one of the nearby towns on Saturdays, to the cinema or rugby matches. There we made many pals among the local lads. Some of them were interested in only what was before their noses—films, girls, football, rugby, and playing illegal pitch-and-toss with pennies in the alleyways, always with a couple of youths on the lookout for the bobbies. Others seemed to be much brighter, and we talked about what was going on in the world, about the Spanish Civil War and the Italian invasion of Abyssinia. So far as I remember, I don't think there was any one of the lads who did not believe that another war was inevitable. They accepted the prospect just as we accept the coming of winter. Many of the older single men who hung around had been in the First World War, in the trenches, and the gory stories they told us did little to cheer us up. They said that the chances of "going over the top" to charge an enemy trench and surviving alive or unwounded were about one in four. I hear a lot these days, a half-century later, about the British desire to appease the dictators. As far as West Wales went, all I remember hearing the ordinary folk talk about was getting over there and clobbering them. It was probably different among the upper classes. It usually is.

"What will you do if they call you up?" Cei asked me as we rode home one Saturday evening.

"Join the navy. You won't catch me in a muddy trench with

a bullying sergeant and one chance in four of getting through it alive," I replied. "What about you?"

"Air force, ground crew," replied Cei. "That's what I'll go for. Learn a lot and no fighting, see? You won't find me getting gassed like your Uncle John or poor old Nye Philips. Anyway, there's plenty of time to make up our minds. There won't be a war for several years yet. It'll take those silly old buggers in London that long to wake up. . . ."

A few days later I rode Caradoc up the valley to the road to meet Rhys-the-Post. He no longer wore the old, flat-topped, double-peaked helmet he used to, with its big brass badge. Now he wore an ordinary-looking peaked cap, like a bus driver or a cinema attendant, and he rode a bicycle instead of a pony. But it was still the same old Rhys, whistling away as he pedaled along the road. "Something for you, bach!" he hollered as he drew up to me in the thin rain. He handed me a brown envelope. I grabbed it. Dad's handwriting!

I shoved the envelope into my belt under my oilskin cape, turned Caradoc, and egged him on back down to our cottage. The pony sensed my excitement and trotted as fast as he could at his age down the rocky track into the valley.

"Letter from Dad, Mam!" I hollered as Caradoc picked his way through the broken-toothed rocks on the lee side of the house. The smell of baking bread wafted through the window where Mam stood, her hair pinned back, her strong features relaxed in the smile she kept especially for me. I jumped off Caradoc, who wandered off into his lean-to stable warm with hay.

"Wipe your feet, bach!" Mam called as the half-door creaked open.

"He's still in Liverpool, Mam; see the postmark. . . ."

Mam took the letter, damp and brown and folded. She brushed the flour off her hands and sat down at the kitchen table to read it.

"What does he say, Mam?" Dad had promised to try to find me a job on the tugs in Liverpool. I doffed my dripping oilskin cape and threw it over the clotheshorse.

"Wait a minute, bach," she said offhandedly as she concentrated on the letter.

I waited impatiently. There were several pages, and Mam read each one carefully, her brows knitted at first, then smiling to herself as she read the last page. Finally she looked up at me and said, "Dad's found you a job, bach . . . look." She read out part of the letter: " ' . . . and Mr. Albert Edward Lee, the captain, I've known for years. He's a good man in a steady trade. The experience will be good for Tristan and will stand him in good stead when we later get him into the Conway Training Ship. . . .' "

I butted in: "What's the ship, Mam? Is she oceangoing? What's her name?" Despite my excitement, I tried to keep my voice low.

Mam gazed at me over her reading spectacles. "Mmm . . . let me see now. . . ." She turned back the page. "Here it is: *Second Apprentice,* out of Harwich' . . . well, that's a good respectable port, plenty of chapel folk there, as I recall."

"When can I go, Mam? Can I go tomorrow?"

For a moment Mam gazed at me silently, showing no expression. Then she said: "Your Dad says next week. He's going to send your fare then. He says it's not legal in England for you to work until you're fourteen anyway, and that's not until the eighth of next month. You'll be off at the end of April. Dad says the boat will be in . . . let's see now. . . ." She gazed at the letter, frowning the while until she found it: " 'Rye.' " (Mam pronounced it "Reeya." It was not a deepwater port, so she'd never been there, and she was speaking Welsh.)

"Reeya; where's that, Mam?"

"Somewhere near London, your Dad says." She looked up at the clock on the mantlepiece above the big old iron stove. "Time for you to be off and meet Angharad. School's out now, and the bus will be halfway here."

I grabbed my oilskin cape off the clothes horse and flung it over my shoulders. Mam came to my side and put her arm around my shoulders. "I'll make you a cup of tea before you go, bach," she murmured.

On the way up the road, perched atop Caradoc, I reflected that it would be some time before I could attend the Conway Training Ship, up in the Menai Strait off Anglesea. I would have to be sixteen before I could go there to study, and then I could go to sea in a merchant ship as an apprentice. Then there would be a further three or four years before I could expect to sit for my fourth mate's certificate. As was the custom in those days, I would have to support myself until I was old enough to go to Conway; what little money my family possessed had been put by for that very purpose. Now Dad had kept his promise: after months of asking and writing to many friends, he had found me a ship.

Angharad was at first pleased and excited at my coming fortune, but then she fell into a pique as Caradoc jogged his way down the valley toward the cottage. She didn't like the thought that I would be going through London and would see the new king and queen, while she wouldn't; but I promised to send her a doll from America when the ship arrived there, and so she forgot about my coming visit to London, the great, grand capital of the mighty world-embracing Empire on which the sun never set.

The new king was not now the old Prince of Wales, who had promised to perform such miracles for his Principality. The new king was his brother, George. There had been a scandal of some kind, but we children had been kept in the dark about it. It was not "fit for children's ears." From what little we knew, an American woman was involved, but her name was never mentioned in adult conversations. Mysteriously, she was always referred to as "That Woman." Now that the old Prince of Wales had gone off and left us to our own devices, "That Woman" was never mentioned at all. It was as though she had never existed. Soon it was as if the prince himself had never been; he too was never mentioned after the new king was crowned. It was as though a favorite son had gone bad and been disowned.

That night, after Angharad had become accustomed to the idea of my leaving home, we lay awake for hours while I told her of the wonders of London, the crown princes and their gowned princesses and Indian *subadhars* wearing diamonds in their turbans and riding Arabian horses, their eyes and medals and scimitars flashing in the sunlight as they trotted along, just as we had seen, our eyes wide with wonder, at coronation time in the penny picture-house in Dolgellau.

"Then you won't want Caradoc anymore!" Angharad pouted, her eyes brimming with ears. "You'll say he's too old and scruffy. You won't want to ride him; you'll leave him until the day he dies."

"Not I, geneth ["girl"] Angharad," I promised her as a tear left her cheek and dolloped onto her counterpane. "I'll never forget Caradoc, nor you, nor Mam, nor Dad; not anything nor anyone in Llangareth. That way, you see, *chwaergen* [little sister], none of you will ever die."

Angharad looked at me, her hazel eyes shimmering, "And we won't forget you, Tristan bach," she whispered, half-asleep. Her hair had fallen over her elfin face, lit by the *derwydd* (druid) moon casting silver dream-drifts over the shadowy, magical hills. Then a cloud-curtain was drawn by the west wind, but gently, over Llangareth, and Angharad slept, *plentyn yng Nghymru,* a child in Wales.

It's a long time ago. Since that night, the first night I ever found it impossible to sleep, the earth has voyaged around the sun forty-three times and has spun on its axis almost sixteen thousand times, and an extra ten spins for the leap years . . . and for luck.

The week that followed was one of excitement mounting and diminishing in turn. Both Mam and Angharad made extra fuss over me, with larger than usual helpings of puddings, and going through my shirts and socks again and again, to make sure no darning was needed. It was arranged that when I went away Cei would look after my chores, and take a share of the garden and stock produce for his trouble. That would help both Mam and the Powell family a great deal.

Each afternoon I was up at the top of the valley, waiting on the road for Rhys-the-Post to bring the letter from Dad. Each day Rhys stopped to chat and tell me all about the wonders of London, which he'd visited for a rugby match ten or eleven years before. And each evening friends called at the cottage to visit and converse with Mam and me. The news had spread around the neighborhood with amazing speed and inaccuracy, and we were only too anxious to set the record straight. No, I had not been left a fortune by a rich uncle in New Zealand;

no, I was not going into service as a stable boy; no, I was not going to work for the post office or the railway (almost every lad's parents' dream at the time).

Finally, after one of the longest weeks of my life, Dad's letter, together with the fare to Rye, arrived. I was wild with excitement and could not understand why Mam and Angharad seemed to be so sad.

"A seagoing vessel trading to the Continent," wrote Dad in his letter, "to France, Belgium, Holland, and Germany, so you will see something of the world and foreign customs. *Second Apprentice* is a good, sound, seaworthy vessel, a ketch-rigged topsail 'boomie,' and Captain Lee is a most respectable, very able gentleman who will teach you a good steady trade and who will look after you as if you were his own son instead of being the well-loved son of your affectionate, Dad.

"P.S. The pay is not much, but it will keep you well until you can go to Conway."

On the same day Dad's letter arrived, so did Davy Harris, the dead widow Carregen's grandson. He had been on a selling trip through North Wales, and he called in at his grandmother's cottage to check that all was well and to have a word with Mam, who was taking care of the place for him until Davy could find a tenant. So far he had not been successful.

Upon hearing that I was bound for London, he offered to take me in his car as far as Newport, in Monmouthshire; then I would catch the train from there to London. It would save a few shillings in fare. Mam jumped at Davy's offer, and arrangements were set for me to be on my way the next day. I was pleased. I liked Davy, who was plump and jolly, even though it was difficult for me to understand either his strange Welsh or his rapidly slurred South Walian English. He was in his late twenties, I guessed, and he had a wife and eight-year-old daughter at home.

The next day, the day of my departure, was fine and sunny. Angharad burst out crying over breakfast, and Mam was quieter than usual. I went into the stable to wish Caradoc a fond good-bye. Cei turned up early to see me off, and was strangely terse and more manly than he had been until then. That was not only because I was going out into the wide world, but also because he was assuming my responsibilities. He carried my new sea bag, which had been sewn up from sail canvas by Llewellyn Griffith, the half-daft lad from Caernon. Mam fussed over me and made me promise to spend my few shillings on a meat pie and sandwiches for the train from Monmouth, to pick a corridor coach on the train so that I could go to the lavatory, to make sure to follow Dad's written instructions on how to get across London, and to be careful not to lose the ten-shilling note that she had secured inside my coat's inner pocket with two big safety pins.

I told Mam not to fret, and said that I would be home at Christmas, and asked whether she would like a green and red parrot in a cage. She laughed at that and hugged me tight. Then she let me go, and I followed Davy Harris into his car and we were off, up the rocky track that led from Llangareth and my childhood, up to the main road and an unforeseeable future. I waved my hand cursorily as the engine spluttered to life, and then I was off, to England and to sea.

As the little motorcar trundled along the road to Barmouth in the early morning, I could see all the familiar places along the seashore and the beautiful, sad shapes of the mountains back from the coast. Now that I was really on my way to a ship and a job, I was not sure that I was so keen on it after all. Now that the dream had become real, the prospect of going to England became less and less attractive.

But I knew that I would have to go to sea sooner or later, and Dad had made a great effort to get me the berth onboard *Second Apprentice.* I would have to persist.

The car passed into the streets of Dolgellau. Davy Harris stopped outside a chemist's shop, took a folder out of the glove compartment, and disappeared into the shop. I sat in the car waiting, watching people pass by. I lowered myself in the seat; I didn't want them to see me. I felt as though I were in some way betraying them. Then I thought to myself that perhaps my feelings had nothing to do with going to England and the sea. Perhaps I was just growing up. Perhaps it was both together, going to England making me know so suddenly and clearly that my childhood was over.

As I sat there in the car, and later, as Davy drove at a steady rate through the valleys of Montgomeryshire, Radnor, and Breconshire, all greens and blues and little whitewashed cottages just like ours, I remembered many things, like the way I had been always drawing faces in books and filling in newspaper pictures from my cheap tin box of watercolors. I'd spent hours like that, on rainy winter nights, with Mam knitting in her wooden chair by the fire, smiling at me now and then. In chapel on Sundays I had drawn the ministers, and the people sitting in the same pew had looked at Mam and laughed quietly.

My mother used to say that I took mostly after my father's father, Johnny Star. Many people have asked me why I first went to sea. Almost always I've told them jokingly that it was because my grandfather was a sailor, and I thought I was being funny. But perhaps what I said was true enough.

As we meandered through the mid-counties of Wales—the farthest inland I had ever been, although we were never, I think, more than twenty-five miles from the sea—I remembered the fuss that Mam had made over me that morning, how she had fried some eggs for sandwiches and wrapped the sandwiches in paper napkins, which we normally saw only at Christmas and Easter; how she had filled her one thermos flask with tea and pressed it upon Davy Harris, pretending it was for the two of us, and her sorrowful dark eyes all the while upon me, and her hand straying to my arm.

We drove on and on, from village to village through the green-gold valleys, with knots of countrymen, threadbare but healthy-looking and ruddy, standing around at the crossroads or before the rises to the tiny, humpbacked bridges. It was tiresome, waiting for Davy. He'd collect his papers and catalogues from the cubbyhole and say he wouldn't be long, but he was rarely in the chemist's shop for less than half an hour. He wouldn't allow me to leave the car so that he wouldn't be delayed by having to wait for me, and I had to sit there, watching people passing now and then in the quiet village streets.

Then we passed over the heights of South Brecon, and in an instant the land changed. Suddenly there were gray slag heaps all around, and the sky above was gray, and the pouring rain wrote bleakness on the side of a mountain below which flowed a river, black and poisoned from pollution. All the green freshness of Wales was gone.

We followed the long, meandering street of black-gray ter-
raced little houses down the valley. Around us were a dozen
pit-wheels, only one of them moving. "Rhondda," muttered
Davy, as he alighted from the car and disappeared into a tiny,
miserable-looking shop with no display in the grimy windows.

"Is this still Wales?" I called after him as he stepped over the
broken pavement. He didn't hear me and went inside.

The rain fell heavily and the street was empty except for a
scattering of figures across the road, the young to the fore, the
aged and crippled to the rear. They had sacks across their
shoulders and under their arms, and they shuffled along in the
rain toward the slag heap, down from which rumbled tip-
wagons. The thin line of coal scavengers—that is what Davy
called them—moved toward the slag heap with the rain falling
like dust upon their bent shoulders. Steadily, as they turned
the corner off the main street and shuffled toward the mountain of mine-spew, they moved from grayness to blackness.
Men and women, old men, children, babes, dragging after
them all kinds of vehicles—battered old prams, bicycles, crude
carts, two planks of wood and a bent wheel—they all moved
slowly or quickly, the seven ages of mankind, loud and bois-
terous, silent and morose, crying children, feeble old men, the
human debris of a hell that we in West Wales could hardly
have imagined, flanked on either side by an amorphous mass
of rust and filthy litter, South Wales's legacy from the "Industrial Age."

"They're allowed on the tip, to scrounge for good coal," said
Davy, quietly, as I watched the thin string of humanity ascend
the dirty, wet mound. They were all bending now, those who
had reached the slopes, scratching in the muck for a few moments of warmth. So they went on, stumbling and falling,
scratching at the wet sludge and on their way back treading
over the richness of the Welsh earth, barred to them forever.
The only right they had was to pick and scratch and curse and
cry through all their days, wet or fine, that curious pathetic
army that now, as their sacks and battered prams were filled,
moved slowly away and began the tortuous journey back
down from the hill of hell.

All the while I stared. I stared at the slag tip, I stared at the
people, I stared at humanity brought down to a shambling

collection of wrecks, and I hated, with all my heart and soul, whoever had caused this to happen in our land of Wales.

A siren blew. As he started up the car Davy murmured to me, "Look, they're coming out from a shift." I turned my head and looked down the gray, woebegone street. The street was suddenly full of black-grimed miners, some of them, with no jackets, walking in their shirts in the thinning cold rain. They went past the stopped car on either side of us, old men and young boys, staring at us with their white eyes. Their faces were thickly grimed, and their lips, pale pink, seemed made-up, like the girl's who worked in the café at Barmouth. The miners all stared hard at us as they passed, and I think both Davy and I got a bit uncomfortable in the presence of these stern lords of the underworld. There was a kind of pride, a challenge, in their eyes. It seemed to me, as I watched them go by, that they were making things very awkward for Davy in his melton coat and motorcar. The miners looked at us as if there was something they could not quite understand, but once they were past us they did not look back. It occurred to me that they were thinking about us as they went back to their tiny gray homes up the hillside street. They had looked at both Davy and me as if we had come from another planet. I felt a distinct relief as the car started and took off down the street, gathered speed and left the town behind.

But even as the rain finally stopped and we emerged once more out into a green valley, I glanced at Davy; I felt that I understood the miners even more than I understood him, and I felt a strange sort of pride for Wales and for myself because of them.

Later, as the car pulled up outside Davy's semidetached house in Newport, and we were greeted by his even chubbier wife and girl-child, I forgot all about the Rhondda Valley and remembered only how London seemed to be such a hell of a long way from Llangareth. To go there seemed a big thing for a lad like me to do.

I never did find out what Davy sold. He wouldn't talk about it to me, but it must have been a medical item of some kind, because on the way to Newport we stopped at every chemist's shop we came across, and, despite the depression, there seemed to be one of those in every sizable town we passed through.

I recall Newport and the train ride to England that night from Monmouth only vaguely, as if it were a long-lost dream. The Great Western Railway train was pulled by a steam engine that would be tiny to American eyes, but it was a great panting wonder to me. I stared through the window as we wound out of Wales (Wales!), through the seven-mile-long Severn River tunnel, and across the dark, moonlit fields of rich-looking England in 1938. In the early morning light the stationmasters all seemed to wear walrus mustaches and gold watch fobs over their waistcoats, and there were fishmonger's carts on high wheels waiting at the station yards, the fine horses rearing at the impatient engine; and the English folk I overheard in the train, those that I could understand, talked of "peace in our time."

2

Tricks of the Trade

Daeth dirwnod i ffarwelio,
Ag annwyl wlad y Cymro,
Gan sefyll am hen dir y Werddon fras;
Fe gododd y gwynt yn nerthol,
Y mor a'i donnau'n rhuthro,
Gan olchi dros ein llestr annwyl las,

Chorus: Dewch Gymry glan, i wrando ar fy nghân,
Fel bu y fordaith rownd yr Horn, rownd yr Horn!
Sef y trydydd dydd o'r wythnos,
Ychydig cyn y cyfnos,
Gan basio ger glân greigio glannau Môn.

(The day of sailing came around,
We were bound to leave our land of Wales,
We were heading out toward green Ireland's shore,
The wind was blowing out the sails,
The seas were running high, boys,
Tumbling o'er the rail with thunderous roar.

Chorus: Come, Welshmen all,
And listen to my tale,
How we sailed our schooner round the Horn, round the Horn!
Third day of the week it was, boys,
When dawn was just a-breaking,
We passed the rocky shores of Anglesea!)

—First verse and chorus of "Round the Horn"

This is a capstan chantey sung onboard Welsh schooners and
South Georgia whalers, which often took on Welsh crews. On
the whalers the second "rownd yr Horn" was usually bellowed
in English—"round the Horn!" The translation is my own. I
have never heard the song sung completely in English.

7

Ships of the Trade

In the late 1930s, working sail-craft the number of on the coasts of the British Isles and Ireland was about five hundred. Their variety was great. Some were employed only in fishing, others in cargo work, some in a combination of both. Now that they are all gone it is easy to be sentimental about the working sail-craft. Many of them were beautiful things, whether at rest or under sail, and with their passing a whole way of life has disappeared. It was a way of life dogged with hazards and dangers, poorly paid and leaving small profit. Very few working sailors led much better than a poverty-stricken existence. Yet the life demanded a skill, agility, and toughness that few other livelihoods call for, with the exception, perhaps, of a circus acrobat or a mountain Sherpa.

The men and youths that I was to meet during my two years in working sail still command my utmost respect for their abilities, competence, honesty, and hardiness. They were probably the hardiest, and hardest-laboring, workers in the whole of the British Isles.

The variety, build, and rigs of the craft were of an astonishing individuality. I doubt that anyone ever saw two working sail-craft that were exactly the same, and each craft, each skipper, each crew had its own idiosyncracies. Each harbor, each creek, each beach around the British and Irish coasts had developed, over the centuries, its own particular type of hull, its rigging, spars, sails, and fishing gear. The craft were rarely fancy; there was little money to spare from meager profits for decorations, but their fitness for a particular job was the core of their appeal, and bestowed on them the very spirit of their beauty. No honest sailor, looking over them, could deny that. None of the working craft ever looked "quaint" to a sailor. For every line, every form, every curiously shaped hull, spar, or sail there was a good solid reason, grounded in centuries of experience in the often tempestuous seas around the British Isles.

There are two kinds of construction employed in the building of wooden sailing vessels. One method, rooted in the tradition of the Vikings, is known as clinker construction. This was used only where plenty of timber was available. The other method is known as carvel construction and stems from an ancient Mediterranean practice.

In clinker-building, a V-shaped groove is cut in a massive wooden keel on either side, and also in the stem (bow) and stern posts, already joined to the keel. Into these grooves, to port and starboard, the first two, lowest planks of the hull, (the "garboard strakes") are fitted. Then the other planks are added on each side, one after the other, each plank overlapping the one below it. The amount of overlap is known as the "lands" and is proportionate to the width of the plank. When a craft ages and gaps develop in the lands, it is possible to patch them with quarter-round fillets of wood nailed along the underside.

Clinker-building, as we might expect from the Vikings, demands little calculation but a fair amount of craftsmanship to get the shape of the hull right. Each plank is fastened to its neighbor with copper, iron, or galvanized nails, clenched or riveted on the inboard side of the hull over washers known as roves. This job requires two men, one outboard with a hammer and the other inboard supporting the rivet head. To hold the planks in position while they are riveted, iron clamps are used. In the old days, wooden pegs, like enormous clothespegs, were used.

As the shape of the boat takes form, wooden "floors," or beams crossing the keel at right angles, are added. These are through-bolted to the keel with either long copper bolts or "trenails." Trenails were common in all types of wooden vessels in the old days. First a deep hole was made through the floor and into the keel with an auger. Then hardwood pegs, usually of oak, were driven very close-fitting into the holes. When the trenails had been driven home another hardwood wedge was driven into its top, forcing the trenail's fibers outward. When immersed in water, the trenail expanded. A good one would stay in place for the life of the ship—sometimes as much as a hundred years—but others, with poor-quality wood or a wedge omitted by some fraudulent shipwright would leave widows and orphans ashore before a year or two was out.

Slightly aft or forward of the floors, the ship's main frames were fitted. These were bent into shape in a steam chest. Apart from tools and a winch or two, that was about the only "capital equipment" in most of the old shipyards. Between the tops of the frames, athwartships, beams were added, and onto these the deck and any superstructure were fixed.

Clinker-built sailing vessels were found everywhere in Britain, except for West Devon and Cornwall. They had many advantages; they were simple to build and easy to repair, and could stand a great deal of very rough handling by both men and the sea. The clinkered planks tended to bend before they splintered.

Carvel construction demands considerably more draftsmanship and design than clinker-building. First the keel is set up; then a series of carefully cut and shaped frames is fixed vertically athwart the keel. Over this rigid scaffolding a skin of planks is fixed, and that shell is then reinforced inboard by another skin of planks called a "ceiling." Each frame is made up of a number of pieces, and a great deal of skill is required to set them up properly. Each plank butts onto the top of its neighbor; then the joints between the planks is caulked with hemp made from old rope. In the old days, after caulking of the hull was completed, iron straps were added over the hull, on which to anchor the standing rigging; decks were laid; and all of the other fittings, such as windlass bitts and hatch-coamings, were added.

Whichever method was used, the old-time coastal shipbuilders rarely made much money at construction; they made more on repairs to hulls that they had already built. Before the turn of the century, the reasons for wood rot were not well understood, and ventilation in the hulls was usually bad. The resulting repair and replacement of rotting timbers kept many an honest shipyard going up to the Second World War, and some even after.

Taking a quick trip around the coasts of the British Isles in 1938, starting just north of London, and seeking only the offshore "coastal" craft, we would have seen:

Essex Smacks, rarely more than thirty feet in length, but very beamy, and with a deep, straight keel. They were all cutter-rigged, with a gaff main and a longish bowsprit. When they were not working the oyster beds off Jersey Island or Holland, they were either poaching oysters from the beds on the coast of Wales or Scotland, or hauling potatoes from France or lobsters from Norway. Of the Essex Smackmen it was said that they would steal a cargo of brimstone from the devil as long as there were two shillings to be made.

From a little further north, on the coast of Norfolk, hailed the *Lowestoft Sailing Drifters.* These were handsome vessels with a straight stem that seemed to disdain the rough waters they pushed through and drifted over. They were about sixty feet long and were yawl-rigged, with a boomless gaff mainsail. This was so that no one, while working the fishing gear on deck, would be clouted suddenly by the boom. A peculiar thing about them was that once the fishing nets had gone over the side, the mainmast was lowered until its masthead was touching the mizzen masthead. The mainmast was then secured to the mizzen masthead, and the mizzen was reefed down as a weathercock to keep the boat's head to the wind while the vessel drifted with her nets strung out from her bow. I saw only one of these, and I think she was being used as a yacht. Modern yachts could well follow their example by getting rid of top hamper in a blow.

The *Grimsby Sailing Trawlers,* also handsome craft, were about eighty feet long, with a beam of around twenty feet. They were ketch-rigged, with a straight stem and a long, deep keel. In the hull, the cod trawlers had both holds for salted fish and wet-wells for live fish. When the cod were caught, their swim bladders were punctured and they were sent down a pipe into the wet-well. In this way, if the market was down, cod could be kept alive in floating pens in harbor, to await a rise in the price of fish.

All around the southeast coast of England worked the *Billy Boys,* said to be the largest clinker-built craft in Europe. They were ketches, and the larger ones were rigged with a square topsail and t'gallants. They were equipped with leeboards for windward work. Their hulls were almost square in section, which allowed them to sit on a beach at low tide to discharge coal into horse-drawn carts, or load bricks, clay, manure, or whatever the cargo was. Having so much sail and spars, they could not sail with an empty hold, and they often loaded gravel on the beaches for ballast.

The *Scottish Zulus* were lug-rigged ketches around sixty to seventy-five feet overall. Over their carvel hulls were fixed three massive iron rubbing strakes. Woe betide any small vessel that got in the way of a Zulu! They and the Fifies were the only vessels I ever saw with horizontal steering wheels, which were set way aft in the sternsheets. When they were fishing they lowered the mainmast into a large crutch alongside the mizzenmast (again an example to modern sailors). Their massive bowsprits were set through a gammon iron, and the heel of the sprit was housed close to the mainmast. Neither main nor mizzen had a boom, and both were lugsails. In 1938 there were very few Zulus about, but those that were sailed as far afield from northern Scotland as Iceland, Norway, the southern North Sea, and the English Channel. They were simply rigged, strong, seaworthy, and magnificent sailers.

The *Scottish Fifies* were double-ended (that is, sharp at both ends). Both the stem and stern posts were vertical when the boat was at rest in calm water, which for the Fifies was a rare occasion. The rig was a high, dipping (lowerable) lug-mainsail forward, something like an American catboat, and a smaller, standing lugsail aft. Like those of most Scottish deep-sea fishing craft, their mainsails had six rows of reefing points that silently told the tale of the rough seas they voyaged. Neither sail had a boom. They carried about twenty tons of stone ballast beneath the fish holds. The frames of the hull were left about eighteen inches above deck level and planked over. This made a bulwark (low wall) around the deck about seventeen inches high, and that was the only thing between the crew and the freezing seas. In 1938, very few Fifies were fishing; those that remained of a formerly numerous fleet were engaged either in coastal cargo-hauling or as yachts. The bowsprit was set to port of the stem post, as in all Scottish vessels and English West Country craft. English east coast vessels always carried their bowsprit to starboard of the stem. There probably was no reason for this except tradition.

On the west coast of Scotland there were still one or two *Gabberts.* These were true sailing barges, built so that their hulls conformed to the dimensions of the locks on the Clyde and Forth Canal. They were seventy feet long, with a beam of twenty feet and a draft of no more than six feet. They were round-sterned and on inland waters carried a gaff sloop rig. When they ventured out to sea in the summer months (the Scottish west coast is no playground) they set a bowsprit and jib. As they were flat-bottomed and shallow drafted, they were the very devil to work to windward, and it was said that half the oaths ever heard at sea were invented onboard the Gabberts.

The waters around Liverpool had been the haunt of the *Weaver Flats,* but by 1938 there were only two of these left. One was named *Keskadale,* but I cannot recall the name of the other. The Flats were massively built of great oak timbers. The lowest planks of the hull were of *four-inch-thick* rock elm. They were always carvel-built, and it was said that they were so long-lived (*Keskadale* was well over a hundred years old) because the salt cargoes they hauled preserved the timber. The biggest of the Flats were about ninety feet long, drew nine feet, and loaded 175 tons. They had a high, peaked gaff-sloop rig, with no bowsprit. The owner's colors were painted rings on the mast above the houndsbands. There were also, working from Liverpool, a couple of *Jigger Flats,* gaff-ketch-rigged vessels of about ninety feet in length, but by the late thirties these had been fitted with auxiliary engines, and used their sails less and less.

Mention must be made of the *Liverpool Pilot Schooners.* Although there were none left in service as pilot boats, there were a couple still remaining as yachts. Along with the Bristol Channel Pilot Cutters, they were probably the most efficient small sailing vessels ever devised anywhere in their time (the 1850's to the 1920's). The Liverpool Schooners, with their yellow upperworks and black trim, could hold their own with any rich man's yacht for looks, just as well as they could hold their stations at sea in any weather while waiting for ships to arrive in Liverpool Bay.

The *Morecambe Bay Prawners* were among the most graceful fishing craft ever built. They were required to work well to windward and yet at the same time be able to lie off quietly while their two-man crew worked the prawn nets; they also had to be able to turn completely in their own length, about thirty-five feet. Their beams were nine feet, and they drew about five feet aft. They were cutter-rigged, with a high-peaked gaff main, a tops'l on a long yard, and a long bowsprit with no bobstay, so that the fishing gear would not be fouled. The accommodation onboard was so simple as to be primitive. Below, there was not even headroom enough for sitting in an upright position. Some of the prawners had a boiler on deck, and the catch was made ready for sale even as the vessel sailed home from the prawning grounds. The profile of the hull was yachtlike, with a rounded forefoot flowing into a shaped keel, ending at a steeply raking sternpost. All of this made the prawners very quick indeed on the helm. They ranged as far as South Wales and Ireland. One Morecambe Bay prawner, *Mink,* however, converted to reasonable accommodations, has made at least two circumnavigations of the world in the years since the Second World War, and I believe she was later to set out on her third. I was to see her in the Seychelles Islands in 1970, and she was then eighty-five years of age.

Another craft frequently sighted on the Irish Sea were the *Isle of Man Nobbys.* These were luggers with a cutter rig and were about thirty-five feet in length, not counting the longish bowsprit. They had a rounded forefoot, a long, straight keel, and a lifting rudder for beaching. The Manxmen, practically all of Viking descent, were daring seamen. They ranged in their Nobbys as far afield as the Shetland Isles in the north, the east coast of England, and the west coast of Ireland, and they landed their catches and sold them wherever they could.

We already know about the *Welsh Topsail Schooners,* but a word or two on their construction. The schooners were built with a full bilge (a "fat-sectioned" hull) so that they could sit upright in dry harbors when the tide went out, and so that they could load as much cargo as possible. They usually had a wheelhouse and a small galley iron-strapped to the deck. Roller-reefing was commonly fitted on both the main and foresail booms. In 1938 three fully-rigged Welsh Topsail Schooners were still working on the British and northern continental coasts, while many more, with auxiliary engines and reduced sail, were also in service. They were between seventy and ninety feet long, and drew about nine and a half feet. Their lines and their rig, and the long voyages they made, as far afield as Newfoundland, Greece, the Falkland Islands, and Argentina, and their reputation for fair treatment of their crews by their skippers, and of sobriety and cleanliness of the crews, made them the cream of Britain's smaller merchant sailing craft during the nineteenth and early twentieth centuries. Those were the good reasons that they were generally referred to as the "Western Ocean Yachts." Later, it would never cease to amaze me that the majority of Welsh and Welsh-descended people, to say nothing of folks of other nationalities, would have little or no idea of the maritime exploits of Welsh sailors in the past. But in the ranks of the great mariners will be found many a Welsh name, as in the names of headlands, bays, and straits the world around, while the entry and departure logs of practically every port in the world, large and small, bear testimony to the old Welsh sea traffic. Wales was, is, and always will be a maritime country. How could it be otherwise, surrounded by the sea on three sides, and not one acre of the country more than forty or so miles from salt water?

From far away on the west coast of Ireland came the *Galway Hookers.* These were to last until well into the 1960s. They were smack-rigged, with a high-peaked gaff main and a dumpy-looking staysail. The bowsprit was carried to starboard of the stempost. They had a rounded forefoot and long straight keel. They were generally built of larch planking on sawn oak frames. The crews were usually two men, or one man and a boy. As the western Irish harbors all dry out, the sides of the hookers had a "tumble-home" (they curved inward at the top) so that the vessel could conveniently lean against the dock when the tide went out. The mast was heavy and short, and supported by only one shroud (wire) either side. The mainsail was loosely laced to the mast. They were no more than forty feet long and drew about six feet. The word *hooker* is derived from the ancient Mediterranean lingua-franca word *urca,* and means a small, far-ranging, fore-and-aft-rigged maid-of-all-work vessel of jaunty appearance (which may also explain the common usage of the word in the United States).

In western England, off the mouth of the River Severn, worked the *Severn Trows.* In 1938 there were only a couple of these vessels—the direct descendents of a medieval type—remaining. They were ketches and carried a long bowsprit that was cocked up at an angle of about twenty degrees from the horizontal. They were gaff-rigged and carried a tops'l in fair weather. Their cargo holds, for some reason which to me is unfathomable, were never covered. They were about seventy feet long, with a beam of seventeen feet and a draft of six feet. Some of the Trows, to improve their sailing qualities, had a removable keel about two feet deep that was fixed into position by means of chains. In 1938, the oldest trow afloat and working was *William of Gloucester.* She had been built in 1808!

From the Severn Sea hailed a type of vessel that, for sea-keeping ability and ease of working, is known and has been acclaimed the world over. These were the *Bristol Channel Pilot Cutters,* reputedly the first sailing vessels ever to have roller reefing and self-draining cockpits. Those two amenities, along with self-steering gear, have been probably the greatest advances of safety and ease in sail-voyaging since the first hull was launched. Although, by 1938, there were no Pilot Cutters still at work waiting to transfer pilots to arriving ships, there were quite a few of them that had been converted to cargo carrying, and they worked all the coasts of Britain, the Channel Islands, and northern Europe. The largest of them were sixty feet long. Their size was limited by the size of their crews. When the pilot had boarded his ship there were only two men, or one man and a boy, to sail the craft home to port. The main features of their hulls were the high bows and freeboard. They had a rounded forefoot and a long, straight keel, and their ballast was shipped inside the hull, usually amidship, although some of the later-built vessels had ballast built into their keels. The great quality of the Bristol Channel Pilot Cutters was their more-than-excellent sea-keeping ability. They could ride winter storms for days hove-to ("stopped"; a "free" ship is never really stopped), head against the sea, with an easy motion that made an otherwise burdensome life a little more tolerable for their crews. Since the Pilot Cutters were usually sailed by one man on deck at a time, the sailing rig had to be simple. The topmast was short and so could stay aloft in the hardest blows.

The last of the working Bristol Channel Pilot Cutters was to continue hauling cargo around the English Channel into the 1960s. She had been built in 1904. It is fitting that her name, *Cariad,* is Welsh for "Sweetheart," and that she is now seeing out her days in the Exeter Maritime Museum.

Another English west coast–bred craft was the *Falmouth Quay Punt,* whose lines were copied, and still are, to some extent, by designers of modern oceangoing sailing yachts. The punts originated as ferry craft to the big square-riggers lying off Falmouth harbor. For this reason their masts were short, so that they would not foul the gear of the bigger ships when the punt lay alongside. With the coming of steamships, competition for the ferry work became so brisk that the punts, now built up to thirty feet long, had to go out far to sea to seek incoming ships. The hulls, as in many Cornish craft, had a greater beam aft of amidships and a sharp bow. The keels were rockered (that is, they sloped down from the bow to the middle of the keel and then were horizontal from there to the stern). The ballast was all carried in the outside keel, as it is in modern yachts. The punts had a low-aspect gaff-yawl rig, and the mizzenmast was set just forward of the transom. The tiller had a "U" bend in it so it could work around the mizzen. Normally, the mizzen was of "leg-o-mutton" (or "Bermuda") shape, but sometimes a large standing lugsail was carried. In the late thirties there were still many punts in use as fishing craft and for taking out tourists, and quite a number of them had been built as yachts.

Also from Cornwall came another type of craft that was seen all around the British coasts, the *East Cornish Lugger.* They were built with very sharp bows, so that they could poke their way into the tiny, crowded harbors of East Cornwall more easily. For this reason they also had massive wooden rubbing strakes along their sides. The hulls had to be very strongly built, for the boats pounded on the harbor ground every time the tide went out and came it. They were the only sailing craft that, as the weather deteriorated, substituted the mizzensail for the mainsail simply by lowering the main, stowing it, and shifting the mizzensail to the mainmast. Then a smaller mizzensail was hoisted aft. Often, in fair weather, they hoisted a mizzen-topsail. The ballast that the East Cornish Luggers carried was inboard and loose. When they went to windward the three-man crew shifted the ballast to the windward side of the hull, so that they could keep as much sail clapped on as possible. They also carried a jolly boat, which when they were headed home on a fast passage, they filled with seawater and rigged on the windward side as additional ballast. The Cornishmen were renowned for their seamanship and fast passages. On one occasion in 1910 three Luggers made the voyage, in ballast, from Mount's Bay, Cornwall, to the fishing grounds off Scarborough Head, Yorkshire: six hundred miles in seventy hours. That was an average speed of about seven knots, not at all bad for vessels only thirty feet in length, and especially in those seas.

In 1938 there were about twenty-five *Brixham Trawlers* working around the northern European waters. Many of these gaff-ketches were still fishing, but a few had been converted to cargo-carrying. They were about seventy-five feet in length, with an eighteen-foot beam, drew eleven feet, and were built with a sweeping sheer (a lovely convex curve of the deck from the bow aft). The sternpost was raked, and the transom was elliptical. The masts had a forward rake, which made them appear at first sight a bit drunken, but this was to make the luff (forward edge) of the sails "bite" better into the wind. One of these fine vessels, *Provident,* was still trading in the mid-sixties, and later was restored to her fishing condition by the Maritime Trust.

Also from Devon and Cornwall came the *West Country Barges.* The few that remained in the late thirties were mostly fitted with auxiliary engines, but they still carried a decent spread of sail. They were gaff-rigged cutters that often hoisted a topsail. Their length was fifty feet and their beam about sixteen feet, while they drew no more than seven feet. They had sharp bows and a good run aft to a shallow (low) transom. The stem raked forward, the sternpost raked aft, and the forefoot was rounded, while the keel was straight.

There were more than twenty *West Country Trading Ketches* working in the late thirties. These were built all over southwest England and in South Wales, too. They were often to be seen, in my early youth, on the open beaches of North and Mid-Wales, and in the harbor at Barmouth between tides, off-loading coal or loading hay or sacks of grain. They were gaff-rigged ketches that carried both main and mizzen topsails and three jibs as well as a staysail. Some of them regularly crossed the Atlantic Ocean on the Newfoundland fish trade, and others made occasional voyages to Europe, but most of them coasted the British Isles. All the sails were small enough to be handled by a master and a mate, or two men and a boy. Most of them had roller-reefing on the main, and some on the mizzen, too. The gaff topsails were set from the deck on a jackstay and were fitted at the head with a long yard. They were not comfortable vessels for their crews; the cooking was done in the poky foc'sle, and on deck there was no shelter of any kind from the elements.

From the waters north of the Isle of Wight came the *Itchen Ferry Boats.* These were gaff-rigged cutters that hoisted a topsail in good weather. They were about thirty feet long and very beamy for their length. They had deep keels so that they could lay to moorings in sheltered waters. Their fishermen-owners worked in the summer seasons as yacht skippers, so the ferries had to be small enough to lay up for the summer and be easily prepared again for the winter fishing season. Competitiveness is the very heart and soul of yacht racing, and this rubbed off on the Itchen Ferry fishermen. The hulls were carvel-built of red pine planking copper-fastened on oak frames, and all the wood in the ship was soaked in linseed oil before it was painted. Many of the Ferries were converted to yachts in the years between the wars, and one of them, *Fanny,* built in 1872, is still cruising as a yacht. Some of the Solent-area fishing smacks were the first British working vessels to be fitted with center-boards, for working their way to windward more efficiently.

The Solent area was also the range of the *Cowes Ketches,* although by the late thirties most of them had been fitted with auxiliary engines. They were carvel-built and double-ended. Their draft was shallow, enabling them to ascend the tiny creeks of the Isle of Wight and the mainland opposite to pick up and discharge cargoes. Both the main and the mizzen were long in proportion to their height. This was to maintain a low sail profile in consideration of the shallow draft (to lessen the risk of a capsize in high wind). One of them, *Bee,* still working in 1938, had been built in 1801!

Around the River Thames and the Thames estuary worked the *Spritsail Barges.* These were to be the very last of all the seagoing commercial sailing craft of northern Europe. They were solidly built, between forty and ninety feet long, and (most important of all) they could be worked by a crew of two. This was made possible by the spritsail rig. The large mainsail practically always remained hoisted aloft, and it was furled by means of brails, which drew the sail up the mast, like a curtain being drawn. The sprit boom also allowed the topsail to remain set when the main was furled, enabling the vessel to be maneuvered under a minimum of sail. Both main and mizzen sails were sheeted to a horse (a rail across the deck), which allowed the sails to go about (shift from one tack to the other) without needing to be handled by the crew. The heel of the bowsprit was set in a tabernacle (a frame with a hinge in it) so that it could be steeved (raised) up vertically when the vessel was entering a crowded dock. Both main and mizzen masts were set in tabernacles so that they could be lowered when passing under bridges. A century ago the "Spritties" could be counted in their thousands. In the late thirties their number was around fifty or so. Their main trade was supplies to the farms up the creeks of East Anglia; bricks to London; and stone from Portland, in Dorset, to towns and cities all over southeastern England. They were able to carry up to two hundred tons of cargo. All the Spritties were fitted with leeboards (that is, outside keels on hinges that could be raised and lowered over the side), and iron winches on the quarters to handle the leeboards. The spritties were built in a simple, boxlike section, with a few grown oak frames or "crooks." They were all flat-bottomed and the biggest ones drew around eight feet loaded, four feet unloaded. When they set off on a coastal trip the Spritties winched onboard a box-galley (kitchen) that was lashed down on deck. The food onboard the Spritties was none too special, as they escaped the Board of Trade regulations for seagoing craft. Most of their skippers had no certificate of any kind at all. But in the estuarial craft these two disadvantages were not grave. Their sailing range was short, and usually bicycles were taken along so that the skipper and mate could go back home in the evening for a good supper and a couple of pints with their pals in their own "local." On the coastal barges, however, the disadvantages were telling. There was no escaping bad food and a bad skipper once beyond the North Foreland or the Naze and out into the rough open waters. For many a young lad before me, especially those from poor families, or families with no connections, or no families at all, a berth on a Sprittie was the usual second step in advancement in a life at sea. The first step was, by rights, either a Stumpie, a Bawley, or a "Mulie."

The least glamorous cargo in the Thames estuary, the garbage and muck from a metropolis of eight million souls, was carried out to sea by the *Stumpie Barges.* They also hauled dull, dirty bulk freight such as timber or cement from the ocean steamers to the building sites around the Thames tidewaters, and explosives from and to the munitions factories up the River Lee and at Woolwich. They were the maids of all work. The crew of two were invariably cockneys, and they could be recognized by their corduroy pants, tied with string at the knee, and their red neckerchiefs.

The Stumpies were so called because they had no topmast. Practically every trip for them was above river bridges, which meant lowering the mast—awkward with a topmast and all its tackle. The Stumpies always worked within tidal range, and because they moved to the tide's orders the lack of a top'sl was not too great a loss. The Stumpies carried a peculiar diminutive mizzen, the mast being stepped on the rudder head. They were, however, despite their mundane cargoes, fancy craft in which their owners took a great deal of pride, much of which came from the fact that a Stumpie's sprit was proportionately longer than the Sprittie's. The hulls were always brightly painted and the transom decorated, sometimes even in gold leaf. The average length was thirty-five feet, with a beam of around fifteen feet, and they all carried leeboards.

There were the fishing craft; the *Medway Dobles* and the *Thames Bawleys,* whose name came from the boilers once used on deck to cook the catches of shrimp before they reached the mooring and market. Hard craft and hard, smelly work.

Last, but not least by any means, there were the *Mulies* and the *Boomies*. Both were ketch-rigged barges. The Mulie, which coast-traded between the Humber and the Isle of Wight, say two hundred miles in either direction from the Thames estuary, was a bastard rig born of combining a spritsail barge and a ketch. Thus the sprit main enabled two men and a boy to handle the rig. The main difference between the Mulie and the Boomie Ketch, however, was that the Boomie had its mainmast stepped on the keelson in the manner of a sea-faring ship, and this made all the difference in the world, both to the Boomie Ketch's crew's attitude to their ship and to the Board of Trade's attitude to the Boomie.

Whereas the Spritties and the Mulies were confined to the coastal trade, the Boomies were granted certificates to trade "foreign." Their skippers were examined for certificates (by 1935), and the conditions of work and welfare were beginning to be regulated by the government; but only just beginning.

The ketch-barge *Second Apprentice* was a *Dandy*, as the Boomies were alternatively, and more commonly, called. I was lucky; instead of having to work my way up from the Bawleys or the Stumpies, and through the Spritties, I was going directly onto a foreign-going Dandy ketch. Dad had found me a berth in one of the aristocrats of British working sail!

These, though I knew little about it at the time—only a few scraps of information picked up from some of Dad's sailor-visitors—were the main material components of the peculiar world that I was entering. These were the ships of the trade.

8

Second Apprentice

The night train from South Wales to London stopped at only one or two places. They must have been Swindon and Reading, middling-sized towns, but to me, a small boy with his face pressed to the steamy carriage window, staring at the lamp-glow and at all the bustle on the platforms, they seemed to be sprawling and enormous, with more people about than I had ever seen in one place before.

Various people alighted at the first stop, and a lady—she seemed very rich and beautiful—came into my compartment with her two children, a boy and a girl, both better dressed than I, of course, but a little younger. In the English fashion, they sat in silence for a while; then the boy asked me whether I was going to London. He spoke refined English, like the BBC announcers on the wireless, so it was not too difficult for me to understand him.

"Ssh," said his mother, flustered and embarrassed. There were a couple of other people in the compartment, silent, hugging their Englishness.

"No, it's to Reeya I'm going," said I, and showed the boy my ticket, which I'd stowed in the pencil pocket of my jacket. The boy looked at me nonplussed for a moment, trying to make out what I had said, then he turned and looked up at the beautiful lady and said, "Oh, mother, I think he's a foreigner."

His mother smiled at me. There was silence for a few minutes except for the noises of the train. Then she delved into her bag and brought out three red shiny apples. She gave one each to her children, then reached across with her gloved hand and offered one to me. I took it, surprised by her generosity and awed by her beauty, but I was so astonished that I thanked her in Welsh—*"Diolch"*—at which her smile broadened wider. *"Il n'est pas de tout,"* she replied softly. As I'd eaten all the food Mam had given me, I took the apple along the corridor and ate it outside the toilet, but by the time I returned to my compartment the lady and her brood had left the train.

The train seemed to take forever to pass through the western suburbs of London, and it was all I could manage to take in each house, building, bridge, and street as we flashed by.

I was staggered. I knew, from what *Mister* Jeffreys-Geography had taught us at school, that there were eight million people in London, but numbers spouted in a one-room school are vastly different from the abodes of hundreds of thousands of human beings, row after row, street after street. By the time the train arrived in Paddington Station my head was in a whirl. A host of passengers left the train and hurried by me to the ticket barrier, but I was too busy staring at the great heaving steam engine and silently hero-worshipping the driver and his fireman to notice them.

Suddenly, amid the hissing of the engine and the clouds of steam emitting from its cylinders, and the dull thrum of noise from the huge station all around, there was a voice at my side. I turned around, and there was a policeman. He was not a big, burly, elderly man like Williams-the-Police back home, nor did he have a bicycle. This one was a young man and thin. "Going somewhere, lad?" he asked pleasantly.

"Reeya" said I, and dug in my pocket for my ticket while the policeman waited, his brow furrowed quizzically. He read my ticket and grinned. "From South Wales, eh?" he asked me.

"No. Merioneth, but I caught the train in Newport."

"Did you now? Well, I'm from Llantrisant myself. Come on, I'll show you the way to the tube train. You have to go to Waterloo. . . ."

"Fe alla i siriad Cynraig." I said that I spoke Welsh.

"Oh, do you? I can understand some, but I don't speak a bloody word of it."

Although the underground train was a frightening wonder to me as it flashed through London far below street level, I felt much better. There really were Welshmen in England. I was not all alone among the *Sais* (Saxons).

The journey through Kent and Surrey seemed to take almost as long as the one from Newport to London, even though the distance was nowhere near as long. In the morning light I peered through the windows at the fields and hedgerows and rich-looking, tidy houses. It seemed to me that in England everything had been put together very carefully and precisely. Compared to this the houses and barns in West Wales were a memory of scraps thrown down higgledy-piggledy by a careless God, jealous of the beauty of our hills. The few acres of arable, rich land that He had bestowed on us were merely a small repayment for our singing. Why, one square mile of Sussex fields seemed more rich than the whole county of Merioneth. There were no rocky outcrops to be seen, no barren uplands, no abandoned farms or cottages, but there wasn't much of the unintended, untended, fierce beauty of Wales, which is beauty in its true state.

Here, in England, the skies were the same blue as in Wales; the clouds the same shape, yet there was something different. There was not the lightening of shades of blue to silver on the horizon, nor did the clouds have the same sinister darkness of shadow on their undersides. The English clouds slid along; the Welsh ones had *charged*.

Finally, after one or two changes of train—I forget how many—I arrived in Rye, stepped forth from the tiny railway station, shouldered my sea bag, and, after asking directions from the ticket collector, made my way along the High Street (the English equivalent of Main Street). Almost immediately I spied the topmasts of four vessels. As I drew nearer I saw that two of the vessels in the river, farther downstream, were upright, floating on the tide in the narrow creek, and two were heeled over at angles, where they had not yet taken the tide.

Folks of whom I asked directions were, it seemed to me, fresh as I was from West Wales, somewhat offhand, but they replied kindly enough even though it was very difficult for me at first to understand their Sussex drawl. In West Wales a stranger would have been escorted to his or her destination, if only for the sake of a chat on the way.

It's all a long time ago, and men have visited the moon, and here I am remembering the cobblestones of Rye quay, and how tufts of grass grew around the bases of the big iron bollards, and the old cast-iron mooring posts made from ship's cannons, and a horse-drawn cart loading up with crates of bottled mineral water, and my first sight of the dandy ketch *Second Apprentice.*

She was one of the two craft that were listing against the quay walls at a slight angle, high and dry above the tide, and all about her hovered the smell of the sweat of the sea—the yeasty odor of corruption and new creation that salt water reveals every time the tide retreats at the bidding of the moon. Her port leeboard, a great iron forging eighteen feet long and eight feet broad at the fan, was drawn up to her gunwale. She was just under a hundred feet long, and her bowsprit stuck out another twenty feet farther. As I lugged my sea bag toward her, my eyes strayed upward. Her main and maintop masts made a total height of about seventy feet above the deck. The standing rigging seemed, to my unaccustomed eyes, to be a veritable jungle of cables, ropes, and ratlines. Her mizzenmast was about forty feet high. On her stern hung a drooping red ensign, almost black with grime.

I reached the edge of the quay and wearily dropped my sea bag onto the paving stones beneath my feet. I looked at the work going on. The gangway onto *Second Apprentice* was no more than a plank, about six inches wide and two inches thick, down which crates of empty bottles were being slid to the deck of the vessel. The shore-side part of the operation consisted of a brewer's dray-type cart, a black-and-white shire stallion with great hairy fetlocks over feet as big as soup plates, an old man atop the cart handing down the crates, and a young lad with tow hair, a bit older than I, sliding the crates down the plank.

I left my sea bag where it was and approached the lad. The stallion gave a sudden start and twitched flies with its tail.

"Good day," said I.

"Wot cheer, come to work, then?" The tow-haired lad stopped work, straightened up, and grinned at me. He was an inch or so taller than me. His eyes were deep blue, and two of his front teeth were missing. He stared grinning at me for a second, then hunched his shoulders, braced his arms, and set to sliding down crates again, still grinning to himself.

I stood there for a short while, as the lad slid the last of this load of crates down the plank to a man on deck, who in turn swung them over and stacked them on top of a net suspended from above by a rope from the end of the gaff, which was being used as a derrick. The man on deck was, at a wild guess, around forty-five years old. He was small and dark, with a complexion the color of a chestnut. He sported a black, bushy walrus mustache and wore a flat cap, an everyday jacket over a collarless shirt, corduroy trousers tied with string just below the knees, and boots. He peered at me through the smoke from a cigarette stuck in the corner of his mouth.

The old man on the cart said, "Got a good berth there, son," flicked his whip at the stallion, and took off along the jetty at a good clip. The stallion was surprisingly agile and fast, considering his tremendous size. As he started to heave the cart his hooves slipped a little on the paving flags, and tiny sparks flew from his massive iron horseshoes. It reminded me of a knife being sharpened on a grindstone.

The tow-haired lad jerked me out of my moment's reverie. "Wanna go aboard then, mate?" (The local accent and those onboard *Second Apprentice* were so esoteric that it would be unfair for me to expect my American readers to follow an attempted rendering of them.)

I plonked my sea bag down on the plank. It slid down to the deck. The little dark man with the walrus mustache grabbed it and winked at me. "You must be the taffy, right, son?" he said. "The new nipper?"

"That's right, sir." I teetered my way down the plank and landed on deck alongside the little dark man, who grabbed me. He saw I was on my feet, then he let me go.

"Take your gear for'rd, right?" he ordered. "There's some tea in the galley. My name's Bert, and I'm the mate onboard this here ship. Tansy's . . . the captain's having a kip. He thumbed aft. "He'll be up when we finish getting this here little lot onboard and stowed away down in the bloo . . . blummin' hold, right?"

"Right, sir . . . er. . . ." I started to say something.

The mate chimed in, "Don't you 'sir' me, Nipper. My name's Bert, right?"

"Right, Bert."

"Right, Nipper, and when you've stowed your gear I'll show you where everything is in the galley, right?"

"Right, Bert."

"Right, Nipper, so now, off you go, on your toes, my son, and make yourself at home, right?"

"Right."

"Right what?"

"Oh . . . right, Bert."

"Right, Nipper, now you go up for'd as fast as Chri . . . as your feet will let you, and get settled in, right?"

"Right, Bert."

"Good lad!" Bert turned again to slinging the crates of bottles down into the hold. As I went forward I heard him mutter, "Blummin' youngsters . . . no idea. . . ."

I made my way forward along the deck, a bit daunted by the seeming complexity of the tackle all around. The mainmast, where it went through the deck, was of immense girth, like a full-grown tree. I saw the scuttle hatchway down to the foc'sle, threw my sea bag down it, and followed it down into the gloom below.

When my eyes became accustomed to the dim light, I found that the foc'sle crew's quarters was a triangular space about twenty-one feet across at its widest, furthest aft. At its longest, amidships, it was about twelve feet in span. There were wooden berths, two on each side, with a big wooden drawer below each berth. In the middle of the triangular space was set a big, shiny, black coal stove with its chimney going straight up through the deckhead (ceiling). Around the base of the stove there were four horizontal brass rails, one above the other, about a foot apart. These, I was to find out later, were for drying wet clothes. From the deckhead hung a large brass lamp with a green glass shade about eighteen inches in diameter. I was to get to know the foc'sle, the lamp, and the stove intimately in the coming months. It was to be one of my chores to clean them daily, regardless of the weather, come hell or high water.

Only one of the berths seemed to be obviously occupied, so I unpacked my sea bag and stowed my clothes neatly in the drawer under the portside after berth. Then, that done, I took another look around the foc'sle. It was all very plain and simple —almost stark—with the rough-hewn timbers of the ship's side and bulkheads fore and aft as the only decoration. It was, however, very clean and tidy, with everything painted white, except for the sole (floor), which was scrubbed. I was soon to get to know that sole very well, too, every square inch of it.

The only daylight that penetrated into the foc'sle was what came down through the open scuttle (hatchway). In the daytime, when work was afoot on deck and the foc'sle lamp was not lit, it was a gloomy place.

Having packed my changes of clothes away and changed my boots for the canvas deck slippers Cei Powell had made for me, I clambered up the hatchway and emerged again on deck out into the afternoon sunlight. I headed aft along the deck toward the galley. This was little more than a wooden box, about six feet by five, and six feet high, strapped to the deck by iron bands.

As I reached the galley door, I saw that another load of crates had arrived on the quay and Bert was again busy lugging them onboard and swinging them down in the net into the dark hold below. I looked down into the hold over the hatch-coamings and saw a cavernous, gloomy space as big as the chapel hall back in Llangareth. It was almost full of closely stacked crates. Stacking them in the gloaming below was a tall, lanky lad of about eighteen. He wore neither shirt nor shoes; only a pair of black moleskin trousers. Under the dust and straw his hair was fair in the English way. As I gazed at him, he suddenly looked up and stopped work, puffing heavily. "Wot cheer, cock?" His grin almost split his face in two. "You the new nipper, then? My name's Ted." I had to listen very carefully to be able to understand what he said. As it was, I must have looked so puzzled that he repeated his greeting twice.

"Hello . . ." I stood there gazing down at Ted until Bert broke in, "Stowed your gear then, Nipper?"

"Yes, sir, I've . . ."

"Bert."

"Oh . . . sorry, sir . . . Bert, I've . . . I've taken the port after berth. . . ."

"Where's your working gear, son?"

"Oh, it's all right . . . Bert; I've stowed that, too. . . ."

"Have you indeed? Stowed it away, have you, Nipper? Well, you just trot back down to the foc'sle and put it on, right? There's work to be done, and look quick about it! Tansy'll be along any minute, and if he misses this blummin' tide there'll be all hell let loose! Now get a move on, f'Crissake, we want our blinkin' tea! Right?"

"Oh . . . right . . . er . . . right, Mister Bert!" I fell back to rush my way forward and below.

"Nipper!" Bert's cry brought me up all standing.

"Yes, sir?"

"I've told you . . . my name's Bert. Now, no more of that highfalutin' nonsense! *Right?*"

"Right, Bert!" I flung myself forward and down the hatchway. In three minutes or less I was dressed in my khaki cotton shirt and bib-and-brace overalls. I made my way self-consciously back to Bert. As I walked along the deck I gazed across the river. A little stumpie barge leaning against the far bank, her decks deserted, lay so still that she seemed to sleep profoundly, wrapped in a hay-scented mantle of soft sunlight and silence, her furled sails like closed eyes.

Bert saw me looking at the stumpie barge. "She's waiting for a load of bricks tomorrow. Her blokes are both at the local, having a pint," he said, somewhat regretfully. Then he grinned at me, sizing me up in my overalls. "That's better, Nipper, nice and shipshape now, right?" he said quietly as he led me into the tiny galley. Inside, the first thing that caught my eye was a big, oblong stove, on the starboard side, all shiny and black with polish, with a coal fire glowing in the center hearth. Everything in the galley was spotlessly clean, except where some fine gray ash had fallen out of the grate into the metal ashpan in the hearth. On the forward and after sides of the galley there were portholes with brightly polished brass frames. The cooking pans were stowed with their handles stuck down behind horizontal wooden battens around the forward side of the galley. Beneath the pans was a potato box to one side, a vegetable box and a flour bin in the middle, and an iron coal box on the other side. Along the portside, beside the galley door, was a long wooden workbench, its top dead white and worn with decades of scrubbing. Above and below the table were cupboards for canned and bottled foodstuffs. Bert opened the cupboard doors. "And make sure you always stow the tins and bottles with their labels showing and the right side up, right?"

"Right, Bert."

"Good. Now we'll have a cup of tea; then, when you've cleared up after that, you can give us a hand with the cargo. We've got to catch the tide tonight, right, Nipper?"

"When can I see the captain, Bert?" I asked nervously, as I filled the gallon kettle with water from the hand-pump by the zinc sink.

"Who . . . ? Oh, Tansy will be around in a while, don't you fret, Nipper." Even as Bert said this, a voice, deep and gruff, rang out from somewhere down aft: "Bert!"

"Talk about the devil . . . there he is now!" muttered Bert. "Yes, Tansy," he hullooed.

"Where the dickens . . . ?" The gruff voice muttered loudly. Then, "The new nipper onboard yet?" I heard the sound of purposeful footsteps treading the deck, coming nearer.

"In the galley, Tansy!" crowed Bert. "Yes, he's here turned to . . ." Bert clapped one hand on my shoulder as I stood back from placing the heavy kettle on the stove top. He was a small man, not much taller than I, but his strength nearly knocked the breath out of my body. It was like being cracked with a snapped steel cable.

"Where?" the gruff voice asked again. The footsteps approached the galley door. The sound was closely followed by the captain of *Second Apprentice,* Albert Edward Lee, Esquire. He stood in the sunshine just outside the galley doorway, bathed in golden light.

At first I couldn't see the captain clearly, but when my eyes accustomed themselves to the glow around him he looked much younger than he actually was. He appeared to be in his mid-fifties, but I later found that he was, in fact, seventy-two.

"Come on out here, Nipper. I want to have a word with you," the captain ordered in a much less gruff tone. I stepped outside, and the captain walked aft along the deck a little way, his hands clasped together behind his back. He had a sailor-man's gait, a sort of stiff roll when he walked. When he turned and stood still, he held his body erect, his feet slightly apart as if he were bracing himself to his ship's movement. His head was lowered, so that he gazed at me from under his dark bushy brows. As I neared him he lifted and lowered one eyebrow. A suspicion of a smile played around his lips. As he stood gazing at me in silence for a few seconds, I, in turn, studied him. He was about five feet ten inches tall, and at first he looked skinny to me, until I realized later that his body was all muscle. His hair, what I could see of it under his bowler hat, was black, streaked with silver. His eyes were a piercing, startling green, deep-set under bushy eyebrows. His nose was prominent, the bridge laced with tiny blue veins, and his complexion was a tanned reddish brown. He wore full salt-and-pepper whiskers around his face, but no mustache. He wore his shore-side suit of blue serge, jacket, waistcoat, and trousers, and in his waistcoat pocket was stuck the stem of a short clay pipe and a heavy gold watch fob. His shirt was blue-and-white-striped, with a white celluloid collar from which hung a narrow black tie. His feet were shod in black, highly shined boots, almost as shiny as the ancient suit he wore. In his jacket breast pocket was tucked an off-white handkerchief that looked as though it had been stuck there for a month of Sundays. He removed his hands from behind his back. They were like steel fox-traps, but their movement was gentle.

"Hmm," said the captain, after he had given me a full twenty-second lookover. "And how was your trip, son?"

"Very good, Captain. . . ." I didn't know what else to say for a moment. Then I went on, "I slept very well on the train, well, for a while . . . and a lady gave me an apple. . . ." I trailed off, feeling embarrassed and childish. I reminded myself to try to keep the tone of my voice low.

The captain smiled more broadly. "An apple, eh? Well now, that was nice of the lady." He thought for a moment or two, then he said, "I hope as how you thanked her, son?" Then, without waiting for my reply, he shot a quick glance over my shoulder at Bert, who was standing behind me. "You shown the nipper around, Bert?" he demanded.

"Yes, well, leastways round the galley," replied the mate.

"Good, good." The captain's green eyes returned to mine. I felt as though I had been jolted. "Now, son," he said in a low confidential tone, "your father and me have been friends for a long time, and if you behave yourself and do your best you're going to get on a treat onboard my ship. It's a lot of work, and at first you won't see much sense in some of it; but stick at it and you'll learn a lot."

"Yes, sir. . . ." I muttered.

"You'll learn more on this blooming ship than you ever thought of at school. It's a bit rough and ready at times, and it's not always cakes and ale, but it's a good, honest, steady trade, and it'll go on for a long whiles yet, because we can get to places where the steamers can't. . . ." Captain Lee thought for a second, his eyes straying up to the rigging. Then he added, "Or where it ain't worth their while to go." He was silent then.

I thought he was waiting for some response from me. "Yes, sir," I said dutifully.

The captain clapped his hand on my shoulder. It was a gentle movement, but his grip was like a vise. "Right," said he. "Now off you go and give Bert and Ted a hand."

"Yes, sir." I turned to take my leave.

The captain's voice, still low, stopped me in my tracks. "Just a minute, son."

I turned around and faced him.

"You know the wages for makee-learners?" He didn't wait for an answer. "Seven shillings a week and all found, and a new set of working clothes every St. Martin's Day?"

"Yes, sir, and Saturday afternoons and Sundays off, my dad said."

"When we're in harbor, Nipper, when we're in harbor," he corrected me, turning to go ashore. As he stepped onto the gangplank he hesitated and again called back to me, "Nipper!"

I was still busy watching him mount the narrow plank. "Yes, sir?"

"When we're in harbor in *England* . . . don't want any of them foreigners . . ." He stopped, then continued: "My name's Albert, and some people ashore call me Captain, and so will you when we're ashore, but my friends and my crew call me Tansy. Onboard you call me that. Then I'll know who you're talking to. . . ." He trailed off and seemed to be thinking of something else. "Ted!" he bawled, after a few seconds.

There was no reply. "TED!" Now the captain's voice was as loud as Bardsey Island foghorn. Ted's muffled reply came up from the dark cargo hold.

Tansy hollered: "We've got a nice leg of lamb for supper! Nip'll give you a hand with it if you show him how. Get supper up early, lad. We want to be out on the tide!" This last as Tansy walked up the shaky, six-inch-wide loading plank as sure-footed as a steeplejack one-quarter his age.

"Right, Tansy!" shouted Ted from the murky depths below. Then he called me. "Come on, Nipper, give us a hand with these bleedin' crates!"

"It's all right," said Bert's voice behind me. "You go and make the tea, Nipper. I'll give Ted a hand. Give us a yell when tea's ready."

Later, when I'd cleared away everything in the galley, I went out on deck with Ted and Bert, and clambered over the hatch-coamings and down the ladder. Stacking the crates was back-breaking labor for a none-too-big lad of almost fourteen, but I was happy. I was in a ship among friendly folk, and we were to sail with the tide. For the next hour or two Llangareth was completely out of mind, at least for the time being. While I made better acquaintance of my new shipmates, down in the dusty, smelly hold in the half-dark, and grunted over crates of empty mineral water bottles, I completely forgot the pain of leaving Mam and Angharad, Caradoc and Cei, Blind Sioni and Goodness Gracious. The hills of Wales sang sadly to me no more for a blessed while, and I was no longer sick for my old home. Such is a boy's way.

By the time all the cargo of bottles were onboard it was almost dusk topside. Dusty and dirty, with sore hands from handling so many crates, and with an aching back, I clambered up the ladder out of the hold. Both Ted and Bert were already washing themselves in salt water, which they had bucketed over the side from the incoming tide.

A few minutes later I was somewhat refreshed and it was time to go into the galley with Ted, and peel potatoes and swedes (rutabagas), carrots and onions, while he set up the leg of lamb for roasting. While the meat was cooking Ted took me below to what he called "the skipper's lobby." This was an-other living space, smaller than the crew's quarters forward, but much more comfortably appointed. On each side of a narrow sort of hallway, wherein was the dining table, there were two small cabins, one for the captain and one for the mate. Here again there was a small coal stove, black with brass trimmings; another hanging lamp, brass with a glass shade; and also a skylight with brass protection rods above and below it.

The paneled bulkheads were of some tropical timber, and varnished. There was a brass ship's clock on the forward bulkhead. At each end of the table was a padded chair fixed to the sole (floor), and along one side was a plain wooden bench. "This is where we eat," said Ted, as he set the table for supper. "All muck in together, see?"

The only time I can remember when we had any kind of relaxation that evening was when Ted and I sat outside the galley for a few minutes while the roast cooked, and over supper.

Tansy came back onboard just after dark with his sailing orders sticking out of his jacket pocket. Soon after, we all ate at the big table in the skipper's lobby. As Ted and I dished out the meal and sat down to eat, the oil lamp over the table just started to budge as the ship's hull responded to the incoming tide. Tansy sat at the head of the table, farthest from the companionway ladder and facing it; Bert sat opposite him at the other end of the table. Ted and I sat on the bench. Ted, being the senior of us two deckhands, sat next to Tansy and I sat next to Bert. Every evening meal onboard *Second Apprentice*, when she was in harbor or at anchor, was taken so, in the small space between Tansy's and Bert's cabins. Tansy said grace before we started to eat, and Bert kept us laughing during the meal, with his tales of all kinds of scrapes he'd been in through his thirty-six years at sea.

But that first night aboard *Second Apprentice*, at supper, although I must have been famished with hunger I could hardly eat for excitement, though I tried to hide it. The captain, the mate, and Ted all ate their food heartily and swigged down their tea, and helped themselves to second rounds. After that they soon tucked down a whole six-inch-deep, foot-wide plum duff, but I could not finish my first plate.

"Not much appetite, Nipper," Tansy observed.

"No sir, I . . . I ate on the train. . . ." I tried to excuse myself.

"A whole apple?" Tansy grinned.

"You'd better go easy, son," commented Bert, who was as thin as a boat hook, "You'll be getting too fat to shin aloft."

Everyone laughed, except me, of course. I was too preoccupied thinking about the ship sailing that night, and how the next day would be my fourteenth birthday.

Then Tansy said, in a softer voice: "Oh, I expect he's a bit shy. First night away from home and all that, eh, Nipper?"

Suddenly I thought of Llangareth. Tears welled in my eyes, but I managed to stop them falling. I was a man now among men. I told myself that I must remember that, and to try to soften my pain I forced myself to think instead about the forthcoming voyage.

9

A Wet Shirt and a Happy Heart

In case, in this "modern" world, much more complex and far more cynical than the world I knew as a boy, my tale reads something like the opening chapters of *Treasure Island,* I must try to explain the reality of it all, the actuality of life in the special world of trade-sailing the narrow seas around Britain in the late thirties.

While words can hardly express the romance of it all in retrospect, so too it is difficult to find sufficient expression for the hard, mean, incessant toil that underlay all the beauty and fitness-for-purpose of the old coastal sailing ships. Toward the life they lived and in the ships they sailed the mariners were deadly serious; they had to be, for not only were their lives and livelihoods at stake, not only were the ships the means of their very existence, they also provided the livelihoods of their families, and the mariners' responsibilities to the ships' owners had to be forever borne in mind.

Some of the people of whom I write might, on the surface, be thought of, in this more glamour-minded age, as "quaint characters," or "salty old sea dogs," or even "semi-retarded illiterates." Some of them may have appeared so, they may even have sounded so, but they most assuredly were not. No one who had navigated, in command or as mate, the treacherous waters around the British Isles for more than a year or two could be anything but well-informed about the waters he sailed, intelligent, crafty, and wily—and these two last in the best meanings of the words.

The fact that I never saw Captain Tansy Lee use a chart, or that he never opened a book apart from the Bible, the accounts book, and the ship's log, does nothing to detract from his intelligence and his experience, so hard won over so many years of silent inner struggle and anxiety. The mate, Bert, while to all appearances a happy-go-lucky skilled laborer, could stow 250 tons of cargo in the hold so expertly that nothing would shift in the hardest gale, and the ship at all times while loading or unloading was kept on an even keel. Tansy and he could warp the ship out of a crowded mooring with the finesse of an orchestra conductor and the responses of a virtuoso. They both, the captain and the mate, had the true sailorman's ability to make even the most complex task or problem seem simple and easy.

In later years I was to see a few instances of sailing ketches and schooners, approximately the same size as *Second Apprentice*, being prepared for sea and making their departure. In all cases they had a much bigger, much more formally educated crew than did *Second Apprentice*; in all cases their equipment, such as sails and cordage, was of modern materials such as nylon and their navigational aids were of a standard undreamed of in the thirties. In all cases electricity had been introduced onboard when the vessels converted to "yachts," together with big diesel engines, and in most cases there was plenty of money among the owners and crews. Often there were voyage sponsors hovering in the background, to come to the rescue should the slightest thing go wrong with the preparations for the voyage or on passage. In most cases, too, there was such a lack of true knowledge and expertise, such a hullabaloo as soon as anything the merest bit unexpected occurred, as to make me wonder how the vessel would ever make any landfall anywhere, or even in some cases reach the offing.

Yet Tansy and Bert could, if necessary just the two of them, quietly warp *Second Apprentice*, engineless, out into the stream, with hardly a word spoken, and that no more than a murmur; punt out; hoist the sails; and be underway with no fuss at all, in silence and grace. They could make a round voyage—a paying voyage—anything up to a thousand miles and more, and be at their destinations within a few hours either side of their estimation. On passage they might emerge from a Channel rainstorm to find the captain of a big transatlantic steamer asking Tansy, in a blinking frenzy of Morse on the big ship's signal lamp, what *his* position was. Nine times out of ten, with a cast of a lead to the sea bottom, Tansy could tell the big ship's master mariner, within a half mile or so, where he was, and ninety-nine times out of a hundred Tansy would be dead right.

The sailormen may seem "quaint" to people of generations that have lost touch with nature, to people whose view of life and the world has been distorted by the false values ground out daily by the "modern" media, but in fact they operated the most cost-efficient transport ever devised.

The sailormen were simple, and many were unlettered. Some were unwise in the ways of the shore world, but all of them, without exception, were true *men* in every meaning of the word. I was not only lucky to know them—I was honored and privileged.

A few words about the ship. For my landmen friends I will try to make them easily understood.

Second Apprentice had been built in Sussex in the 1890s. Her hull, except for the bows and stern, was a boxlike structure of oak with a flat bottom. She was ninety-five feet in length and twenty-three feet in beam, and her hold was eight feet deep. She loaded a maximum of just over two hundred tons, and when deep-laden her draft was seven feet six inches. This meant that when she was fully loaded, as she often was in summer, there were only six inches of her hull above water level.

The bowsprit was almost twenty feet long, tapering from a diameter of about six inches at the outboard end to approximately eighteen inches inboard, where it was stepped into a double bitt (stout vertical timbers rising from the forefoot, through the deck to just above deck level).

The bowsprit bobstay was triced up while in harbor. The standing end of a short chain pendant was shackled to a plate on the cutwater at the waterline. The other end of the pendant had a single block shackled onto it. The standing end of the running part of the bobstay was shackled to the lower eye of the cranse-iron tack and then went down to the block on the chain pendant, back to a block on the bowsprit, and from there inboard. The bobstay was slackened off in port and triced up by an inhaul. There was a patent iron windlass, hand-worked, for raising the anchor, which weighed about a quarter of a ton and more. The anchor chain (or cable, as we called it) was stowed in two lockers in the forepeak. Each locker had sixty fathoms (360 feet) of 5/8-inch cable, made up of four fifteen-fathom lengths. Thirty-five fathoms of anchor cable were always, except in heavy weather, laid out on deck from the port locker. The reserve cable was in the starboard locker, with one link out from the chain pipe on deck, ready to be hauled up. Very low gearing on the windlass permitted one man (or two boys) to weigh anchor in fair weather, and one man and a boy in contrary conditions.

Just abaft the windlass was a dolly winch. This was used for warping in and out of harbor. The wire on its barrel was 6/19 of an inch, eighty fathoms (480 feet) long.

Stowed in the forepeak were also: thirty fathoms (180 feet) mooring rope of six-inch coir, thirty fathoms of towing rope of seven-inch coir, eighty fathoms (480 feet) track line of 1 3/4-inch cotton, sixty fathoms (360 feet) horse line of 2 3/4-inch cotton. (The track and horse lines were used for warping in and out of harbor.)

A little abaft the windlass was a scuttle (hatchway) with a sliding roof that led down to the crew's quarters in the foc'sle. There were two hatches to the hold—the fore and the main. The smaller forehatch was just forward of an iron horse on which the foresheets worked. On either side of the mainmast were barrel winches for the halyards. A little further aft was another barrel winch for working cargo with a block swung on the mainmast. Right across the deck, between the two hatches, was an iron lug-plate, on which the leeboards worked, port and starboard. The main hatch, with three-foot-high coamings, had fourteen cover boards, each thirteen inches wide, three inches thick, and fourteen feet long. Forward of the mizzen-mast was an iron box in which the mainsheets worked, and to port and starboard were the leeboard winches, hand-worked. From them the chain falls to the leeboards passed outboard through small sheave holes. To starboard of the mizzenmast was a galvanized iron water tank that held about a hundred gallons and was strapped down onto the deck with iron bands. There was a skylight over the captain's flat, and aft of that was a small deckhouse. The open forward end of the deckhouse was roofed over and housed a brass-decorated steering wheel. A small enclosed head (toilet) was to starboard of the wheel. Abaft the helm-dodger was the galley, and to starboard of that was the companionway down to the captain's flat. On the port quarter were the boat davits, where the jolly boat was rigged when the ship was underway.

As for the sail plan, it was very simple. There were three headsails, which were set out on the bowsprit; a staysail; a gaff-headed main topsail; the main and mizzen sails; and a mizzen topsail. A squaresail was also carried, and when the wind was directly astern this was set up from a yard. The whole squaresail rig, sail and yard, were sent up as far as the main houndsbands when required for running before a hard breeze. Then the mainsail was handed and furled. The main-mast was raked forward, and the topmast had a pronounced curve that to the uninitiated made it seem that the forestay had been set up too taut. The flying jib was hanked to the topmast stay, but the jib halyards all led to the masthead cap, so that the upper part of the flying jib gradually left the topmast stay, making the upper part of the luff of the sail appear to be bent aft. There was a good reason for this. It enabled the sail to be carried much longer in a stiffening breeze. If the flying-jib halyards had been led to the head of the topmast, the strain in a good blow, had the skipper kept the sail up too long, would probably have broken the topmast, if not the mainmast.

The sails on *Second Apprentice,* and on all the dandy ketches, were left their natural canvas color, as distinct from the other coasting barges, which had red-dyed sails. Another difference was that on ketches the topsails were set to port and the jolly boat's davits were on the port quarter instead of the starboard.

Both the main and mizzen booms had roller reefing, but unlike modern practice, this was managed by means of a wire reeved around a "gypsy" at the heel of the boom and then through a block aloft, which was secured to a burton from the houndsbands. Apart from this, all the running rigging was manila rope.

On each side of the mainmast were four galvanized iron shroud-wires as well as a running backstay, which was set up on the windward side. Hemp ratlines were clove-hitched to the shrouds, one foot six inches apart. Also lashed to the shrouds, outboard, were two lifebuoys painted in white and red, with the ship's name painted on them in black. These were within easy reach of the deck. Above these, the kerosine-fueled navigation lamps were fitted, red to port, green to starboard. The mainmast heel was set into the keelson, and, unlike most of the other types of coasting barges, the masts were not made to be lowered for passing under bridges. For this reason the boomies or dandy ketches were considered by the authorities to be fully fledged seagoing vessels, and so could trade "foreign."

The mizzenmast was stayed forward by a burton (a "forestay" that could be tautened by heaving on a line led through a block), and had two shrouds either side. When cargo was being taken on or discharged, the main boom and gaff were swung out over the ship's side (usually to starboard) out of the way. A small, thick gaff was used as a derrick for hoisting and lowering cargo into and out of the hold if no shore derrick or crane was handy.

The ketch rig first came into use in the early 1700s, in the Royal Navy. Special vessels were needed to carry huge bomb-mortars, which weighed several tons and, when fired, almost shattered with their recoil the very hulls which carried them. The mortars, therefore, had to be mounted well forward in the ship. In full-rigged ships it was found that when the mortars fired their heavy shells the shock did tremendous damage to the forward mast, yards, and rigging. The foremasts were then removed. This left a vessel with only two masts, a main amidships and a mizzen aft. In time, square-rig sails gave way to fore-and-aft-rig. This is the reason that the two masts in a ketch or a yawl are known as the main and mizzen, while in a brig or schooner they are more sensibly called the fore and main.

The dandy ketches, like *Second Apprentice,* and their cousins the spritsail barges and the mulies, had much in common. All three types had a boxlike hull, and all used leeboards when hauling to windward, but in the ketches the hulls were far more fit for heavy seas. They had higher bows with a bolder sheer, much more powerful for throwing off steep seas. In the ketches, the lines of the hull forward were finer, and they carried a false clipper cutwater (a heavy, triangular-sectioned timber balk for parting the seas). *Second Apprentice*'s cutwater was decorated with gold scrollwork. This, apart from the gold-leaf ship's name on each bow and on the counter, was the only decorative work on the otherwise all-black hull.

Aft, *Second Apprentice*'s lines were less sharp than forward, and they finished in a well-rounded counterstern. Some of the other ketches which we saw, especially those built in Kent, had a square transom.

Along the sides of the deck ran a deep bulwark, about four feet high, to keep as much seawater where it belonged, in the sea, and not so much on deck when the ship was deep-laden. As we shall see, these bulwarks were also handy in stopping the crew from being washed over the side in heavy weather.

The construction of *Second Apprentice*'s hull was . . . massive. Some idea of this can be gained from the dimensions of her main timbers (which I noted during my time on board and quoted in a letter to my family). The keelson (inner keel, along the length of the hull), fourteen inches by fourteen inches, Oregon pine. The floors (bottom frames), eight inches by six inches, oak, on twenty-one-inch centers. The keel, twelve inches by four inches, elm. The ceiling (the deck above the floors), fourteen by three inches, pine. The futtocks (side frames), six inches by six inches, oak, on twenty-one-inch centers. The outside planking, double, two-inch-thick pine, carvel-built, caulked with hemp and oakum. The stem and stern posts were nine inches by twelve inches, oak. The stem was twelve feet six inches long.

As near as I recall, the sail areas were as follows: mainsail, 255 square yards, No. 1 flax canvas. Main topsail, one hundred square yards, No. 2 flax canvas. Foresail, ninety square yards, No. 1 extra G flax canvas. Mizzen, forty square yards, No. 3 canvas. I cannot recall the areas of the three jibs, but combined it must have been about one hundred square yards. This gives a total of about *5,300 square feet,* all to be handled by one man and two boys! The squaresail was about 180 square yards in area.

On the stern rail were fitted two sweep irons. Into these the rowlocks for the thirty-foot-long sculling sweeps (oars) were fixed, for moving the vessel when there was no wind, or for maintaining a slow headway over a current when the tide carried the ship.

The steering gear was a massive worm-gear arrangement connected by rods and chains to the steering wheel, which was about three feet in diameter and made of teak. It had eight turned spokes and was decorated with brass strips. Below the steering wheel, on the deck, were two ringbolts to which the wheel could be lashed down in an emergency in case the wheel brake failed. The compass binnacle was also brass and was secured to the deck immediately forward of the wheel. Inside the binnacle was a small oil lamp, which exhausted through a little chimney in front of the binnacle. From the top of the deckhouse protruded the chimney from the galley stove. This was known as the "Charlie Noble," but no one could ever tell me why. The deck locker on the stern, where various spare blocks and tackle, coal shovels, and deck brooms were stowed, was known as "Yarmouth Roads," after the mooring ground off the east coast port. I suppose that in the dim past someone with a wry sense of humor must have named the locker so because he thought that all the odds and ends found their way to Yarmouth.

From about 1850 onward, large numbers of sailing ketch-barges had been built on the English east and southeast coasts. Their main trade, in the heyday of sail, before the First World War, and to a much lesser extent between the wars, had been hauling coal from the staithes (small jetties) of northeast England to the harbors and beaches along the east and south coasts. Flat-bottomed, the ketches could run right up the beaches on the tide, with a kedge anchor run out astern to haul themselves off again on the next high tide. Once on the beach they unloaded their cargo onto horse-drawn carts, or if the weather threatened to deteriorate they dumped the coal onto the beach, to be picked up at leisure by the purchasers. Often the skippers sold the coal cargo piecemeal to the rural locals. This was a great benefit to many isolated communities. It meant cheap coal, and they could exchange for it their farm produce, which was eagerly sought after in the ports of northern England, so near to the great industrial centers.

Several ketch-barges made transatlantic voyages, mainly to

engage in river trading in what was then British Guiana, and one or two of these were still to be at it after World War II.

Most of the barges that voyaged far abroad were schooner- or barquentine-rigged. The largest of these, *Eliza Smeed,* loaded 750 tons, and it was said that she logged ten knots easily. She ended her days driven ashore in a hurricane on the beaches of New Jersey, on a voyage from New York to the West Indies.

In the late 1930s the ketches took whatever cargo they could get. It might be coal from Yorkshire down to the Thames or round into the English Channel to one of the many havens there; it might be pitch to France; cement or bricks to anywhere; Portland stone to London; or farm produce, grain and such, from a creek on the east coast to the Pool of London for transshipment onto lighters or onto big steamers bound abroad. It might be cowhides—a stinking cargo—or gravel, or scrap iron, or even manure for fertilizer—and everything was loaded and unloaded by hand.

On my first trading voyage we were lucky. Ours was a comparatively easy cargo—about two thousand wooden crates of empty mineral-water bottles closely stacked and lashed in the hold, atop about fifty tons of scrap iron—all headed for Germany.

By modern standards there was very little ease or pleasure in the lives of the crew of a small trading sailing vessel. What there was of both of these abstract notions was almost always serendipitous—an occasional delay in the delivery of a cargo, the ship caught in harbor on a Sunday, a chance day of fair wind and fine, sunny weather—but mostly it was hard slog, slog, all day and all, or much of, the night. Even when we were held up for cargo, or fog-bound, or at anchor waiting for a favorable wind, there was still maintenance work to be done onboard, wood and iron to be scraped and painted, bilges to be pumped out, masts to be painted, rigging to be oiled, wires and cables to be spliced, sails to be repaired, and, for the boys, always cleaning, cooking, cleaning, in between all the other jobs. Even in the fog there was a lookout to be kept, the bow bell to be tolled every minute.

Most of the coasting sailing barges were, despite their low

freeboard and flat bottoms, very seaworthy craft that could take any amount of punishment from the often vicious winds and seas of the English Channel and the North Sea, and still remain tight as bottles. Many a time I was to see *Second Apprentice* still being driven along with all her working sails aloft, when motorcraft were seeking shelter or making very hard going.

The captains of all the coasting barges were highly respected. Most of them had been at sea all their lives, and many of them had held command since their early twenties and were well known in practically every port in the British Isles. Many were recognized in European ports, too, from Hamburg, Germany, to Bordeaux, western France, and a few even farther afield. When he went ashore the captain always wore a good shorego-ing suit, and when he returned onboard he usually went down into his cabin and did not emerge until the ship was ready for sea.

A sailing vessel trading only in British waters required only a master qualified by hard-gained experience. He needed no official certificate of competence, unless he was to be the skip-per of a fishing smack of twenty-five tons or over. If a boy wished to eventually rise in the trade by gaining a master's certificate he sought out a berth in the dandy ketches, like *Second Apprentice,* which were considered by the authorities to be fully recognized as seagoing vessels, and whose masters needed Board of Trade certificates. A berth in a dandy ketch was, by the late thirties, very hard to come by; I was very fortunate that my dad and Tansy had been friends.

At the other end of the scale from the captains were the boys. Even though we lived almost cheek by jowl with the master, a great chasm separated us. Boys from poor families, or from orphanages, usually went to sea first on a fishing boat —and generally the only things they possessed were the clothes they stood in. Onboard the bawley or the smack they worked all the hours that God ever sent. Their quarters below were no more than a filthy shelf in a floating slum, their pay no more than would just keep them alive.

Between the two extremes there was a wide range of pay-ment and living conditions, but for all at sea, sail-in-trade life, whether underway or in harbor, whether in fine weather or foul, was in the main little but arduous, unremitting toil.

Among all the seamen I met whose craft had been converted from sail to power I cannot recall any one of them ever complaining about it. Without exception they all considered it a blessing, but they were also extremely proud of the ability and skills that they had gained under sail. When they spun a yarn, it was invariably a tale about blown-out sails, or clawing off a lee shore with no engine below.

In the fishing boats they still carried on the indentured apprentice system for boys. They had an even grimmer existence than did we lads in the ketches. Their main job was to coil the trawl warp down below in the fetid, tossing, stinking warp room each time the long, wet, freezing-cold tarry warp was hauled in, which might be several times a day. The only thing to remind them of the light and the sky and the sea outside was the steady clink, clink of the pawls on the windlass barrel and the hiss of escaping steam from above. In between spells in the dark, heaving warp room, they peeled the potatoes, made tea, helped pack the fish catch in boxes, helped stow the heavy boxes in the hold, coiled lines on deck, and, if there was a fog, stood for hours on the freezing bow tolling the fog bell. The fisherboys had only one consolation for their baleful existence —they had a tiny share in the profits from the catch. It rarely came to more than a few pennies, but the thought of how their share would be spent ashore kept many a poor little fourteen-year-old going as the never-ending warp came snaking like a cold, wet serpent into the gloomy warp room. In the ketches we had no share in the profits, but a good skipper would work a small bonus into a boy's pay if a fast passage had been made. It was hardly ever more than a shilling (twenty cents), but it made all the difference to a good or a bad voyage.

By the late thirties most of the coastal sailing vessels still in trade were owned by companies, but there were still a few, like *Second Apprentice,* that were partially owned by the masters. British vessels are apportioned, for God only knows what reason, into sixty-four shares. This has been so from time immemorial—probably since before Stonehenge was built—and it still is so. The thirty shares not owned by Tansy were owned by a ship's chandler and sailmaker in Harwich, a coal merchant in Deal, and a captain's widow in Ramsgate. In the days before the government started to get its sticky finger into everything that worked well, this was in many respects a good thing, a forerunner, if you like, of syndicalism (worker-owned businesses). For instance, if a skipper was trying to skimp on the crew's food and pared down on the meat for meals, then the butcher who arranged the supply of meat was going to want to know why. Our sails, when we replaced them—which was rare—were obtained from the sailmaker in Harwich at a decent discount, because he was making sails partly for himself. It was the same with blocks and rope and such from the chandler. The coal merchant arranged for *Second Apprentice* cargoes of coal from Gateshead, County Durham, to Kent or Sussex whenever we were seeking a cargo, so the ship was very rarely without gainful employment. As for the widow, each time our ship was to call at Ramsgate, she brought delicious meat pies down to the jetty for us in china bowls covered with blue cloths—and she had a pretty young daughter, besides.

The food was always the responsibility of the owners. There were a few cases of skippers starving their crews, but these episodes were soon advertised around the coast, and those captains would be lucky to find themselves another crew, or with anything but an incompetent rabble clambering onboard, desperate for work and incapable of securing a mooring line properly, much less making a fender from old, worn-out rope.

The sailors in the coasting trade, while they were probably the hardest-worked laboring people in or around the British Isles, were also probably the best fed, at least while the ships were in harbor. At sea things were different, as it was not easy for a young boy to prepare a gourmet meal in a bucking, tossing, tiny galley only five feet by six square, with no refrigeration onboard. After a few days at sea the ship's biscuits were broken out. They were about four inches square, gray, smooth on one side, and rough on the other. The sailors called them "Portmadoc pantiles," because they looked a bit like roofing slates, but I was proud that the little port in West Wales, once the home of a great sailing fleet, was still remembered here, far away in southeast England. Later I was to find that Portmadoc was remembered the world over, wherever a sailing craft wandered—with English spoken onboard and ship's biscuits in the galley locker.

Within a few hours of joining *Second Apprentice* I had learned the dandy ketches' slogan: "A wet shirt and a happy heart."

10

Underway

That first evening onboard *Second Apprentice,* no sooner was the supper eaten and the pots and pans cleared out of the skipper's lobby than preparations started for getting underway. By then the ship was well afloat on the tide, which was just about to turn. There was a fitful southwesterly breeze, which meant that it was more or less against us until we got out of the river and gained the offing. The night was fine, with moonlight illuminating the stream between fleeting clouds.

The captain, mate, and deckhand were in no hurry, or at least they seemed not to be to me. Ted delved into Yarmouth Roads —the big deck locker aft—and brought out the side lights, green and red. They were brass lamps about a foot high. In the galley he filled their kerosine reservoirs with oil and lit them. Then he jerked his head, signaling me to follow him. Soon he had both lamps lashed to the sideboards, which were secured to the main shrouds. The red and green lights cast an eerie glow on each side of the ship, the green one on the leaves of the trees which lined the jetty, and the red one on the waters of the river. Little midges and other flying life darted about in their beams, like sparks off a slow match. These emerald and ruby iridescenses on each side of the dark ship gave an aspect of unreality to the scene.

Meanwhile, Bert had secured the last of the cargo-hold cover boards and covered them with tarpaulins, which he wedged in firmly to sockets in the hatch-coamings with a sledgehammer. Next, he and Ted, with me watching and helping where I could, gathered up all the running rigging, which had been temporarily displaced to be out of the way while the cargo was being loaded, and put it back in its proper position, flaking it out on deck or belaying it to the correct cleats. Then all the spare ropes and spars were laid out neatly fore and aft along the top of the main cargo hold.

That done, Bert went aft to the captain's companionway and called softly, "Right, Tansy, all squared away!"

There was a muffled, gruff reply. A minute later Tansy emerged from down below, still wearing his bowler and his watch fob. His clay pipe was between his lips, with the bowl upside down. "Nipper," Tansy peered at me, "you stay alongside me, seeing as how it's your first trip." Then he turned to Bert and nodded with a slight movement of his head.

Bert moved aft, while Ted ran forward. Silhouetted against the red, green, and silver moon glow, they moved like sprites in the night. Ted let go of the forward mooring warp, which he quickly ranged aft along the starboard side-deck, and hopped to the main-topsail halyard, ready to hoist the high sail over the mainmast. As soon as the forward mooring warp was let go the breeze caught the mast's spars and rigging and slowly pushed the bows out into the stream. Bert then let the after mooring warp go and hopped onboard, and we were underway. As soon as the tide moved the ship forward, Ted hoisted the topsail. I thrilled as I stood beside Tansy at the wheel and the moonlight shone on the white sail far above us.

The anchor was still hung out over the bow, below water, but clear of the bottom. As the ship approached the other bank of the narrow river on the starboard tack, the anchor caught the bottom mud and brought the bow to a halt. The ship pivoted on the anchor, and the stern carried on swinging towards the far riverbank. To my novice eyes this was very disturbing; I thought we were going to collide with the bank. But then, as soon as the wind caught the port side of the topsail, Tansy spun the wheel to starboard. Bert and Ted were on the anchor windlass and pumping away for all they were worth, raising the anchor again. The ship moved forward on the port tack, toward the jetty bank from which we had departed minutes before, but about fifty yards downstream.

This maneuver was repeated about a half-dozen times, until we had a fair breeze to make the harbor exit on a broad reach (that is, with the wind at right angles to the sails). The anchor was left cock-a-hoop (hard up against the bow), while the mainsail was hoisted. As I watched the man and the youth hoist the heavy main gaff right up to the houndsbands, Tansy said to me, "We call that jilling."

With the mainsail set, the ship seemed to give a start and a sort of sigh as her pace quickened. Now we were passing the outer harbor light, and ahead of us I could see only the gleaming sea, restless under a fitful, gibbous moon. As I turned to Tansy for a fleeting moment, *Second Apprentice* felt the clear scent of the sea, and she became a living thing, the sum of all the life that had ever been bestowed upon her by generations of sailormen. It was impossible that she could be merely a sailing barge on her way to the Rhine with empty bottles and scrap iron. She was a quinquereme, a galleon, a caravel; she was a carrack bound for the rainbow lands of gold and precious stones across a sea of silver and azure, with a cargo of dreams and poetry. Tansy repeated, "We call it jilling, Nipper."

"What's that, sir?"

"Tansy," the captain reminded me softly.

"What's that, Tansy?" I asked him, my eyes back absent-mindedly on the white mainsail, now pregnant with the wind and shimmering ghostlike under the moon.

"What we did with the anchor back upstream. There's another way to do it, called dredging, but we call it *drudging,* because it is a real blessed drudge, especially for those who have to raise and lower the anchor every time we want to come about."

By this time the mate and Ted had the foresail hoisted, and were busy hauling up the two jibs. Tansy looked around into the night. Then he said to me: "Hold the wheel a minute, Nipper. I'll just go and hoist the mizzen."

I stared at the great brassbound wheel in Tansy's grip, not moving. I must have looked like a rabbit gazing at a snake.

"Come on, Nipper, it won't bite you," said Tansy. "Catch ahold of this here spoke and keep her heading just like she is. See the compass?" I stretched a little on my toes and peered into the binnacle. I was accustomed to the tiny compass on Morgan Whistle's lugger. This was a much bigger one, but the principle was the same. The heading was east-by-southeast.

"Yes, sir."

"Tansy. Well, keep her on that there heading," ordered the captain.

"East-by-southeast, Tansy."

"Good boy!" Tansy's face shone softly in the subdued glow from the light of the compass binnacle for a second; then he was gone into the shadows aft. I gripped the wheel with a tight, nervous fist and stared for all I was worth at the compass card, which hardly moved, even when Tansy hauled the mizzen sail up. Soon the captain was back again at the wheel. "Now," he said, "you've had a long day, Nipper, what with traveling and all. You go forward and get a good sleep."

"Oh, I'm all right, Tansy. . . ."

"That's an order, Nipper." His voice was stern.

"Yes, Tansy." I started to make my way forward on the gently heeled deck, marveling at the tautened shrouds and the bellied mainsail, which looked like a gigantic seashell seen through shimmering water. I heard Tansy's voice behind me. "Careful how you go, son. Good night!"

"Oh . . . good night, sir . . . Tansy!" I saw Bert and Ted working away up forward. Before descending down the scuttle to the foc'sle, I paused to watch them as they brought the anchor onboard to lash it down on the cathead. They were both wet with spray. When the anchor was safely catted Bert went aft to relieve Tansy. Ted looked up from securing the anchor with the iron cat-stopper. "You'd better get your head down, Nipper. You've got a long day tomorrow."

I looked out into the night, at the moon's reflection leaping from wave to wave between the blackness of the cloud shadows, and dimly to starboard; over the green coruscation from the sidelight playing on the sea; at the coastal lights, a steady gaze here, like a nurse watching her charge, a slow gleam there, like a fond farewell, and quick stabbing flashes in the low blackness of the horizon; reminders that the sea does not gladly suffer fools or idlers, and that we must look to our duties.

Reluctantly, yet sleepily, I headed down the ladder into the foc'sle, where Ted had already lit the swinging lamp and the dying stove gave off a soft golden glow on the sole. Wearily I climbed under my two blankets and lay my head down on the pillow, close to the ship's side. Even though the side planks were four inches thick, I could hear, as the bows rose and descended gently, the trickling wavelets as they washed against the moving hull. It was like the sound of young girls gossiping and giggling. I fell to thinking about Angharad and Branwen Powell back home in Llangareth. Then I remembered Mam and Caradoc and Cei, but before I started to cry I fell asleep, half sad in my homesickness and half mad in my joy. That is the way boys are.

In between being half-wakened a couple of times in the next few hours by thumping and clattering overhead, I slept soundly through the night until Ted roused me at daylight. "Come on, Nipper, work to do!"

I clambered sleepily out of my berth and squared away my blankets. Ted was cleaning out the ashpan of the stove. The foc'sle was rearing up and down, and the bows were banging away quite merrily. I hung grimly on to the ladder.

"You missed all the bleeding fun," said Ted, without looking at me.

I looked at him. He was still wearing his blue shirt and tattered oilskin jacket. His hair was tousled. "How's that, Ted?"

"We was running free all night, from just after you turned in. We dropped the main and hoisted the square sail. We came up past the Downs (the Dover Strait) like a dose of salts. Then, when we was off the foreland we got a northwester, and we've been biting the bloody wind ever since—heading hard to windward. It's a bit lumpy up there. You want to wrap up nice and warm—cold as a fish's tit . . . and you'd better get aft as quick as Christ'll let you. Tansy's waiting for his breakfast."

When I reached the top of the foc'sle scuttle it was as though I were on another ship than the gentle vessel of the night before, or rather it was as if the ship were in another world. The first sensation I had was a stream of cold spray all over me, but I was in my oilies, so there was little harm done, apart from the stinging shock of North Sea water.

The ship was heeled over so much that the port bulwark was half under water half the time. The mainsail was closehauled (hauled in tight, so that its luff and plane grabbed and bit into the wind) and pulsing like a living thing against a gray, overcast sky. The only land to be seen was a thin blue line on the horizon on the port quarter.

Over my head and behind me the staysail and two jibs drummed away like an army of martial angels, and the wind in the rigging zinged. I peered skyward. Tansy still had the topsail set on the main, and it was as full as an elephant's belly. Aft, the mizzensail had been reefed a couple of points so as to avoid having too much weather helm (the tendency of the aftersail to keep pushing the ship's head into the wind). I clumsily made my way aft along the sloping deck and passed the helm as I headed for the galley. Tansy's hand was on the wheel, and he sat on an upturned barrel, with his pipe still upside down and his bowler perched on his head.

"Morning, Nipper."

Even as the captain greeted me gruffly, Bert emerged from the after companionway and hailed me. "Had a good kip? Wait for Ted in the galley. He'll show you the ropes for breakfast, and after that you and him scrub down the decks, right?"

Breakfast was porridge, cooked in a great iron pot, smoked haddock and bacon, with two fried eggs apiece, and, of course, tea. It was my first try at cooking a meal in a small galley that was heeled over and jerking with every judder of the mainsail and jolting with every shudder of the bows against the seas, but somehow or other, under Ted's supervision, I managed it all right without spilling too much porridge or tea. By the time we had shipped the fiddles on the table in the skipper's lobby there was quite a decent spread. (Fiddles are wooden battens that are pegged into the sides of the tabletop to stop eating gear from sliding off when the ship is heeled or rolling hard.) As Bert sat down to eat we could hear the noise of the thousands of empty bottles in the hold, forward of the bulkhead, all clinking away. "You a good bottle-washer, Nipper?" the mate asked.

"You have to do that before we put the bottles ashore in Germany," broke in Ted, his face serious.

Bert looked at Ted. "Don't tell him that, you'll put him off," he said, also serious. "I told you not to tell Nipper about washing them bottles until we got to Remagen. . . ."

Now they had me worried. I stared at them both; then I burst out: "What, wash all those bottles? Why, there must be a million of them!"

"Well, you wouldn't want them there Jerries filling dirty bottles with mineral water, now, would you, Nipper?" Bert replied. They they were both silent, as they piled into their food and tea, and left me shattered at the prospect of cleaning all the bottles. They kept the jape up right until the crates of bottles were slung ashore, and they had me worried every time I thought of it for the rest of the trip.

Scrubbing the decks took an hour or so. Ted and I did this despite the water streaming over the decks every time the ship plunged into the cold humps of the North Sea. As the forenoon wore on, though, the sun came out fitfully, and then, even though the seawater was painfully cold on my bare feet, the sights and sounds of the hull and sails driving through the sea and the wind, and the rigging humming with effort, were glorious.

Towards the end of the deck-scrub we sighted a spritsail barge heading north, also beating into the wind. As we caught up with her the sun shone. The sprittie was about seventy feet long, and her bluff bows shouldered the green-blue seas aside, occasionally rising to come down again with a resounding crash that sent showers of iridescent spray whizzing over her foredeck, drenching her decks and hatch covers, and soaking the lower cloths of her dark red mainsail, already almost black with brine. As *Second Apprentice* overtook her we saw her name on her counter—*Lady Mary*.

"She's one of Everard's boats," commented Ted, as he casually turned away to stow the deck-scrubbers in the afterlocker.

I watched the play of purple shadows on *Lady Mary*'s russet sails and the shining whiteness of her jib as it strained at the bolt-ropes. Her brightly varnished topmast gleamed as it whipped to leeward under the pressure of the wind in her huge topsail. Her weather rigging, on the far side from us, was as taut as steel bars, and her sails were all hard curves, except for her mizzen, which was half brailed up to the mast.

As we pulled ahead of her, the sprittie came about (went on the other tack, so that the wind would be on her other, starboard, side). She was only about fifty yards away from us. I could clearly see her helmsman pushing the wheel over hard —she had no deckhouse. *Lady Mary* wound into the wind with a thundering slatting of canvas that we could hear plainly even over the drumming of our own. Her great sprit spar (which held her mainsail out) lurched to and fro for a few seconds, her head paid off from the wind helped by her foresail held a-weather with a bowline, her topsail began to fill, her foresail was released and smacked over to leeward with a sudden explosion. Then she stood out on the starboard tack, a vision of graceful curves and shadows, her golden transom rising and dipping in the creamy froth of her wake as she streamed away from us toward the English coast in the west. I see her in my mind's eye now, so long ago and far away.

At sea, Tansy wore—under his yellow oilskin coat if it was wet—an older, more worn version of his shoregoing suit, but the same bowler hat. His seagoing suit was single-breasted, and when the light caught it edge-on it shone green. At sea he wore calf-length rubber boots inside which he tucked his trousers. When the weather was warm enough—which was not very often—he doffed his jacket and shirt collar, and rolled up the sleeves of his thick flannel shirt to his elbows. His trousers were rigged with both suspenders and a two-inch-thick leather belt with a great brass buckle. On his left forearm, the muscle like a steel cable, was a single tattoo, blurred with age—crossed flags, the British Union Jack and the American Stars and Stripes, and, below, a scroll on which was engraved the words "Death before Dishonour." With his clay pipe and waistcoat, there he was, a typical barge skipper, one of the last inheritors of a tradition going back almost to the dawn of human navigational history.

"Where does Tansy come from, Ted?" I asked as the deckhand and I prepared dinner that day.

"He lives in Sandwich, leastways he's got a cottage over there," Ted replied. "His missus died four years ago. He don't hardly go there anymore. Got a nice daughter, though, Daisy. She comes down and visits us sometimes when we're in Kent or Sussex. A real, bloody good hand is Daisy, but she don't stand no nonsense, leastways not from the likes of us." Ted stirred the soup on the stove, tasted some from the spoon, smacked his lips, and went on: "Like I said, he don't go home much now—stays onboard most of the time when we're in harbor. Well, at holiday times it saves him having to pay a bloody watchman, don't it?" Ted stirred the soup again, balancing himself against a beam overhead as the ship bucked and jolted against the head seas. "He don't stand night watches, Nipper. Tansy, I mean. It ain't the custom for skippers to do that, not when they got two other bleeding helmsmen onboard." Ted stuck out his thin chest slightly as he said this. "But he always keeps the forenoon watch while Bert—he keeps the morning watch from four till eight, see, gets his head down—has a kip, and I clean up. 'Course, now you're onboard it'll be a bit easier for me. We been without a bloody nipper for over a month, ever since the last one fell from the gammon iron [at the top of the mainmast] and cracked his skull."

I was astonished. I hadn't heard of this accident before. Ted grabbed the soup dixie (a pan with a bucketlike handle) and started ladling out a rich leek broth. "Oh, he was a silly little sod, wouldn't listen to no one. Came from bloody Stepney, didn't he? Reckoned his old man was a waterman on the Thames lighters, but he was as thick as two bleedin' planks."

"Do you think I'll be able to take a trick on the helm, Ted?"

"Well, you want to ask Tansy about that. I expect he'll let you take it while he's on watch, for the first couple of trips, anyway. Here—take these down to the skipper's lobby. . . ." Ted handed me the dixie and spoons, which somehow, God knows how with the ship bashing away and jolting like a startled carthorse, I managed to set out on the table without spilling more than half the contents.

Over dinner, Bert told me that I could spend an hour or so on the helm, and this I did, after the meal was cleared away and he had relieved Ted. The afternoon sun shone gloriously over a greenish-blue sea. As I gripped the wheel and held it steady (it was surprisingly sensitive) I could hear behind me, on the other side of the galley bulkhead, the pots and pans banging and rattling in their battens as they jarred and racketed to each plunge of the hull. Each time *Second Apprentice* met a sea up, up the foredeck climbed, yawing and surging and quivering, and then, with a clear, sickle-like swoop it plunged down into the seas. I could plainly hear, above the thrum of the sails and the screeching of the dry blocks, the flaring bows as they cut down into the water below them and *squelched*. Then there was a pause each time the bows reached the bottom of their scend, where the divided waters rose above the bowsprit and came down heavily onto the foredeck like a volley of grapeshot. That, each time, was followed by the tinny, clinking rattle of thousands of bottles in the hold below, a hundred grunts and squeals and swishes from two dozen blocks and twice as many lines, a yaw as the vessel slid off the sea, a punt, and a kick. Then *Second Apprentice,* before my wondering young eyes, half-blinded by spray, gathered herself together again to repeat the motion. Pickle, smash, and rinse; pickle, smash, and rinse. Beating to windward, it's called. All the time the endless seas tramped toward us from the north, one after the other in serried millions, never ending.

That evening, just before supper—it must have been about seven o'clock—Tansy came out on deck, leaned against the port, weather bulwark, and stared at the horizon for a minute or two. He came over to Bert, who was about to take the helm over from Ted, and said, "We'll bring her round now, Bert."

I stared around at the horizon and the sea. I saw nothing at all that was different from what it had been an hour before.

Tansy took the wheel and turned it to starboard. The bows turned away from the wind, Bert and Ted eased off the sheets, and the ship headed more or less southeast, with the wind on her port quarter, almost running free (going directly away from the wind). Quite suddenly, it was as though *Second Apprentice* were in another time and place. Now the wind apparently eased from half a gale to a modest breeze, the seas gently caressed and nursed her hull with fond massages from astern, and the ship's bow rose in and out of the troughs sedately, fitting into each trough cozily, rising on each crest modestly.

"Now we'll have a nice easy run into the Maas," murmured Tansy. "If this here wind keeps up we should be off Voorne in the morning at first light." With the wind aft, and in the calm shelter of the helm-dodger, he turned his pipe bowl right side up, and, as Bert and Ted adjusted the main, fore, and mizzen sheets, he puffed away contentedly. "Go and get the supper up, Nipper."

Before I went into the galley door I looked all around. Dusk was upon us. It was a fine night, with little cloud for that part of the world. From astern of us, out of the blackening horizon, came the music of the elemental symphony of wind and water. The breaking tops of the seas glowed whitely in the glare of our stern light, like little corpses rolling in their shrouds. The ketch moved gently enough to cause a shower of silver sparks to break from under her stern and dissipate in her wake each time her counter lifted atop a sea. Sometimes *Second Apprentice* paused for a moment as the wind varied, and the seas seemed to stop, too, before once more taking up their charge.

The noises were much more subdued than they had been all day. They were mainly the noises of the moderate wind and what it encountered, rigging or spars or canvas; or the play of a slack rope; or the bubbling of the water along the side; or the slight groaning of the hull timbers as they worked, each against the other. Nothing is ever still at sea. I stepped over the sill of the galley door and set to, boiling four pounds of potatoes for supper.

Around the table later, there was little sign of all the activity topside, all the wonder and immensity of sea and sky. In the gleam of the swinging lamp, reflected on the varnish of the bulkheads all around us, with the little coal stove glowing, the talk was mainly of ports along the rivers Maas and Rhine, where we were now bound, of cargoes taken in and discharged, of friends in Holland and Germany, and of when we could expect to be back in England. That is the sailor's way.

After supper was cleared, there was not much for me to do but stand by Bert at the wheel and wonder at our passage. We had no newspapers or magazines onboard—they were too expensive for the meager funds of the captain and crew, and Tansy would not have allowed a wireless set onboard, even if one could have been afforded. "Too much bloomin' noise onboard already," he had told a fellow captain who had proudly displayed his radio receiver. Fortunately, I had with me my *Oxford Book of English Verse,* which I read for a while in the dim light of the foc'sle lamp; but I wanted to see the night, even though it was quite cold topside. After an hour or so of silently gazing at the sails and rigging dimly lit in the fading moonlight, it was time for me to turn in. I fell asleep trying to recall the names of all the ropes and tackles that Ted had shown me that day. It didn't take me long to slumber. I had been on the go practically since dawn, making breakfast, dinner, tea, and supper for four hungry people, one of whom (Ted) ate like a horse; cleaning the galley each time a meal was finished; scrubbing the decks and the foc'sle and the skipper's flat; tidying both the captain's and the mate's tiny cabins; giving a hand wherever I was asked to; and making a tremendous effort to learn and remember a bewildering number of different things, their proper places, and their uses.

The next morning, just before dawn broke, I was roused again, but to a very different scene than the previous morning. All around the sea was almost calm. The wind was a mere zephyr, but still from the northwest. Above, the topsail bellied slackly, but the main hung half-empty, while the jibs drew almost no wind at all, shielded as they were by the bigger sails. Dawn came up in fiery red splashes that bathed the eastern horizon and shot stabs of golden light through the tops of light blue seas with a sandy cast to them. As I headed for the galley, Bert, on the helm, lifted his chin ahead and grinned at me. I looked forward of the bowsprit . . . and saw my first foreign shore. It was a long, sandy rise shining in the early sun, all along the southeast horizon. On it, a couple of miles away, a stark white lighthouse held up an admonishing finger before my astonished eyes.

Second Apprentice was holding a course more or less parallel to the shore, which was about two miles off, and we were heading for the headland, which, as Bert explained, led around into the mouth of the Maas River.

By the time I had four kippers grilled, and a dixie of porridge and a gallon of tea prepared, I could hear Bert cursing at the wheel. Next I heard Tansy's footsteps mounting the companionway from his cabin. Right away, Bert's language moderated.

"What's up, Bert?" I heard our captain ask the mate.

"The bloomin' wind's changed, Tansy—we're headed!" I

poked my head out of the galley door. Suddenly we had got an inexplicable steady breeze right in our teeth, from the northeast.

"No sense in it," I heard Tansy mutter. "It don't fit this season, and it don't fit the sky." All the while the mainsail and jibs slatted away, until Bert shoved the wheel over and we headed northwest again, out to sea, away from our destination.

"Someone's got it in for us, Tansy," I heard Bert say.

"Reckon so," agreed Tansy, as the easterly breeze rose to a hard blow and *Second Apprentice* heeled over, sailing in the diametrically wrong direction from her destination.

"Be just right, this here wind, if we was out on a pleasure sail," commented Bert after a while.

All at once the breeze dropped, and we were left in a dead flat calm, rolling away, with the ship's bows turning where they willed, and no headway on the vessel.

"Damn and blast!" cursed Bert.

"The Lord provideth," said Tansy, quietly, as *Second Apprentice* pitched and tossed on a windless sea, three miles out from the beckoning, tantalizing rivermouth.

11

Magic Moments

For an hour, as we clumsily consumed breakfast *al fresco* around
the galley door, the ship wallowed and rolled like a drunken
dinosaur. Bert and Ted had already handed (lowered) the
mainsail to stop the gaff from slatting about, but the foresail
and jibs were left hoisted. Every time *Second Apprentice* heeled
this way or that in a sickening lurch the canvas slammed over
with a great hollow *thud.* In the galley it was as much as I could
do to keep everything from sliding off the stove top and table
onto the deck. Every so often the ship's bows came round and
headed into shallow hills of undulating sea. Then her movement became wonderfully gentle as she slowly, leniently
pitched and tossed for a few minutes; but as the bow turned
again off the seas she gave a sudden lurch sideways, sending
everything in the galley toppling.

After an uncomfortable breakfast yaffled standing on deck
braced against anything handy (what they would call these
days a balanced meal), Bert and Ted unlashed two thirty-foot-
long pulling sweeps from their stowages along the side bulwarks and shipped them in the sweep-iron rowlocks just forward of the helm shelter. Then they commenced to row the
ship, with Tansy steering.

As Bert hauled on his sweep he called to Tansy, "How's the
tide?"

Tansy stooped and peered through the skylight, just in front
of his feet, to see the time on the lobby clock below. He ambled
over to the side-rail and looked directly down at the sea for a
minute. "She'll be on the flow in about an hour, Bert." On

many occasions since, I have seen various yachting skippers reckoning up the tide, usually scrambling and fretting as they read out the figures in the local tide tables, their electronic calculators beeping, and I always remember Tansy and *Second Apprentice* in the North Sea off the Maas River so long ago. It was as though they were both part of the tide and locked into the tidal influences. Tansy just *knew* the tide was going to change.

For an hour Bert and Ted heaved and pushed away at the sweeps, each giant oar as long and thick as a young tree trunk. Then it was my turn to relieve Ted for half an hour of back-breaking toil. My sweep was so long that it took me three or four steps backward and the same forward to get the full range and half the power of the oar. The ship hardly seemed to move. We were merely holding our own against the outgoing tide for the first half an hour. When the tide turned, though, it was clear that we were moving at about one knot, and with the tide helping us the toil at the sweeps eased off greatly. All we had to do now was maintain steerage-way over the tide.

While all this was going on we were practically surrounded by other craft, big and small, sail and power, entering and leaving the Maas. There were a couple of small tugs lying off the mouth of the estuary, but a tow cost money, and *Second Apprentice* was working on a small enough profit margin as it was. A tow, unless the ship was in grave jeopardy, was out of the question. We might just as well have expected the crown jewels for Christmas!

As the inflow of the tide decreased the speed of the current of the Maas River, our ship moved a little faster through the water, and by noon we were well inside the Maas estuary. When the tide slowed down again, in the early afternoon, Bert and Ted were still pulling away at the sweeps. Tansy steered the ship over toward the north bank of the river, just downstream from Maassluit town.

As we approached the low, gray bank I could see no houses on the shore, nor any land behind the riverbank wall. This puzzled me until Tansy told me that the wall was in fact a dyke and the town behind it was all below sea level. There was nothing to see all around but high, gray walls lining the riverbanks, and hundreds of barges, sail and powerboats, dumb-lighters, tugs, and other work boats, moored all along the sides of the river.

Just as *Second Apprentice* changed course to head for a mooring, a slight breeze sprang up again from the northwest, blowing directly in from the sea along the river, setting up a crinkled sea. The opportunity was grabbed. With hardly a word spoken, the two long sweeps were pulled inboard and laid along the deck. Bert and Ted hauled on the mainsail halyards, heaving the sail up for all they were worth. Tansy sheered off and headed upstream, and we made slow but steady progress against the river current for the rest of the afternoon.

I was amazed at the number of craft navigating and moored along the Maas River, everything from the biggest class of ocean steamers down to tiny sailing smacks; it was two long processions of vessels heading both ways along the river, past hundreds more anchored and moored along the banks and in the great docks of Schliedam and Rotterdam, which seemed to sprawl for miles and miles. Often, where ships had been taken down through the locks to berths below sea level we could see only a forest of mast-tops over the top of the dykes.

Going upstream on the Maas, though, was not a sightseeing trip for me or anyone else onboard. There was still the ship's work to be done: oiling the windlasses; scrubbing the galley and toilet; polishing the brasswork on deck and down below; scrubbing out the foc'sle, the skipper's flat, and the captain's and mate's cabins; changing the officer's bed linen; laundering; and preparing the supper. There were very few minutes of relaxation, and, of course, all the while I was wearily anticipating having to wash all the empty bottles in the hold when we reached Remagen. I'd even worked out the number of bottles by now—thirty thousand, give or take a few hundred.

Second Apprentice "went" to moor ("brought up" is the correct term) just before dusk off the town of Ridderkerk, which is on a branch of a stream joining the River Maas to the River Waal. Bringing up was more or less the same process as getting underway, only in reverse order. First the mizzen was handed, then the main, and the leeboards were hoisted while the captain eased off the headsail sheets. The jibs were handed as the ship crept up to the mooring under topsail and foresail only. Next the foresail was lowered, rolled up and lashed like a sausage, and hauled again up the forebrace clear of the fore-deck. As the bows slowly approached the mooring buoy, Ted went over the bows, clinging onto the bowsprit with one hand, mooring rope in the other. When the ship was near enough he reeved the mooring line through the ring on the buoy and passed the fag-end back up onboard. That done, the topsail was lowered with a clatter, and another mooring line, with a shackle in an eye on the end, was passed over to Ted, who shackled it onto the mooring buoy. Then the first, looped mooring line was either eased off or brought back onboard. It was not easy, handling four-inch tarry coir ropes while hanging over, under, or onto the bowsprit, but Ted made it look easy, and within a few weeks I was doing the same thing myself.

The Dutch customs inspection at Ridderkerk was no more than a handshake and a greeting between the inspector and Tansy. They were obviously old acquaintances.

Like any boy I would have loved to be able to go ashore. I stared longingly at the little town, so clean and fresh in the clear May evening. There were trees and flowers growing all along the riverbank, and people young and old strolling along, but for my first six months I was allowed ashore only on Saturdays. In any case, by the time the ship was moored, and the supper cooked and cleared up, I was so weary that I could just about drag myself forward to the foc'sle and turn in, like everyone else onboard, with the prospect of rising at five o'clock the next morning and getting underway again.

The daily routine of ship's chores was almost always the same, whether at sea, up a river, or alongside, except that alongside it was much more strenuous; the crew handled all their own cargoes out and into the vessel. First there were the decks, the galley, and the toilet (or "head") to be scrubbed white and a score of bits of brass to be polished. Then breakfast to prepare. After breakfast was cleared up Bert told Ted and me what our tasks for the forenoon were; chipping paint, varnishing (varnishing!), tarring, splicing, or sewing; or, if the weather was too wet to work on deck, unlaying old rope for Bert and Ted to make up fenders or sennits or baggy-wrinkle. These last were pads made of old rope that were laid around the standing rigging wires, where the sails tended to chafe against them. The standing rigging always had to be kept taut, and we were forever cleaning and painting the ship's structure, even when underway in calm waters. Alongside, if we were waiting for a cargo, the ship's side was scrubbed and painted where necessary, and every block was overhauled and greased as far as possible.

Hull bottom cleaning was carried out twice a year, and it was two days of hard labor for a man and two boys to scrub and then apply two coats of black varnish to the whole three thousand square feet or so of the underwater hull. Daily, every few hours at sea, there was the hull to pump out, for wooden ships always take in a certain amount of water, no matter how tightly they are built. No harm in that—salt water keeps the wood fresh.

It was little wonder that at the end of a long day, even in a place as pretty and attractive as Ridderkerk, none of the crew showed much eagerness to go ashore, and were only too pleased to crawl into their berths.

Later, I was to find that sometimes it was a relief to be out at sea in bad weather even in winter, because, apart from standing watches in fog, snow, and rain, the weather conditions and the movement of the vessel made most kinds of work impossible, and then, when I was off watch, in between preparing and cleaning up meals I could catch up on sleep and restore some of the strength I had lost working in port.

The next morning we got underway as soon as the night sky started to lighten. There was no breeze, so it was sweeps again for Bert and Ted while I cooked breakfast. That lasted until about seven o'clock, when a nice, steady southwesterly breeze roused itself. We were not alone; about a dozen other sailing barges, and many more motor barges, all started off upstream and downstream at the same time as *Second Apprentice.*

Most of the Dutch barge skippers sailed with their families onboard, and their vessels were real little family homes, with flower-boxes around the windows of the deckhouses and children scampering around the decks. The Dutch boats were invariably clean and shining as new pins; they always seemed to have been freshly painted that very day. They were big vessels, many of them much longer than *Second Apprentice,* with huge, bluff bows and a tremendous sail spread. What with the flowers and the youngsters and women on deck, and usually with lines of laundered clothes hanging out on the sterns, when a flotilla of Dutch barges got underway it was more like a regatta than anything else.

Quite a few of the Dutchmen knew Tansy and Bert. When they encountered us on their way downstream, or passed us going up-river, they shouted greetings and waved. Going up the Maas and the Rhine in *Second Apprentice* was often like a triumphal homecoming. Many a time at a mooring, someone would row over to our ship and offer a bottle of schnapps, but Tansy always gently and courteously refused. He would not countenance booze of any kind onboard. On these occasions Bert usually looked on, silently ruminating. Both Bert and Ted liked a drink, but they drank only ashore, and that was invariably beer, which was all they could afford.

That day's wind took us a good fifty miles by dusk, up as far as Zaltbommel, in Gelderland. All the way, as I worked, I stared fascinated at the life of the river. There were vessels from practically every country in Europe—German, Danish, Swedish, Norwegian, Belgian, French, Swiss, and Austrian— even, much more rarely, Polish, Finnish, and Hungarian. Bert explained the different ensigns as the barges motored or sailed past.

Upstream from Rotterdam we saw few, if any, of our own flags, as the British small-craft trade with the Continent, especially under sail, had been almost throttled to death during the First World War. Now there were very few British vessels heading up and down the Rhine, apart from the two or three engaged, as we were, in the mineral-water and scrap-iron trade. There was a trickle of coal going out from the German Ruhr, but not much—Welsh coal was cheaper and better for use in ship's boilers. There were also a few cargoes of wine from the Rhineland, although before the Second World War the British drank much less wine than they do now, especially German wine.

Besides the depredations of the First World War on British sail, the northern Europeans, especially the Danes, Swedes, and Dutch, who had been neutral during the conflict, had built up fleets of motor coasters powered with diesel engines. These were hardy steel vessels, which might take little or no account of weather conditions. By the late thirties they had seized practically all of the European coastal trade, even into the Mediterranean, and they were small enough to sail a great deal of the European inland navigational system of rivers and canals. Diesel fuel, in those days, was cheap and plentiful. Each cargo of oil landed in northern Europe tolled the death of yet another sailing craft, or at least the conversion of a thing of beauty into a mastless hulk that plodded the coastal waters and the rivers as if ashamed of itself.

On the way up the Maas and the Rhine we saw dozens of sailing-craft hulls that had been converted to power, and not one did we see that was not ugly; not one did we pass without feeling a strange pride, despite their overtaking us ten times out of ten. Subconsciously we knew that *Second Apprentice* was part of the elements, of the winds and the waters, and that she was not forcing them, but bending them to her will without hurting or destroying them. We were as much a part of the sea and sky, the river and the trees, as the birds on high.

The next day we were headed—that is, the wind was against us—but despite this, by tacking back and forth across the wide river we were able to make good about thirty-five miles, up to Druten. On that day Tansy let me take the helm in the afternoon, after I had finished my morning chores. I was surprised at how easily the ship came about through the wind. There was not much tending of sheet-ropes because we carried no jibs then, and the foresail, topsail, mainsail, and mizzensheets all worked on horses (iron bars across the ship), so they worked themselves. At first, the slam of the iron horse-travelers, to which the sheet-ropes were attached, was alarming, but soon I got used to it, and after a while I gloried in sending the ship's bows through the wind as sharply as I could. It was a bright, sunny day, and I can still see the owner's pendant streaming back in the breeze from the topmast cap, and round, woolly clouds driving across a blue sky, and on each side of us the tidy, green fields of Holland, with Frisian cows, all black-and-white, grazing on the green slopes, so different from the dark, rugged hills of Wales.

All the time we were tacking upstream we were accompanied by other sailing barges doing the same thing, as far as the eye could see ahead and astern, and many a racing match developed. We always tramped past the smaller vessels, but we were hard put to keep up or pass Dutch ships of the same length as *Second Apprentice,* and I don't recall our beating any bigger vessel, though I expect we probably did, because some of them were under-sailed for their size. The Dutch botters, as heavy and ungainly as their hulls appeared, were surprisingly fast and handy, and they could turn in practically their own length. When they went about they seemed to pivot more than travel through the eye of the wind.

The following day, *Second Apprentice* was again headed for much of the time by an easterly breeze, but we managed to make Millengen, just on the Dutch side of the frontier with Germany, passing Nijmegen on the way, where there were, it seemed, a thousand river craft either moored, or busy loading or discharging cargo.

Millengen was an appealing town, and we fetched there in the late afternoon. Much to my envy, Ted got ready to go ashore with Bert to buy fresh vegetables and a leg of pork. By "got ready" I mean that Ted slicked his hair back with some water and put his shirt and shoregoing boots on. I went topside to see them row ashore in the jolly boat, which I helped to lower into the water. My face must have been as long as a wet Sunday in Aberdeen, so long that Tansy called over to me, "Nipper, you lost a shilling, or what?"

"No . . . Tansy . . . I . . . I. . . ."

"What's up, son?"

"Noth . . . nothing."

"Want to go ashore for a spell with Ted?" Ted sat in the boat grinning.

"Oh . . . could I . . . please?" I was still in my grubby working gear.

"Well, it's not a Saturday, but seeing as it's Holland . . . and you've been a bright spark, considering . . . yes. But hop to it and be quick. . . ." Tansy turned and clomped down the companionway to his cabin.

It took me no more than three minutes to fly forward, slide down the foc'sle scuttle, and change, as fast as I could, into my shoregoing rig, the one I'd arrived onboard in at Rye five days before. With my working clothes still strewn about my berth, and my boots in my hand, I took off up the ladder, still buttoning up my shirt. I tied up my bootlaces while I was in the jolly boat, with Ted rowing it to the landing stage. There I set foot on a foreign shore for the first time in my life, in Millengen, the last town on the River Waal in Holland, before it becomes the Rhine.

We three, the gallant crew of the British Registered Vessel *Second Apprentice,* rolled up the steps from the landing stage and crossed the riverside wall. It seemed strange to be on dry land again, on a deck that was not moving. Just before we turned a corner to go into the town, so neat and clean, I turned to take a look at our vessel. She sat gracefully at her mooring like a mother swan patiently awaiting the return of her cygnets from a waddle on the bank.

Once we were out of sight of *Second Apprentice,* the first place that Bert made for, with Ted and me traipsing alongside, was a bar. Unlike a British waterside pub, it was very light and airy inside. The walls were covered with white tiles with blue pictures on them, of sailing ships and windmills and such. Bert boldly plonked a British shilling down on the marble counter. The owner, a stout, bald man wearing a blue-and-white apron, a bow tie, and a huge blond mustache, perked up, inspected the shilling, nodded his head slightly and slowly, and poured Bert a beer, at the same time greeting him in very guttural English. It was obvious that Bert was a repeat customer of the establishment. The mate also bought a beer for Ted and a lemonade for me. We sat back like freshly arrived ambassadors to the court of Kublai Khan, in the unaccustomed luxury of padded chairs, taking in the sights and scenes all around us and, through the windows of the bar, watching the people go by, some of the men and women, boys and girls too, wearing wooden clogs. Practically all the men smoked big-bowled pipes or big cigars. To my surprise, many of the boys, some even smaller than I, did so, too.

On the way to the greengrocer's and the butcher's I saw quite a few strange sights, like dogs pulling little milk carts, and people carrying loads suspended from wooden yokes that they wore over their shoulders. It was a bit like a modern tourist picture of Holland, only then, in the thirties, that is the way it really was. I had felt strange in England, where I could barely understand what was said, but there, in eastern Hol-

land, I felt as though I was visiting Mars. The language spoken
was rapid and guttural, but Bert seemed to make his way quite
easily by simply turning English back to front. "I the potatoes
and carrots want. . . . I the beef for the stew want. . . ." The
shopkeeper smiled and seemed to understand perfectly as they
reached for exactly what he had ordered.

All the way along the streets and in the shops, Ted ogled the
girls. As he was not a bad-looking lad, as English lads go, the
girls usually returned his look with a bright, bold smile. This
made Ted go red in the face, look away, and talk to me about
his favorite soccer team, Arsenal, and how they were doing in
the Soccer League. I noticed that he didn't swear while he was
anywhere within hearing of a female, even though he probably
would not have been understood.

We could only have been ashore for an hour or so—it was
still bright day when I rowed the jolly boat back to the ship
—but I still recall clearly the surprises and wonders that I saw
in Millengen; the clean, tidy houses, most with flowers in
boxes around the walls; the well-tended gardens, all shipshape
and Bristol-fashion; and the trees in bud along the riverbank;
the green grass and the flowers, so new and fresh after a week
at sea seeing nothing but wood, iron, canvas, soup, salt beef,
potatoes, carrots, plum duff, tea, rope, sky, and water.

From the Dutch-German frontier to Remagen as the crow
flies is about a hundred miles, but by river, with all the twists
and bends, this increases to about one hundred and eighty. It
took *Second Apprentice* another four full days to make the passage
upstream against the current. We had a fair westerly breeze
most of the way, but at times, especially in the lee of the hills
along the western side of the river, we lost the wind. Then it
was a case again of what we called "Armstrong's Patent Pro-
pulsion System"—in other words, getting out the long sweeps
and rowing all three hundred tons or so of *Second Apprentice* and
her cargo against the might of the Rhine. Sailing up past places
like Duisberg and Düsseldorf, the scenery was nowhere near
as pleasant as it was on most of the river. The smoke from the
furnaces of those great industrial cities blackened the sky and
often made night out of day, besides settling a layer of soot all
over the ship and her sails, which had to be cleaned off each
time.

We passed through customs inspection just inside Germany, and the inspector was friendly to Tansy, but his crew were surly-looking and offhand with us. The customs boat wore a swastika flag on the cross-trees, as did many of the German vessels we saw. South of Düsseldorf, we passed very close to a couple of motor barges with their decks crowded with people, mainly youngsters, it appeared, all wearing brown uniforms, shouting and singing at the tops of their voices, apparently having a rattling good time. The adults with them also wore brown uniforms and swastika armbands. Some shook their fists at us—some waved. A band was playing on deck very loudly and oompah-ish. "What price the Salvation Army now, Tansy?" joked Ted.

"Silly blighters . . . silly, stupid beggars . . ." Tansy replied quietly.

Most of the German bargees were friendly to us when we passed them, or moored by the bank in the evening, and the officials who came onboard to log us in or out acted very correctly. One or two, who wore war medals on their uniforms, even saluted our Red Ensign when they came onboard or left the ship.

We had a broad reach most of the way upstream from the frontier to Remagen (that is, the wind was at right angles to the ship, usually the fastest point of sailing). We clipped along at a good rate when we were not shielded from the wind by a high hill, and arrived at the confluence of the rivers Rhine and Ahr nine days after sailing from Rye. We had carried almost 250 tons of cargo (about twenty-five truckloads) without using one drop or lump of fuel, apart from what we put into the lamps and stoves, and without any wear, tear, or damage. The only cost had been captain's and crew's wages (about $9.60 at the rate then) and food (about the same). The soap, paint, and other material used on the voyage would have cost about eight dollars. For a total expenditure of less than thirty dollars we had transported our 250-ton cargo almost five hundred miles from dock to dock. That's a freightage cost of roughly *twelve cents* per ton of cargo.

At the confluence of the Ahr we were met by a man with two big stallions. He had arrived at the behest of a pal of Tansy's who had telephoned from Bonn. Our tracking ropes were attached to the horses' harnesses through brass rings on the top, and the horses, with the topsail helping them a mite, towed us along the Ahr River, plodding steadily at about two knots, the few miles up the river to the Apollinaris loading dock.

As we approached the dock, in beautiful rural surroundings, with trees and meadows all around, Ted appeared on deck with a metal bucket and a piece of wire with a bit of rag seized on the end. He put them down beside me, as I stood at the galley door staring at the passing scenery. I looked down at the bucket.

"That's the bloody bottle-washing gear," said Ted. "You'd better get some hot water ready and put a bleeding decent gob of liquid soap in it, too, Nipper. We'll be humping the fucking bottles out very shortly."

I put the largest kettle on the stove and did as Ted had bidden me, wearily reckoning up how much time it would take me to clean the thousands and thousands of bottles. As *Second Apprentice* approached the dock nearer and nearer, I saw many children running down to the riverbank, there to stop and stare at us, or shyly wave. Then, with a dull, soft thump, we were alongside the dock, Ted and Bert cast on the mooring lines to the dock bollards, and my first voyage was over. I stepped out of the galley and looked around. I saw the big shed where the mineral water was stored ready for loading, and a steam crane on the jetty, and how our cross-trees had been steeved up so they would not be damaged by the overhanging trees on the river bank, and how, on the way up the River Ahr, our hold covers had been taken off and all made ready for work to commence as soon as we docked.

We arrived at the Apollinaris dock in the middle afternoon. The unloading started right away, as soon as the ship touched the dock and was secured. Ted and I went down below, hefting the boxes onto the skip. Then, on deck, Bert and a German had transferred the boxes from our skip onto a kind of pallet, which the steam crane on the jetty hoisted up. The pallet was then unloaded by Germans ashore. It was impossible, Ted explained to me, for the steam crane to hoist the boxes straight out of the hold because its boom was not long enough to reach over the top of the hold.

When darkness fell, the Germans, being nothing if not efficient and thorough, rigged up an electric floodlight over the hold so that Bert, Ted, and I could go on working. By the time the hold was empty of boxes, my back and shoulders were almost breaking and my hands were so blistered that I could hardly haul myself up the ladder when the last box had left the hold. I was so thankful and relieved that I didn't have to wash the bottles that I completely forgave Ted and Bert their jape.

Over a mug of tea, which Tansy had made while we finished work, we found that the scrap iron was to be unloaded a mile further up the river, early the next day, then *Second Apprentice* would shift back to the mineral-water dock to load with full bottles of that liquid so necessary, evidently, to the upper drinking classes of England.

By the time we had drunk our tea, it had started to rain, and it was becoming a downpour. Weary as we were, the mate, Ted, and I hefted the heavy hold-covering boards into position so that the hold would not flood too much with fresh rainwater, which does wood no good. Then Ted and I set to making supper. It was a quarter to midnight when we finally cleared up the galley and dragged ourselves forward to the foc'sle. It was cold down there. We'd been too busy all day to light a fire in our quarters, but I soon got warm under my two thick blankets and fell asleep, exhausted.

We unloaded the scrap iron further upstream very early the next day. That was easier than the boxes of empty bottles had been—there was a long-boomed crane that picked up the great jagged pieces of boiler-plate directly from the bottom of the hold, so all Ted and I had to do was to secure strops around the iron. It was very dusty in the hold, and we had to be careful not to tear our hands on the jagged metal, but it was a walkover compared to the empty-bottle boxes of the day before—or at least I thought so until we started loading the full-bottle boxes, all 4,500 of them, back at the Apollinaris dock. That was what the Americans call a real goddamn ball-buster, and by the time Ted and I had the boxes all securely stowed under Bert's expert eye I was just about ready to die; but I put thoughts of expiring out of my mind and got on, somehow, with peeling the potatoes.

We sailed at first light next day, and now that we had the current with us we carried on downstream day and night until we reached the German-Dutch frontier, which, with the fair breezes we encountered, took us a mere day and a half. From the frontier we made it out to the Estuary in another day and a half, emerging from the Harengvliedt mouth of the Scheldte River. Out in the North Sea we found a good northwester blowing, so we were on a close reach for most of the two-day sea voyage back to Rye, until we passed by the foreland and into the Straits of Dover, when we were headed by a south-wester. That meant a couple of tacks on either board for a whole day.

It was a glorious day, the sunlight clear and strong. As we ploughed the Straits the waves of the Channel seemed to know that *Second Apprentice* was coming home. The waves met her charging at them to dash them into myriads of sparkling gems that hovered about her at every surge. Every drop of water she threw into the air became a gem, and *Second Apprentice,* pounding forward, grabbed diadem after diadem from the air about her bows. Rainbow after miniature rainbow she flung out from her bow, time after time, as if she, too, knew she was bound for the green, gently rising hills of home.

We finally made our way into Rye harbor entrance five days after leaving the dock at Remagen. The whole round trip of about nine hundred miles had taken *Second Apprentice* just two weeks, and I had made my first foreign voyage. The following day was a Saturday, and I was given leave to go ashore in Rye for the afternoon, with a strict order from Tansy to be back onboard by nightfall. I felt rich as I went ashore with one of my two shillings (the remnants of my pay) in my pocket, and I must have looked at the other boys in the street and in the cinema with some disdain. I was a fully fledged seaman now, so I thought. I strolled along with a slight swagger, or leaned back manfully in my cinema seat. The prospect of all the thousands of boxes of full mineral-water bottles waiting to be unloaded on Monday morning completely left my mind for a few blessed moments.

12

In My Element

The amount of work expected of a young boy onboard a ketch-barge never ceased to amaze me. I had known from conversations with old seafarers at home that the boy was cook as well as deckhand, lookout, steward, cargo-handler, makee-learner helmsman, rigger, sailmaker, and painter, but I had never realized quite how much continual effort was involved, nor how much of this was taken up by the cooking. The worst of that job was that unless I thought about it deeply, I could never see any result. No sooner was a meal ready and served than it was consumed. There was left only a pile of plates and pots to be cleaned, and that in itself was another job. We had no such thing as washing detergent. Soft soap was, in our straitened circumstances, always in short supply. I used to do most of the galley cleaning with salt water and sand.

With the amount of work to be done by everyone onboard it was vital that the crew be properly fed. After the first trip, when I had worked in the galley under Ted's tutelage and with Bert's eagle eye often on me, I was left more or less alone to get on with it as best I could, though the mate and deckhand were always willing to help me if I had a problem.

On the short passages we ate pretty much as we would have done ashore; porridge, bacon and eggs, and tea for breakfast; plenty of bread brought from ashore; butter; potatoes, onions, carrots, cabbage; and fresh beef, lamb, or pork. There was always a good supply of tea, condensed milk, and sugar, too.

On the longer sea passages, when we sailed, for example, up to the northeast coast or south to the Channel Islands, where we might expect to be (and often were) becalmed for a few

days, it was a different story. Then we stowed away salt fish
—usually cod or haddock—potatoes, rice, dried peas, "Portmadoc pantiles" (hardtack biscuits), margarine, and salt beef.
Unlike some of the other coastal sailing craft, we salted down
our own beef. Tansy never trusted the quality of barreled salt
beef bought ashore. Before a longish trip he took time off from
all his other duties, such as dealing with the paperwork, the
factors, and a couple of dozen other entities, to go along to
a local butcher (who was usually a pal of our butcher-
shareholder in Harwich). There he selected his own cuts of
beef—flank, brisket, chuck, or sirloin. When the butcher's
white-aproned errand boy showed up with the meat in the
basket of his bicycle on the jetty, I carried it down below to
the meal-table in the skipper's flat, still in its muslin wrapping.
There, Ted and I rubbed coarse rock salt into the beef until all
the salt had been absorbed. Tansy never let Bert take part in
the beef salting, though I never found out why. It might have
had to do with an old sailor's superstition that only virgin boys
could do it; otherwise the beef was supposed to go off. As far
as Ted was concerned, I wasn't so sure that Tansy was on the
right track. From the yarns he spun to me when we were alone
in the foc'sle Ted was far from a virgin, if he was to be believed.
Our beef almost always stayed good, so I presumed Ted was
exaggerating about his conquests.

After we had salted the beef, we took it back topside, to
where a big salt barrel was lashed on the port side of the
deckhouse. This was known as the "harness barrel," since the
meat looked like horse harness. The brine inside the barrel was
so salty that a wooden tackle-block would hardly submerge in
it. The beef was held down in the brine with a broom handle
until it stayed completely immersed, and it was left to pickle
for several days before it was taken out and cooked. Then it
was either delicious or rank; it was a matter of luck. We had
a lot of luck. We never called it salt beef; the sailor's name for
it was "old horse." The name for salt fish was "yellow peril."

By the end of a hard day's work loading or discharging cargo,
or standing watches at sea, everyone had a good appetite. Ted
ate like a shark—anything and everything put before him. I
have never seen anyone since who could eat like tall, thin, wiry
Ted. A great steaming helping of roast beef, potatoes, and

greens, all piping hot, along with duff pudding, rhubarb and custard for afters, and two or three pints of hot, sweet, milky tea would disappear as if by magic after Ted sat down to his evening meal, and he always asked for second helpings of plum duff. Both Tansy and Bert had good appetites, too. Cooking for them was, as they would put it, "a dockyard job."

After we had been at sea for a few days, the baker's bread, bought ashore, would either be used up or moldy. Then the hardtack was broken out. The Portmadoc pantiles were so steely that Bert, who had lost a few teeth when a boom smacked him across the deck in a past, well-recounted gale, used to take a jackknife out of his jacket pocket to crack the biscuits. He soaked the pieces, as hard and sharp as slivers of glass, in his mug of tea for a minute or two before he attempted to consume them. It was said that if you fed pantiles to a pig they would cause internal bleeding, and the animal would roll over and die. The biscuits were so rock-hard that after eating them for a few days our gums became sore and started to bleed. Then we couldn't eat them anymore and had to make do with watered porridge for our cereal intake. This never happened to Ted. He could consume hardtack forever and a day with no evident difficulty. When he cracked the hardtack he even looked as though he enjoyed doing it.

There was much more to cooking salted food properly than at first met the eye. If it wasn't pickled properly and then steeped in fresh water for a good spell before cooking, it brought out salt-water sores on our bodies. Salt fish and salt beef were mostly boiled, but after a while I learned how to make ground beef for shepherd's pies, fried fishcakes, and suet dumplings. Those dumplings, with boiled beef, carrots, potatoes, and onions, made a good, nourishing stew, which we all thoroughly enjoyed. "Bloody good grub" was the invariable opinion of Bert and Ted.

With rice I made curried beef and rice, and rice pudding liberally dosed with currants and raisins. Sailors called that "soldiers in a snowstorm," or "1812."

In bad weather, in the tiny, hot galley, with the door shut to keep out spray and wind, it was like all hell let loose. I had to sit on the seat over the coal bin and try to keep the pans from skittering off the heaving stovetop. I was scalded quite a few times, but fortunately never seriously. The wind blowing down from the mainsail blew the smoke back down the chimney, or "Charlie Noble." When the galley was full of fumes and I was forced to poke my head out of the door in order to breathe, then I usually got a good dollop of freezing spray over my face and a gallon of seawater swirling over the galley deck. Then I had to mop that up, as well as try to keep the pans on the stove.

In rough weather, when the food was ready, a difficult job was to get it down below and onto the lobby table without losing it or getting it dowsed in cold seawater. After a couple of minor disasters I learned the tricks and managed quite well. One of these accidents was quite funny, though at the time it didn't seem so at all. I was juggling a tray of boiled salt fish and a dixie of soup down the companionway. Topside it was blowing the devil's pants off. Bert and Ted had just gone down below for their supper. Ted was already sitting down, waiting, fork and spoon in hand, in the glow of the lobby oil lamp. Suddenly the bows hit an extra-big sea. The ship lurched like a Grand National courser going over the sticks. I lost my footing and went slithering down the companionway with an almighty crash. The tray and the soupcan went flying out of my hands and smack into Bert, covering him from head to foot in fish and soup. Fortunately, he had his back to me while he took off his oilskin coat, and he was still wearing his sou'wester hat, so no real damage was done—but he was lucky. Bert took it in his stride—he merely turned to me with the "yellow peril" and soup dribbling and dripping from his oilies, and growled, "That grub smells nice, Nipper, but next time put it on the table, please."

I scrabbled around for the pieces of fish and put them back in the dish. They were still reasonably warm and edible, and the sole of the lobby was so clean and scrubbed you could have eaten the fish from it. Bert and Ted both declared that it wasn't worth the trouble of cooking another meal, and they made do with the rescued yellow peril while I mopped up the soup. I was thankful that Tansy was on the helm when this happened. By the time he came off watch I had another piece of fish fried up for him. I never forgot the lesson. I never again tried to carry more than one hand could hold from the galley down to the lobby in rough weather. Ever afterward I bore in mind the old sailor's saying, "One hand for yourself and one for the ship."

On the very few occasions when the salted meat went bad, we used some of it for fish bait, with varying degrees of success. On one trip to Bordeaux with cattle feed we were becalmed for more than a week with a barrel of stinking beef onboard and caught nothing but a couple of small fish. We had to make do with potatoes, margarine, and hardtack, until we finally arrived off Royan. There Bert went ashore in the jolly boat and fetched back a box of tomatoes and a leg of lamb. Tansy never went ashore in France if he could possibly avoid it. He never said why, then, but his expressions whenever a Frenchman was in sight showed that he was not exactly a Francophile. I'll never forget how good those fresh tomatoes and roast lamb tasted, though, after more than a week on hardtack and boiled spuds.

It was onboard *Second Apprentice* that the value of fresh water was driven home to me. At home in Llangareth, fresh water had to be pumped from a spring, but there had always been plenty of it. At sea, fresh water can be worth its weight in gold. In *Second Apprentice* we had a hundred-gallon tank on deck, beside the galley, and another three-hundred-gallon tank down below in the "cupboard," as the after-end of the main hold was called. One of my jobs was to keep the deck tank full by pumping water up from the main tank. Before I could do that, however, I had to ask Bert to unlock the pump handle, which was secured by a padlock and chain. Then, when the deck tank was topped up, I had to ask Bert for the ready-use tank spigot handle, which was detachable. Without the spigot handle no water could be drawn from the ready-use tank. More often than not, Bert, in his capacity as mate, stood over me while I drew what fresh water was necessary for whatever galley job was in hand. For the captain and mate the daily fresh water ration was one-and-a-half gallons in a bucket, and they took alternate first turns at washing and shaving in it. It was the same for Ted and me, except that we had to make our water last two days. This was considered by all to be fair, because neither Ted nor I shaved then. In harbor, where most of the dirtiest work was done, it was different. Then we could find a tap or a pump ashore somewhere and wash away to our heart's content, or if the ship was in a fresh-water river and the water was not too filthy, we could sluice ourselves in that.

Apart from galvanized steel buckets, the only other toilet facility onboard *Second Apprentice* was the lavatory, or "head," as mariners call it. This was in a very poky little closet open to the sky alongside the helm position. It consisted of a wooden box inside which was a sort of large metal funnel, mouth-up. To the bottom of the metal funnel was fixed a pipe that led at an angle straight down through the ship's side just below seawater level. Ullage ("waste") was sluiced down with a bucket of salt water. It worked very well until the ship started to labor in any kind of heavy seaway. Then, unless we were very wide awake and jumped up in time with the ship's move-ment, our transoms were liable to be slushed with a few gallons of cold seawater swishing up the pipe. Of course, I didn't know about this. The first time *Second Apprentice* started working heav-ily, in the North Sea going hard to windward on our way to the Maas River, I had gone into the "kaasy" (a gypsy-Romany word), as the bargemen called the head, and all three of my shipmates had waited gleefully for me to come shooting out again, my trousers around my knees, spluttering and dripping salt water.

"We always uses the chains at sea," said Bert.

"The chains, Bert?"

"Yes, up forward on the bow. You'll probably get a wet arse up there, too, hanging on the cathead, but at least it'll be when you expect it!" (Which explains why the ship's toilet is called the "head.")

Sometimes, if we had good salt beef remaining in the harness barrel after a voyage that had been faster than we had ex-pected, we let the townsfolk know, and they came down to the ship to buy it from Tansy; his reputation for the excellence of his salt beef was so good. This was so particularly in the ports of Ramsgate and Margate. Tansy always put the proceeds of these sales straight into an old biscuit tin in which he kept the food kitty, for further food purchases.

There was always plenty of coal onboard, which is not sur-prising, considering the amount we used to carry as cargo. We also did very well for cheeses, as we took a couple of cargoes

of Edam and Gouda from Holland to Harwich that first summer. We didn't pilfer the cargoes—what we had was given to
us by the Northumberland coal wharfingers and the Dutch
cheese merchants. Tansy used to take with him gifts, such as
a couple of boxes of Whitstable oysters, to present in return
for the gifts we were given. Tansy—being as he was, as straight
as a die—would never have countenanced anything like pilfer-
ing, not even one lump of coal or a basket of coke.

Although stowing and unloading cargo—boxes, sacks, coal,
housebricks, stone—was hard enough work for young boys,
the heaviest job, as far as I was concerned, was anchoring and
getting the anchor up again when getting underway. Going to
anchor, the first job was to haul about several cables (say, 150
feet) of anchor chain out of the lockers down below, through
the spurling pipe, and range it along the deck forward of the
windlass. Another several cables were then hauled up and laid
in two wooden mangers, one on each side of the forward main
hatch. As the ship approached the anchorage, the anchor,
which was catted up to the bow (that is, hauled up with its
shank horizontal) was lowered until it hung vertically from the
hawse-pipe; then the anchor was "apeak." This done, Bert
stood by with a crowbar. When Tansy nodded his head to
order the anchor let go, Bert released the cat-stopper tumbler
—a sort of big pelican hook—with his crowbar, thus releasing
the anchor. Down through the hawse-pipe the chain went,
with a roar. If extra chain needed to be let out, to increase the
scope, I flung a turn over the windlass barrel, and the weight
of the chain already over the side heaved it out steadily. We
had to always be careful that we didn't lose a finger, or even
a hand, especially on a dark, windy night at an open anchorage,
with *Second Apprentice* yawing and veering, pitching and tossing
like a maddened steer. We had to watch our feet, too, to see
that they were clear of the wildly running chain as it surged
through the hawse-pipe.

The worst job of all—the most exhausting—was heaving up
the anchor, especially if we had let out a lot of scope. It needed
all the strength of Bert, Ted, and my puny self. The windlass
was worked with a lever, like a pump, and it brought the wet,
cold chain onboard link by link. The chain piled itself up on
deck as it came in and had to be cleared back into the manger

every so often. This we did with a chain hook, something like a meat-handler's hook.

After interminable pumping, the anchor chain was at last straight up and down. Then we hoisted enough sail to move the boat, depending on what the wind and sea were like, and from which direction they were coming at us. As all three of us pumped up and down on the windlass handle, Tansy sheeted the sails in and worked the ship's head off the wind, thus using the ship's weight to drag out the anchor from the seabed. All the time we pumped away on the windlass handle until the anchor stock broke the surface of the sea. Then, with the anchor still half underwater before the bow, we hoisted more sail, so as to get clear out to the offing. As the ship moved we hauled in the anchor and catted it; that is, we slung a line with a hook on the end of it around the anchor stock and hauled the anchor up onto the cathead high enough so that another chain, called the cat-stopper, could be fastened onto the anchor, to prevent it from being accidentally let go. That done, the hook was shifted to the anchor crown and the anchor was then "fished" tight on the outboard side of the bulwark, where it was secured with yet another line called the shank painter, and then with the cat-stopper. By the time that was done all of us were sweating, no matter what the weather, and breathing very hard indeed.

We often also let out a second anchor, called the bower. Then there were two anchors to be weighed, and sometimes they might both, the main and the bower, be fouled on other crafts' anchors that had dragged over ours, or over which ours had dragged. Imagine the work involved in unsnarling such a fuck-up on a moonless night with the rain blowing hard in the wind, especially if the wind was blowing onshore, leaving the captain little sea-room in which to maneuver the ship! This happened on more than one occasion, especially in the wide, open harbor of Dover. What with heaving up our own two anchors and perhaps another besides, and at the same time hoisting the sails, a good foredeck hand needed to be a cross between a circus strongman, an acrobat, a steel-erector, and a ballet dancer. After six months onboard *Second Apprentice* my back, belly, leg, and arm muscles were like steel cords. I was, as the sailors say, "like an Afghan greyhound—all prick and toenails." I also developed an appetite like Ted's; the only difference between our eating capabilities was that I couldn't tackle the hardtack as voraciously as he could.

It was just as well that my muscles developed as they did, because hoisting anchor or the big heavy main gaff, with the huge mainsail weighted on it, needed all the strength that Ted and I could muster.

Being at anchor, especially in open roads when we were wind-bound—waiting for a favorable wind—meant standing night anchor watches. In the summer these were quite pleasant, and I sat on the forward windlass humming to myself or trying to remember a poem or a passage I had read, all the while keeping a lookout for other vessels coming to anchor, or our own or other vessels dragging. In wintertime, though, anchor watches could be purgatory. I stood or stamped up and down the foredeck (if Ted wasn't asleep down below) or the sidedeck trying to keep warm, or in the rain or snow, trying to keep dry, with my oilskins streaming wet and trickles of cold water oozing down from the scarf tied around my neck. It was useless to seek shelter—there was none, and if there had been it would have obscured the necessary all-round view. My favorite anchor watch was the morning, because it was the shortest; at daybreak I could dowse the anchor light and turn in. My least favorite anchor watch was the middle, from midnight until 4:00 A.M. The nights were at their darkest, there was little or no movement in other ships, and the hours never seemed to end. The worst time of all at anchor watch was during a fog. Then, every noise from outside the vessel was a nightmare; it might be a big power vessel bearing down at us, we might be dragging our anchor, we might even be drifting near to the shore; I never knew for sure what was happening much of the time as I strained my eyes searching, trying to penetrate the thick fog and ringing the fog bell every minute or so. Sometimes in a fog the cold was so damp that it penetrated even a set of oilskins and two thick wool jerseys, right through to my bones. During my first few months onboard I woke Bert several times with false alarms in fog, but he never chastised me for it. He always said that it was better to be mistaken and safe than to be cocksure and dead.

There was still a lot of work to do, even when the ship was

fog-bound or wind-bound. There was still the galley and the cleaning, the scraping and painting, and every time the tide changed the anchors and cables had to be tended, to make sure, as our bows changed their attitude to the wind and as our ship and all the other ships in the anchorage slowly swung around, that we did not foul any other vessel's ground tackle, hull, or spars. Even so, we had several close shaves, and it was only by fast and judicious use of the sweeps that we were able to keep clear. We had to keep good anchor and tide watches; repairs were expensive, and money was in short supply. But it wasn't the thought of having to spend money that made good seamen —it was the fact that for them there was only one way to do anything: properly and well.

The easiest cargoes to handle in and out of the hold were bulk cargoes like grain or coal. They were usually loaded on-board down a chute. Then all we crewmen had to do was wait at the bottom of the chute, but well clear of it, for the stuff to come hurtling down, a whole wagon at a time, and redistribute it around the hold evenly with our shovels. It was so dusty when the commodity poured down that we had to wear neck-erchiefs around our mouths and at times could hardly breathe. The worst for dust was coal ("all or nothing"), and the fine black powder got everywhere. Our shovels were eighteen in-ches across the blades, and with them we could lift about twenty pounds at a time at first, but soon that dropped to ten pounds.

Getting the coal and the grain out of the hold when we discharged cargo was a different matter. Then we used "skips," shallow boxes with an iron lifting-ring at each corner. They were lowered down the hold one at a time by Bert operating the spare gaff as a derrick by means of the dolly winches and blocks and tackles. As each skip came down we loaded it with our shovels as fast as we could. When the skip was heaped full —about half a ton each load—Bert hauled it up and on deck. There, most times, the gaff tackle was unshipped from the skip, the shore-crane tackle was bent on, and up it went, onto a pile of grain or coal ashore, or into a railway wagon or horse-drawn cart or lorry, depending on where we were.

Flour, potatoes, and cement were shipped in bags, each weighing forty pounds. By the time a thousand or so of those had been chuted down the hold, and humped up in stacks as tight as we could get them, you can imagine how our backs ached. At that time cement had started to be shipped in thick paper sacks, but the manufacturers had not quite developed sacks strong enough to never break when they slid down the chutes. Usually, cement powder flew everywhere. Each time the hold was unloaded and empty, it had to be cleaned out, to be ready for the next cargo, whatever that might be. That was a good two-hour job for Ted and me, first with brooms and shovels and then sluicing away with a hose. And after that the hold bilge had to be pumped out.

The worst cargo of all was house bricks. We usually carried them to the Channel Islands from Southampton or Portsmouth. None of the brick-loading docks had a crane, and we had to handle fifty thousand or so bricks by hand each time we loaded and discharged. This involved five people. One man, on the wagon ashore, threw the bricks down, five at a time, to his mate on the jetty. He in turn threw the bricks, still in fives, down to Bert on deck. Bert slid the bricks down a wide plank into the hold, where I caught them at the bottom of the plank. I was supposed to throw them, five at a time, to Ted, who stacked them in the hold, but at first my hands were too small and soft. I could only manage three bricks at a time, and consequently a pile of bricks grew at the bottom of the plank. Then, while the men topside took a short breather, I had to continue clearing the heaped-up pile of leftover bricks at the bottom of the plank. It was months before I could handle five bricks at a throw, ten thousand throws a load. We were not provided with gloves, and we wrapped our hands in rags, but by the end of the day, after fifty thousand bricks had passed through them, I had hands like bloody pieces of meat. It took weeks for them to harden enough to handle bricks without stinging and bleeding.

I don't blame the skipper or the mate for this; it was partly my fault that I suffered so. I was too proud to complain. If Ted could do it, so went my reasoning, so could I. In a way I was right, because after a few months I could stack bricks as fast as he could. On subsequent visits to the Channel Islands in the years since, I have often looked at the neat brick-built houses that were constructed just before World War II and wondered whether the inhabitants had any idea of the torture involved in getting those bricks to the islands.

The cargoes back from the Channel Islands were usually cattle or sheep hides. These were dried and heavy, and the sharp edges were excruciating to handle with unhealed hands. We didn't usually have many hides, but they generally were accompanied by barrels of animal offal, which stank to high heaven; so much so that when we docked to unload them in Poole or Gravesend other craft slipped their cables and shifted berth or went out to anchor, to get away from the stench. When the hold was at last clear of hides and offal, Ted and I scrubbed away for hours to get rid of the smell.

It wasn't all drudgery, though, and there was many a fine day out in the Channel, with the wind fair and easy. The times I enjoyed the best were when, after a few weeks, Tansy let me take regular tricks on the helm. At first these were during his watch, the forenoon or "dog" watch, so that he could keep an eye on me. One fine, sunny day, in September I think it was, there was a cold snap in the air, and we were bound cross-Channel with a cargo of bricks for Jersey. I was tending the helm, while Tansy sat on his upturned barrel, smoking his pipe, alongside the wheel. The wind was almost dead on the beam, from the northwest, steady and not too strong. *Second Apprentice* was wearing every stitch she had but her squaresail, and she was hammering along through the short, choppy seas like a steam engine, on a broad-reach. Astern, the coast of England still guarded us; ahead, there was nothing but blue seas stretching to infinity, shining and cold. The sky was clear, except for a few solitary gun-puffs over on the western horizon.

I was half-alert, watching the curve of the sails, the lines of the luffs, the gentle pitching of the bowsprit, and half-daydreaming about the immense silence of the sea and of its voice. I was thinking how strange, what a paradox it was, the sea, its voice, and its silence; yet how true. The noises we could hear as *Second Apprentice* ploughed on toward the rim of the world were not of the sea. They were of the encounter between the sea and what it met—the ship's hull, her rigging, the strain of her timbers. The sea is more reserved unto itself, more solitary, than any other phenomenon known to man. I reflected that the land lay inert; the land, except for what life in its myriad forms imparted to it, was dumb. The sea had a life of its own. Even if there were not one living thing in the depths of the sea, even if all life left the Earth, yet the sea itself would live, and the sea would speak still in her masked voice of silence, like one of the oracles of the Gods, the essence of mystery, eternal.

I was wakened from my half-reverie suddenly, as a seabird cried over the starboard quarter. I turned my head to see it. Tansy was no longer there on his bucket; he must have crept away down the companionway and left me to steer the ship alone. There was no one else on deck. I was in command of the ship. Silently, without a word, the accolade of trust had been bestowed on me, and I knew then that I was considered to be more of a man than I thought myself to be. Almost mechanically, I peered down into the compass binnacle. The ship was a point off the course. Joyously, proudly, I shoved the helm over, lifted my head, and checked the wind and the sails. They seemed, at that moment, to share in my pride and joy. There was an instant urging in the wind, an instantaneous stiffening of the sails' curves, a prompt angling of the hull a little further to leeward, a brisk acceleration of the bowsprit's pitches and tosses for a minute or so. Then the wind eased back into its regular strength. The ship regathered her sedateness about her and plodded on. But I knew that *she* knew, and that in the bygone moment we had been one entity, the wind, the sea, the ship, and I. I was in my element.

13

Ted

To many a city businessman, as he watched the sailing coasters ply London Pool, the Thames estuary, or the Solent, the life of a sailor must have seemed replete with romance, perhaps with a spicing of hazards. Many an office boy on his way across Tower Bridge with a message, or a clerk going home after a boring day at the office of a law firm, must have felt a pang of envy when he saw two or three spritties, ketches, or stumpies rafted together, waiting for a change of tide, or for the arrival of cargo to be loaded. The captains might be sitting together on the stern of one of the craft, yarning, as he thought, telling tales of faraway places and sunny shores; more likely they were comparing notes as to what cargoes were waiting, where, or what vessel had foundered, and why, and who had survived, or what ship had been laid up in the breaking yards, or what trade our heavily subsidized continental competitors had broken into.

As his eye ran over the hulls, our city gentleman would perhaps have noticed the red sails of a sprittie brailed up to the mainmast and wondered why they looked so sloppy and untidy. His eyes would have ranged over the mainsail of a ketch and noted the varied hues of the patches on her mainsail. But the main cause of his envy would have been the evident casualness with which the crewmen carried on their tasks. Unless they were maneuvering the vessel or handling cargo, the bargemen rarely hurried. They must have seemed to move slowly, as if they had all the time in the world, as if they had brought into the very heart of the twentieth century the leisured pace of centuries gone by.

We could hardly have expected our city man to realize the truth of the matter: that the mainsails were brailed up loosely in readiness for shifting the craft; that the ketch mainsail had been patched because new mainsails cost money; that the crewmen moved slowly because they were probably exhausted after unloading a 250-ton cargo of cement by hand in the little time available between tides, or while a dumb-lighter (a towed or rowed, nonpowered vessel) was available; that the cook was gasping for air after sweating in the poky galley for hours.

Sunday in port was the only day when we perhaps deserved to be envied. If *Second Apprentice* was anywhere within reach of the southeastern suburbs of London, Bert went home to his wife and family, but Tansy, Ted (who had no home), and I stayed. In the morning Tansy put on his best shoregoing suit and went to chapel, if we were anchored or moored within decent reach of one; if not, he stayed in his cabin and read his Bible. Sunday was the only day I didn't tidy and clean his cabin. On the shelf beside his bunk the sole objects were a faded picture of his dead wife and a collection box for some Methodist mission in West Africa. The only other books he had in his cabin, beside his Bible, were the ship's log and the accounts book, in both of which he made his entries in graceful copperplate handwriting. Two of my weekday early-morning jobs were to see that his ink pot was half-full and that his boots were shined every morning, even at sea.

While the captain was at chapel or down in his cabin on Sunday mornings, Ted cleaned up the foc'sle and topside; I looked after breakfast and prepared the midday meal. In port this was always a bit fancier than the weekday fare, perhaps pork with apple sauce or a stuffed hen, with a gooseberry tart and custard.

After dinner, when everything was cleared up, Ted gave us a few tunes on his mouth organ as we all sat on the cargo hatches. If we were laid alongside other coasters we might go and visit them, or their crewmen might come onboard *Second Apprentice*. Often there was someone with a banjo or a concertina, and the bargemen usually came onboard after the pubs shut at two o'clock. Then the landsmen must have really envied us, as they strolled along the jetty with their families on their Sunday-afternoon outings. Sometimes, if there were several ships lying together, perhaps the spritties *Cambria, Genesta,* or *Sirdar,* which all had lively crews, there would be quite a gathering, with anything up to twenty sailors and captains, mates, deckhands, boys, ship's cats and dogs (on the shore), and, on rare occasions, even a wife or two and a few sailor's offspring, all enjoying Ted's rendering of "Lambeth Walk" or "Tipperary." He was a discordant musician; his music was barely recognizable, but everyone enjoyed themselves anyway. Someone would bring out a tin whistle, someone a Jew's harp, and soon a pretty full orchestra was under way. They always, out of courtesy, played Tansy's favorite tune—"Goodbye, Dolly, I Must Leave You." We young lads soon found ourselves humming or whistling along with the music, and we forgot the back-breaking drudgery of the weeks gone by and to come, for a short while at least.

In this way I met many bargees and coastal sailors, some from as far away as Ireland, Scotland, and Liverpool. Some of them, in their younger days before the First World War, had been seamen in the old square-riggers, the Cape Horners like the ships of the Garth Line, and some, as boys, had even sailed on the American Black Ball Line, the hardest-driven ships ever in the history of sail. I cannot remember any one of them who was at all loud or boastful, though God knows they had the background to be. I was always surprised—and, I suppose, as a boy would be, a little disappointed—to find how modest, pragmatic, and conservative they generally were. After several voyages, I came to realize that these traits were necessary to ensure happy and safe passages under sail, and that they were almost invariably balanced by a bigness of heart, a generosity of soul, an almost childish freshness of outlook, and a knife-quick sense of humor that was both ribald and mischievous. They were expert at practical jokes.

A few of our sailor-visitors loved a drink, but (perhaps fortunately) their pay did not run to much more than a pint or two of beer a day when they were in harbor. The common landsman's impression of professional sailors as a rowdy, drunken lot is completely in error. It might have been true of a few— a very few—of the seamen from bigger ships, suddenly let loose on the shore after weeks of being pent up in the dreary confines of a steamer or under the rigid discipline of a warship, but very rarely was it true of coastal or estuarial sailormen, and especially in the cargo trade. Their pay was too low, their work too arduous, and the risks too great. As the sailors used to say, "Only fools and passengers drink too much." As for the long-passage sailors in the old days, the reason they took to hard drinking between passages is simple—it was to insulate themselves from the appalling conditions of their existence ashore. It wasn't easy to be a homeless, shipless sailor on the waterfronts of Liverpool, London, San Francisco, Valparaiso, or New York. It still isn't.

We were also visited by various shoreside friends of Tansy's —a farmer, a butcher, a ship's chandler, perhaps an innkeeper or two—but to me those visits were nowhere near as enjoyable. The main topics of conversation seemed to be supplies, cargo, and money, and the tradesmen rarely, as the sailors almost always did, seemed to treat me as anything other than a small, unintelligent being meant to be either patronized or at everyone's beck and call.

Sometimes, if we were moored anywhere near Sandwich, Tansy's daughter Daisy came to visit us. She was in her middle teens, and it was obvious to me that Ted had taken a shine to her. Daisy, however, treated him with a certain aloofness and sought out my company. I don't know why this was—I was nowhere near as tall or "handsome" as Ted. I suppose it must have been because I liked her as a person just as much as I liked her as a girl. She reminded me of Branwen Powell back in Llangareth, on whom (I realized when I'd left Wales) I'd had a secret crush for a couple of years. Also, unlike Ted, I didn't try to change the subject when she talked about what were supposed by Ted to be "girlish" things like books and poetry, music, and painting. By any standard, Daisy showed promise of becoming a real beauty. She was slim, she had golden hair, she had April in her eyes and music on her tongue. Several times I ached to ask her to come for a walk, but always I desisted for Ted's sake. I had to go to sea with Ted, sometimes cooped up with him for days on end, and I depended on him to "show me the ropes" when it came to most jobs onboard. I think I acted on intuition; I don't think I was any wiser than my years would allow. Daisy, anyway, was a year older than I and one year at fourteen is like ten years at thirty. But Ted and I always looked forward eagerly to Daisy's visits, and we both spruced ourselves up for hours before she arrived, though I doubt that anyone would have noticed it except ourselves. The other thing we looked forward to were the dainties that she brought each time she visited us, things like jam tarts, apple pies, treacle toffee, and homemade jellies. What I appreciated most were the books she brought me, everything from *Mister Midshipman Easy* by Captain Marryat to *Nostromo* by Joseph Conrad. After our first conversation, Daisy always brought me at least half a dozen books and a few newspapers. I devoured them eagerly, at sea, hunched up under the foc'sle lamp in between cooking, cleaning, tricks on the wheel, or cargo handling. As Tansy had predicted, I was to learn a lot more onboard *Second Apprentice* than I had at school.

Another source of books was the Missions to Seamen launch, *Flying Angel,* which cruised the Thames estuary, bringing a small lending library along with spiritual comfort for those in need. Each time *Flying Angel* came alongside, the clergyman onboard stayed in the launch, in consideration, I suppose, of the old sailors' superstition about having a "man in black" onboard one's own craft. Tansy chatted with him for a few minutes over the side-rail. Ted and I seized the opportunity to dash onboard the holy-roller's launch and down below to a tiny cabin where books and papers lay higgledy-piggledy in a large crate, in the custody of a severe-looking young man wearing rimless spectacles. Ted sorted out several comics, those that weren't too tattered, and I scrabbled around for anything above the level of *With Gordon in the Sudan* or *What Katy Did.* Sometimes I came across a treasure trove, books like *The Autobiography of a Supertramp* by W. H. Davies or *The Call of the Wild* by Jack London. (Since I read the first page of that I have remained a devotee of London.) The variety of old magazines that the Seaman's Mission launch brought around never ceased to amaze me—there seemed to be everything from *The Tatler* to *The Farmer and Stockbreeder,* from *John O'London's Weekly* to *Tit-bits.* Sometimes the magazines were years old, but we enjoyed them all the same. I once even discovered one of Havelock Ellis's manuals on sexual behavior, which had evidently escaped the eagle eye of the Mission librarian. I shoved the book under my jersey quickly and smuggled it onboard *Second Apprentice.* Ted and I eagerly tried to decipher its esoteric Victorian language. At first I was pleased with my find—I'd actually interested Ted in a *book*—but after one or two sessions hunched over the book with furrowed brows of deep puzzlement, Ted gave up on Havelock Ellis. "Too bleedin' long-winded," was his verdict. "Blimey, if I wanted to get a bit of khyfer (sex) and stopped to read all that bloody rubbish my bird would have it away on her toes before I got through the first fucking page!"

Apart from girls (or daydreaming about them), Ted's only other shoreside interest seemed to be cowboy films and soccer. His prize possession onboard was an old football, which, when we had a rare idle hour, we used to kick around on the quayside, sometimes with the lads and men from other craft joining in. This we did rain or shine. His dream was to be center-forward for Woolwich Arsenal soccer team, or, failing that, outside-right. His job onboard, and the life he led, he seemed to consider to be temporary, a brief episode before a life of soccer and women that was to somehow miraculously come about "when I'm bleedin' twenty, by Christ."

I had very early learned the unwritten law that onboard a ship of any kind a person's private life, his origins, his family, were completely his own concern, and that I should never ask any questions about those matters. It took several months before, from what he volunteered to me, I could piece together scraps of Ted's life story.

Ted's mother, so he said, was Irish, and she had been an assistant cook in a big household in London: "Bleeding house full of toffs up in the West End," as he put it. She had fallen for a soldier, who, after she discovered that Ted was to be bestowed on the world, promptly deserted her by wangling a transfer overseas (one of the conveniences of Empire). How Ted knew this was a mystery to me. It seems that Ted's mother farmed him out to foster parents soon after he was born and paid for his keep. Eventually, when he was about four years old, his mother disappeared. Whether she had gone away with another man, killed herself, or returned to Ireland no one ever knew. Ted was sent to an orphanage near London, and he remained there until he was old enough to work—fourteen. "Bloody place—I was in trouble half the time—you know, smoking in the shithouse and that kind of thing, and I spent

bloody hours nearly every day polishing the floor in the hallway—at the posh end of the house, see? Polished my bleeding
arms down to the fucking elbows, I did. They used to make us
all dive into a bath full of bloody cold water every morning
when we got up. Never knew why. I suppose they thought it
would stop us getting a hard on—that and the bleedin' cocoa
every night. They laced that with some stuff to stop us wank-
ing [masturbating], but Christ, you could hear the bloody beds
squeaking and rattling all sodding night."

From the orphanage, Ted had been sent to work in a pub as
a live-in porter—cleaning up and carrying crates of beer down
into the cellar—but after a week or so he was discovered drinking ale on the job and "sent up the road" (fired). The relative
of a youth whom he had befriended was the deckhand of a
shrimp bawley sailing out of Southend in Essex, and he got Ted
a job as deckboy. Ted's duties were to help cast out the shrimp
nets, make tea, haul in the nets, and help to cook the shrimp
on the way into port. If that sounds a fair employment for a
young lad, see how Ted expressed himself about it: "We was
out day and bleeding night, the bloody boat was only twenty-
four feet, and sometimes the fog was so thick and the rain so
fucking heavy you could have stuck your arm out and made
a hole in it. The skipper was a right stingy geezer, as mean as
Old Bill [a policeman], and he docked our pay anytime we
ripped a net, or was late getting back into South-bloody-End.
I didn't have nowhere ashore to stay, and my pay was bloody
sixpence a trip, so I couldn't afford a doss-house. I slept in the
fore-cuddy, about as big as an ordinary fucking dog kennel,
and got fish and chips from ashore for the first few weeks. The
bleeding skipper found that I'd been pinching a handful of
shrimp to eat, and docked me a week's bloody pay. Then I
started cooking for myself on the little stove where we used to
boil the sodding tea water, and when he found out about that
he charged me for lodging onboard, three bob [shillings] a
week, the fucker, and him not married, neither. Pity any poor
woman that married a geezer like that. She'd be paying him
bloody lodgings and giving birth to fucking cash registers, and
living on bloody boiled shrimp for ever and a fucking day!
Come to think of it, the sod had a face like a bleeding boiled
shrimp! Then a mate of mine got me a berth on a mulie, so I

told the shrimp skipper to stick his bleeding bawley where the monkey sticks his sodding nuts. It was tons better on the mulie, though. I was onboard her for about six months. But the bleedin' cargoes—all the shit from every bleeding horse in the Household Cavalry and at Whitbreads Brewery, and from Carter Paterson's furniture wagons. It wasn't bad working with the brewery people, though; they always used to send a crate of beer down with the horse shit. The grub was much better too, and the mulie had a proper foc'sle. It was like bleeding home from home. Then, through another pal, I met Bert, and here I am. Of course, I won't be at sea all my bloody life, no fear! I'm going to find a nice little pusher [girl] and have a home and kids and everything. . . ."

At first I was wary of Ted. He was a rough-looking kind of youth, despite his handsomeness; I had been warned in Wales time and again about the dishonesty of Londoners, and how they would rob their own mothers. But Ted never stole anything from me in the eighteen months or so that we sailed together. True, he might, in jest, hide my sea boots, or surreptitiously cut the buttons off my watch jacket while he stood talking to me in the darkness on deck, and then hide them, but those were normal japes among lads anywhere. Neither, as far as I know, did Ted ever pilfer from the cargoes we carried, although sometimes the stuff we carried, like bags of sugar or boxes of tomatoes, could easily have been broached and some of the contents sold ashore. That would have been very risky, because most of the waterfront folk of the small ports in Britain were finely attuned to any activity that was in the least bit unusual. No doubt word of any misdeed would have reached Tansy's ears before the ship sailed, if not upon her arrival at the next port, or upon her return to the scene of the crime.

Ashore, to Ted, however, was a different matter; ashore was another world, and, to him, landsmen merited a separate set of morals. Never, I think, did Ted go ashore for a walk in the town and around in the summertime without returning with his pockets full of apples or plums filched from some good yeoman's trees. Never did he go shopping on an errand for Tansy and not come back with a couple of bars of chocolate or a bag of sweets, or a packet of Woodbine cigarettes that he had shoplifted. Ted ashore was like a magpie; anything that wasn't cemented to the ground, lashed down, or nailed down was fair game. He never stole from the shops where he bought things for Tansy or Bert—that would have been against his peculiar sense of morality. Instead, he went to the bigger department stores, such as Woolworth's or Marks and Spencer's. That he was never detected and caught is a wonder. When he slithered down the foc'sle-scuttle and triumphantly displayed combs and pencils, candy and chocolate, cigarettes, and even, once, a fancy shirt, I always wondered how he had managed to hide it all. Once, in Ramsgate or Margate, I had a bad cold and no money to buy cough lozenges (I sent most of my wages home every time I was paid). Ted disappeared into the rain ashore "to buy a paper, Tansy, I want to see how Arsenal got on." He returned a half hour later with two packets of cough lozenges filched from a news-agent's counter. How Bert never knew that Ted was doing this is a mystery, because it was obvious that on a deckhand's pay he couldn't afford a shirt like the one he stole. Perhaps Bert did know, and turned a blind eye. That would have been Bert's way, except that I'm pretty sure the mate would have had a "quiet word" with Ted.

Ted borrowed small sums of money from me from time to time—sixpence here, a shilling there—but he always paid me back as soon as he himself was paid his wages.

We could draw advances on our pay at any time in port, but I was wary of doing this in case I couldn't send my mam her regular five shillings (about a dollar) a week. That left me with two shillings (about forty cents) spending money, or roughly threepence halfpenny (about six cents) a day. That wasn't bad, in those days, for a lad of fourteen, because a bar of chocolate was only twopence, and the entrance ticket to a Saturday after-noon cinema show was never more than threepence. However, by the end of July I had started to save up for my railway ticket home to Wales at Christmas, so that just about halved my weekly pocket money down to one shilling (twenty cents). Out of that I had to buy an oilskin coat (I'd lost mine over the side through my own negligence) and a new pair of shoregoing boots—the ones I had worn from Wales were ruined by salt. (The romance of sail-in-trade!)

Ted's cursing lessened a great deal once he got to know me better. I observed that it was his habit to curse a great deal more

when he was with strange, newly encountered people, especially other boys whom he didn't know very well. I put it down
as a cover-up for shyness or for inarticulateness. Where others
said, ". . . er . . ." or ". . . hmm . . ." Ted said "bleeding,"
"bloody," "fucking," or "sodding." He meant nothing by it.

Ted was, despite the often dirty labor, a very clean lad. Even
on the coldest days, as soon as work was finished he sluiced
himself down, bare to the waist, in sea or river water hauled
over the side in a bucket. I soon found myself doing the same,
though I hated the coldness of the water. The shock seemed,
somehow, to be too much of an intrusion into the depths of my
being. Perhaps I had been subconsciously thinking of Ted's
cold baths in the orphanage.

After a while I never read anything but papers or magazines
when Ted was in the foc'sle. He seemed to be uncomfortable
when I was reading a book. I did my best not to sound better-
read or more informed about what was going on in the world
than he appeared to be, but it was a hard job. I had to be on
my guard most of the time I was with Ted, so as not to lose
his fragile friendship. To put him at his ease, I never lost any
opportunity to ask his advice on how something should be
done—coiling a line, or how to make a knot or a splice. This
pleased him greatly, and then we were very close pals. Indeed,
we became such good friends that at Christmas that first year,
1938, I invited Ted to go home with me to Wales; but Bert had
already made arrangement for him to visit his family in London. I had to be careful how I invited Ted. He was sensitive
to any suspicion of pity about his circumstances. For weeks I
boasted to him about how much more wealth, how much more
friendliness, what better soccer players, what prettier girls we
had in Wales, until he was ready to put a bet on it and even
agreed to come to Llangareth to see for himself. Fortunately,
because of Bert's invitation, he couldn't come. I would have
either lost the bet because I'd lost the argument with Ted, or
lost a friend, so in the end it all worked out for the best.

Ted was one of the nimblest-fingered sailors I ever saw. His
deck-seamanship was—there is only one word for it—professional. In the fourteen months or so that he had been onboard
Second Apprentice he had learned a lot from Bert, and had even
surpassed him at making eye splices and long splices in wire

rope; his knowledge of knots and hitches was surprising in one so young. The average bargeman used only a few knots—the reef, the sheet, the figure of eight, the bowline—and about the same number of hitches—the clove, the timber, the Blackwall, the Liverpool, the round-turn and two half-hitches; but Ted knew knots and hitches that even surprised Tansy at times, and he could run up a foot or two of baggy-wrinkle (sail protector pads), out of scruffy old rope, in no time at all. Ted loved working with ropes and wires. He disliked keeping watches at the helm. He said it bored him. Often I stood an hour or even two of his watch, while he stood in for me in the galley. Ted was the kind of person who always had to be doing something with his hands and was not happy unless he could see the results of his effort. When he made a sennit (a fender from old rope) the look of absolute concentration on his face while he was busy making it, and of satisfaction when it was done, were sights to be remembered. Whatever Ted had made looked as though it had been purchased brand new at a chandler's.

Apart from making things, another activity Ted enjoyed was shinning up the main shroud ratlines whenever a job had to be done at the mainmasthead, such as lashing up the topsail when it was handed, or keeping a lookout for a buoy or a marker. Then he looked completely *en rapport* with all his surroundings; he was unconsciously what all boys who ever dreamed of going to sea would like to be—fair, handsome, healthy, strong, mostly willing, clever in his own way, ingenious in a pinch, well-liked, and good-humored.

If everything went well Ted would advance in life, slowly perhaps, but he would advance to at least a mate in the trade. He might even rise to master some day, if he could keep his language, his childlike impulses, and his man's passions under control. If he could not, then he was doomed to a life of toil, privation, and debauchery. This was one of the things about himself that Ted knew, as he confessed in the small dark hours, but the one thing he did not know was fear or self-pity of the whining kind. Ted was doomed to be one of those who are man enough to scorn any who might pity them. His life, hard as it was, was his own, and to live it was, to him, a privilege. He was a child of the sea, and knew of no other affection or love. He was one of a type whose tradition goes back to the youth of the world, a type without which the mighty civilizations and empires of the past could have been only dreams; without which the human race would probably still be sitting by fires in caves.

It could be said that Ted's cultural replacements are the skinheads and the punk-rockers of today, but they are a lot less innocent than Ted was, not quite as colorfully profane, and much less believing. They have learned how to make themselves heard, but they have also learned how to whine and complain. That Ted never did—he would rather have thrown himself over the side. He knew all about cruelty, coldheartedness, and exploitation—if anyone ever knew about man's inhumanity to man, Ted did. But he never once showed spite in his heart, nor even resentment. Even when he cursed the memory of some bullying or meanness toward him or others, it was always with a hint of wry humor. Now Ted's ilk are middle-aged, and those of them who survived the war are comfortably ashore, probably fully paid-up members of some trade union or other.

The generation after generation of boys and men who labored on the seas in vile conditions for a pittance have all gone, forgotten except by a few, a very few, who are honored to have known them—and who loved them.

14

Bert

Sometimes *Second Apprentice* was very pleasant lodgings, as when she was moored in a little rural creek or river like the Stour, the Hamble, or the Medway. Sometimes, when she was made fast to a tree, birds sang in her rigging and spiders weaved gossamer webs in her shrouds so that they looked like ratlines for elves, fairies, and goblins; and green, red, or golden leaves, conkers, and acorns fell on her deck. At other times, we hauled the bower anchor ashore and sank it into softly waving green grass. Then Ted and I ran on the banks and swung on low tree branches. There *Second Apprentice* might wait for a whole tide mirrored in a pool, her decks spangled with dew-drops under the moon, her black rigging and sails towering into the night sky, probing the domain of the driving clouds and the swinging stars. Then, when we lads crept silently down the forescuttle, the foc'sle was snug, warm, and without drafts. The oil lamp lit up brightly in a second or two, and all in the calm water was undisturbed, without dirt or noise, and with no landlord's bill to pay. On those days and nights, very few and far between, I would not have exchanged homes with the king of England.

Gradually, as the weeks of my first year onboard passed, the ship became more and more my home, and she became a part of the men in her, so that the men in her became part of my home. Abaft the deckhouse, *Second Apprentice* was like a replication of her captain—quiet, tidy, stern yet at ease, severe yet relaxed, and honest as she was sturdy. Forward of the helm she took on certain aspects of Bert's personality. At sea or in port, to a trained eye everything about her midships section was shipshape; everything was how, where, and when it should be; all the halyards, the sheets, the burtons, the lazy jacks, the downhauls and falls, the clean decks and paintwork, all was exactly as it ought to be in any well-run ship. But to the novice or the landsman, unaccustomed to the ways of working sailcraft, it would have all seemed a chaotic pickle, with a plethora of ropes of all different lengths and sizes hung, strewn, and coiled in all sorts of places, so that he would wonder how anyone could ever sort out the mess. So appeared, too, our ship's mate, Bert, to anyone who didn't know him well.

Everything that Bert did onboard *Second Apprentice* he did with a perfection that is almost unattainable this side of the pearly gates. If Bert heaved the weighty gaff of the heavy mainsail up in a howling breeze, the halyard needed no extra swigging; it was *up, chock-a-block.* If Ted and I with our combined strength could not lift another link of the anchor cable and Bert grabbed the windlass lever, the anchor came *up.* If Bert made an eye splice in a two-inch-diameter wire rope, it was finished as neat as a roebuck's eye, and that wire would part before the eye splice failed. If Bert stowed an awkward cargo of barrels, sacks, boxes, or timber, and the weather played up hell on the passage, the cargo *stayed stowed.*

But often, perfection breeds paradoxes. Everything that Bert did, he seemed to do awkwardly. Even when he walked along the deck it was with an awkward gait. When he ate his meals he seemed to be all odd angles, and his missing teeth did nothing to help him seem symmetrical. It wasn't the shape of his body; hard labor had kept Bert trim enough, as it did most of the working sailors (except a few of the very old cooks). It wasn't lack of dexterity; I saw Bert many a time flick a round turn and two half-hitches over a cleat or a mooring post so fast that my eyes could not discern his movement. It wasn't that he did not have a sense of fitness or tidiness; God knows he instilled that into us lads so deeply that it remains with me until this day. In his movements he resembled one of those men who, despite the neatness of their form, no matter how much they spend, can never find and wear a well-fitting suit of clothes. It took me several days of working closely with Bert to finally discover what it was about him that made his movements seem so awkward. It was very simple. Bert was left-handed, "clack-handed," as the sailors put it. It was also obvious after observing him for a while that his left-handedness did not stop at his elbows but extended up to his brain, and therefore it affected the way he saw everything. Trying to learn from Bert was a little like looking in a mirror. You know that what you see is your reflection, and you take it for granted that this is what you look like. It is only after a few weeks or months of acceptance of this that you realize that what is in the mirror is actually the reverse of what you look like. The image is true, but only for your reflection, not for you. Everything that Bert taught us or showed us, every technique, was correct for him. But we had to reverse the whole process so as to make it correct for us. The miracle to me was that it worked. Bert, once he had taught us anything, no matter how complex, made it stick in our heads, and I for one never forgot it.

As mate, it was one of Bert's duties, by the unwritten rules, to teach us youngsters practically everything except the domestic chores. Those, like street rhymes and hopscotch, were taught by our immediate predecessors on the ascending age scale—in my case, by Ted.

There were no formal lessons in seamanship and navigation, as there would have been on a big oceangoing vessel. It was all "hands on" training, as the Americans so vividly express the method. If I wanted to know how to do something, I did it, and Bert stood over me to correct or congratulate me. To do this he had two stock phrases—"Not that way, you silly bugger," or "Good show, cocker! Now do it again!"

One of the first aspects of navigation that Bert taught me was the "Rule of the Road"—the rules governing the navigation of a ship by night and day when other craft are in the vicinity. He did this by making me repeat rhymes over and over again until I could have repeated them backward:

> When both lights you see ahead,
> Starboard turn and show your red.
> Green to green, or red to red,
> Perfect safety, go ahead.
> If to your starboard red appear,
> It is your duty to keep clear,
> To act as judgment says is proper

To port or starboard, back or stop her;
But if upon your port is seen
A vessel's starboard light of green
There's not so much for you to do
For green to port keeps clear of you.

Steamers, white lights on the mast,
A sailer no such light will cast,
But if she shows red over green
Then a sailer you have seen.

Two black balls or red on red,
Then you know her rudder's dead.

Green on red, three whites on high,
And you know a tow goes by.

If moving white light you discern,
Then you know you see her stern.
One or two white lights and stopped,
Be sure her anchor she has dropped.

Green over white—trawling light,
Red on white—catch fish they might.
Two black cones their points a-kissing,
By day you're sure that she is fishing.
A third cone, point up, like a cuckold,
Then your course well clear you hold.

Three black balls to heaven bound
Shows that vessel is aground;
If by night to ground she's wed,
Two white lights and red on red.

A sailing craft, cone pointed down,
Her engine's pushing, homeward bound.

Nothing could be an easier method for learning and remembering the basic safety rules of nautical traffic. The official written rules were so complex as to be almost beyond the comprehension of the average barge makee-learner.

Other rhymes were:

For two sailing vessels meeting with the wind on different sides:

> When the wind is on your port
> Then of wisdom don't be short,
> Like the ladies of the street,
> You'll avoid them when you meet.

For two sailing ships with the wind on the same side:

> If you are closer to the wind
>   [always pronounced "wynd"]
> Of her stay clear and peace you'll find.

For a sailing ship and a powered vessel meeting in confined waters:

> No matter if you're a big three-master,
> If she's got power she is faster;
> A barquentine or sleek square-rigger,
> If she's got power she is bigger.
> To yourself you always say,
> "She has power—and right of way!"

For a sailing ship and a powered vessel meeting in open waters: (Note: Except for the last line, this rule no longer applies.)

> When well clear and in the offing,
> The steamer's cap to you she's doffing;
> To you the right of way she'll give—
> But keep well clear and you will live!

Right from the first trip, when we arrived at Remagen, I helped Ted to rig the cargo derrick under Bert's supervision. Even after six months onboard, when we had rigged it innumerable times, Bert could still do the heavy job alone faster than we two lads. A spare gaff, which was lashed to the bulwark when not in use, was mounted on the mast by a locking ring on its heel. Then a single whip was led from the dolly winch at the base of the mast through a big block on the outer end of the gaff. A cargo hook was moused to the end of the whip. That was the heaving line. Then two guyropes were bent on the outer end of the gaff. One of these led through another block lashed up high to the shrouds. To the end of that guyrope we lashed a heavy weight—the bower anchor was usually employed for this, but if we were alongside a lighter, at anchor ourselves, then we used anything that weighed heavily enough —bags of potatoes or sacks of coal. This weight was known as the "deadman."

The cargo was hoisted up in skips by Bert, working the dolly-winch handle. This hauled up the hooked whip, which pulled the loaded skip up above the hatch. The shoreguy was then heaved by the man or boy on the jetty, and the gaff-end was pulled over the cart or wagon being loaded. This movement pulled the shroudguy, thus hauling up the deadman weight. The skip was then lowered onto the cart by Bert unwinding the dolly winch. The carter unloaded the skip and shoved it, empty, back toward the ship. The return of the gaff-end over the hold was aided by the weight of the deadman as it sank again. Then Bert unwound the skip-whip, thus lowering the empty skip once again into the hold, where Ted and I waited to reload it. Each haul and return of the skip, once we got into the swing of things, took about three to four minutes, and each loading of the skip, depending on what type of cargo we were handling, took between five to fifteen minutes. So it went on, up and down, all day, mostly in sweaty silence except for the rattle of the dolly winch, the squeaking of blocks, the puffing and hooting of railway engines, the neighing of horses, and Ted's shouts each time the skip was loaded and ready to be hoisted: "Heave away, Bert!" or "Up she goes, my hearty!" and Bert's yell each time the skip was swiftly lowered: "Watch your heads!" or "Come on, I thought you'd filled the bloody thing!"

Getting ready to sail was, for us all, a relief from the grinding work in harbor. Then Bert was in his glory. If we were all sitting at a meal, perhaps breakfast, waiting for the tide to rise, Bert disappeared early from the table, usually without saying a word, or only, "Well, I'd better go and have a shufti [look] up top. . . ." By the time I had cleared up the pots and plates, and Ted had squared away the skipper's lobby and the foc'sle, Bert, always humming to himself when he worked alone, had the cargo-hatch covers, all heavy long boards, in place, and the loose gear such as the huge sweep oars and the punt-poles, and loose mooring lines, all lashed down on top of the hatches, the running rigging lines all flaked out on deck ready for hoisting, and the topsail sitting on the main truck ready for hauling up. When the time came to let go the mooring lines, Ted or I was already at the top of the shrouds, ready to let the topsail loose from its gaskets. If there was a strong wind blowing this was a risky business. I always remembered that my predecessor had been killed doing that job when he had fallen, or been blown, to the deck fifty feet below. As if I needed reminding, Bert always warned us, as we shinned up the ratlines, "Take heed —one hand for yourself!"

Only when the mooring lines were ready to be slipped, and the last topsail gasket was being taken off, did Tansy appear on deck. He stood by the helm studying the mastheads for a minute or so, gauging the weather; then he silently nodded. The mooring lines were thrown off the bollards or the buoy, or the anchor was brought onboard, the last gasket came zinging off the ballooning topsail, and it was hoisted up, gaff and all, until it was apeak. The power in the topsail, considering its size compared to the main, was amazing. No sooner was it apeak and sheeted home than all ninety feet of *Second Apprentice,* if there was any breeze at all, started to gain steerage way. By the time I had regained the deck, the mate and Ted were already hoisting the mainsail. I guess that the time from when Tansy took hold of the helm and nodded his head to when we were under full working sail was no more than about twelve to fifteen minutes. That was main, main topsail, foresail, two jibs, mizzen and mizzen t'sail. Often I caught glimpses of people watching us from the shore, or from other ships moored along the jetties or at anchor. Then I always felt proud and important, and not at all envious of the watchers.

Bert always kept his eyes on the sails and rigging when we were entering or leaving harbor, and much of the time at sea. I suppose that is one of the main differences between true sailors and town dwellers—the sailor's head is generally *up.* If there was a tricky exit, or a headwind entering a narrow harbor, Bert watched the sails and rigging, leaning over this way and that to watch a luff, or to check the run of a sheet. His blue eyes squinted almost closed, and one hand stroked his walrus mustache. Being novices, Ted and I generally followed the captain's gaze in tight corners, but Bert always watched his charge, the rig, and when he moved to correct the set of some sail, he moved like quicksilver. I guessed his age at about forty-five, but when he was in a hurry his movements were those of a lad of twenty. Bert usually had a cigarette, lit or not, stuck in one corner of his lips. He was the dandy of *Second Apprentice*. Being the only married man onboard, he changed into a wife-laundered shirt every two days, but he never wore a collar unless he was going ashore for a message or a pint in the evening, or to his home. Both he and Tansy, in port, generally went to a pub where they were known, for a bath once or twice a week. We lads, not being rich enough, or, in my case, old enough to drink, had to make do with cold sluice in a bucket, or, if we were near a fresh-water supply, a hot-water "rubdown" from a large bucket heated up on the galley stove.

Except at the meal table, Bert wore a flat cap, in the peak of which was stuck a faded, tattered Armistice Day poppy. The cigarettes he smoked were Woodbines at fourpence for ten, and he gave me the cigarette cards each time he opened a new packet. They were of footballers, and I treasured the whole set for years, until I lost them years later in the *Two Brothers* disaster. They would be worth a small fortune now, but that's not why I saved them; we'll come to that in time.

The only occasion that Bert didn't smoke on deck was when we carried ammunition during the early part of the war, explosives, or fodder. Then when he needed a "fag" he puffed away down in the skipper's lobby, safely away from any danger of fulminant fumes. Ted told me that Bert smoked and wore his cap even in bed, when he was asleep, and I believed him, until one morning I discovered Bert sleeping off a hangover.

Ted smoked Gold Flake cigarettes, at sixpence for ten, but he didn't give me the cards. He swapped them ashore, and onboard other coasters, for two cigarettes apiece.

It was obvious to me, after a few passages, that Bert loved *Second Apprentice*. He must have; he'd had one or two offers of a captain's berth on river-plying spritties, but he was content to stay with our ship. When we were in harbor or when Tansy was not on watch, Bert was completely in charge of the ship's sailing and working. Bert never seemed satisfied unless the ship had called from him his utmost exertions, and he had called from her all her power and strength. Both he and the ship repayed each other by a faithfulness, a loyalty which was often to be tried to the limits of endurance and beyond. He watched every flutter of the sail-luffs as though they were entering his very being. Every murmur of the water alongside seemed to delight him. He was, when his hands were not occupied in some task, always resting them for a moment on some piece of the ship, as if he were fondling her. In those moments his eyes veiled momentarily, as if he were suddenly dreaming, as if he were at that instant living more intensely than we have ever known, as if the ship were his ideal of beauty and perfection.

I once mentioned this offhandedly to Ted. "Let's face it," said that stalwart, "he's bonkers about the bloody ship. If his missus could see him—blimey, it's like he was on the vinegar strokes[having an orgasm]—she'd do her bleeding nut [go mad]!"

Whenever the ship was underway and Bert was on the wheel, he was somehow bigger and taller, and it was only when Tansy came on deck that he reverted to his real dimensions, and the color of his complexion and clothes faded. But that was only in the imagination of a small Welsh ship's boy. Ted said that Tansy had "tasted bloody salt water before Bert was bleeding breeched. Bert's one of them blokes what always has to have someone over them. Tansy's a master, and that's why they work so flipping well together, see?"

"What do you think I'll be, Ted?" I asked him.

"A bloody tally clerk, that's what you'll be, if they don't bleeding hang you first!" Ted grinned when he said that. I was reading a book. His face fell serious in the low glow of the foc'sle. "You reading all that fucking bullshit. Fill yourself full of that and you won't know which way is sodding up!"

Toward the winter of 1938, we arrived at Greenwich on a Sunday morning with a cargo of coal, and Bert took Ted and me to his home nearby. It was a gray, overcast day. I was astonished at the transformation in Bert when we stepped ashore from a neighboring coaster's jolly boat. From being a man in charge of all he surveyed, from looking as if he cared for everything he saw, from being an erudite source of esoteric information about everyting from airing holds to refitting windlasses, from avoiding the Goodwin Sands to wearing the north foreland, he was suddenly transformed into just another rather funny-looking little man in a shabby raincoat, black boots, a flat cap, and a mustache much too large for his face. As we waited for a bus he no longer talked of "sheeting home" and "being in irons," and ships he'd sailed aboard that had been "stiff as a church but mean as a pawnbroker's clerk." Now all his talk was of how his wife might be annoyed with him for taking us home to lunch without first warning her. "She'll do her flipping lid. I hope the baby's got over that whooping cough. . . . I'd have taken you for a couple of pints, but if the missus smells it. . . ." As we boarded the double-decker bus (the first one I'd ever been on) he turned to me as he reached the top of the stairs. There were other people waiting impatiently to go down the stairs to dismount at the next stop. Bert said: "How about you blokes giving me a hand in the garden this afternoon? Last time I was home the missus played up merry hell because it's in a bit of a pickle. . . ."

We alighted at the end of a long street, as straight as a rifle shot, lined on both sides with houses that all adjoined onto one another, like a long row of stacked mineral-water boxes, all looking exactly alike. They all had the same shape of gable roof, with the same kind of wooden fretwork under the eaves, and the same type of iron railing in front, around tiny gardens that looked, from the end of the street, like a long array of dwarves' spears. Every so often, along the mile-or-so-long street, there was a lamp post, each one exactly the same as the next. The only things out of place on that street were Ted and me, and a pile of dung left by a milk-cart horse that slowly traipsed from gateway to gateway wearing a bored look on its face.

As we wended our way to Bert's house, he told us that he was related to one of the old river families who had been in the barge business since the days of Henry the Eighth, "and probably before that. I started my working life on a dumb-barge owned by my father and went from that to a sprittie; that was before the last war. Then, when old Jerry started his fe-nangles I volunteered for the Navy and went into mine-sweep-ers. I was lucky; I never got into any real trouble. We was based in Scapa Flow and pretty well out of the way of it all. But it got me hooked onto the sea. When I was discharged I didn't want to be on the river no more, see? So I looked for seagoing coasters. I was in several of them, first as deckhand and then as mate. Let's see, there was *Torment;* she was a sprittie, but she sailed up as far as Yarmouth and Lowestoft. Then there was . . . *Sepoy,* till we lost her off Cromer—1933, that was. . . . *Goldfinch* . . . she was a schooner, a real beauty, that one. . . ."

Bert reeled off the names of ships one after the other. It was like a roll of honor of many of the most famous British coastal sailing vessels between the wars. As he reeled off each name, we passed yet one more front gate exactly the same as the one before. The contrast between our surroundings and Bert's ac-count staggered me.

Ted stared around him the whole way; I supposed he was looking for any girls that he could ogle. His luck was out. It had started to rain, and the young lasses were probably all at the cinema with their boyfriends who had good jobs in the City or at the bank or post office.

After we had walked along the endless street past the houses all lined up and expressionless as Grenadier Guards, Bert grabbed one of a hundred iron gates, this one covered in faded green paint. "Here we are, lads," he murmured perkily, "wel-come to home sweet home!" He fumbled in his pockets for his door keys and finally extracted them, attached to the ring on top of his clasp knife, the one with the small marlinspike down one side that both Ted and I coveted.

Bert inserted his key into the green-painted front door. A thin treble voice called out loudly from the depths of the house. I fully expected, when the door opened, to see a cargo hold yawning open in front of us. Instead there was a dark, narrow hallway that smelled of cooked cabbage. Up one side of the small hallway was a flight of narrow stairs; on the other wall, which was disguised by wallpaper covered with a design of latticework and roses, was a coat hanger rack.

"Hang your hats up here, boys—hulloo, angel!" Bert cried

loudly in a rising voice, as though he was ordering the topsail handed. But neither Ted nor I had hats. The treble voice quavered again from a room at the back of the short passage: "Who's that with you I've told you not to bring any of that crowd from the local why didn't you send me a letter saying when you'd be home I promised my mum I was going to see her today who's this?" Mrs. Bert was a pale, thin, whispy-haired woman with a birdlike face. I guessed that she was in her late twenties. She was dressed for the street and looked as though she needed a long sea cruise. As she inspected Ted and me her expression softened just a mite. "Hmm . . . that lot from the ship?"

"Yes, Nora. . . ." Bert was about to reply when a noisy wail came through the back door, which let directly from the kitchen, where we were, into the backyard. "How's the babby . . . ?" Bert trailed off.

Mrs. Bert sniffed. "Oh, Hermione's all right look I'm late already I promised Mum I'd be at her house by one o'clock I thought you might be home I've left your dinner in the oven if they want anything . . ."—she looked generally in our direction—"you'd better show them where everything is and they can help themselves only don't touch the ham and the butter or the jam and the sugar and leave the milk and the lamb chops alone. . . ." With that Mrs. Bert exited out the back door and soon returned with a tot's baby carriage with a fat, runny-nosed infant of about eighteen months. With quick, jerky movements, as Bert looked red in the face and Ted and I stared in amazement, Mrs. Bert maneuvered the stroller around the kitchen table, past the sideboard cupboard and out through the inner kitchen door; slamming it behind her, she was gone. Bert's offspring's wail diminished in reverse ratio to her mother's progress through the front passage, out of the green-painted door and the green-painted iron gate into the street.

Bert removed his raincoat and his cap and sat down. "Well, boys, make yourself at home. Plenty of stuff in the cupboard. Have a fry up if you want to. . . ." He poked his fork at the gas-stove.

Ted and I cooked up some fried bread and egg, with milkless tea, and hungrily consumed it in very short order. As we finished our repast Bert said: "Well, like I told you blokes, there's nothing like a nice little home ashore, with a missus and family. I was a bit wild when I was your age, but since I found Nora and got tied up I've never been so well looked after." Bert's face was deadly serious as he said that. Ted's face was a study in surprise, and I did my best to keep from bursting out laughing. From above us assorted diapers and baby clothes on the clothes-drying rack dripped water onto my collar.

After dinner was cleared up, Bert showed us his family photograph album: oval sepia picture after oval sepia picture of chubby-looking Victorian and Edwardian ladies with their hair done up in buns and lace around their necks; stout, serious, respectable looking, black-dressed, mustached and bearded gentlemen in waistcoats and watch-fobs, holding bowler hats on their knees, and lacy-drawered little girls all desperately trying to look like Alice in Wonderland. Then we helped Bert tidy up his small back garden. There wasn't a lot to do—dig up an old bicycle frame half-buried in the earth and clear up a few leaves—but it was good to be out in the fresh air, even if it was a couple of miles away from the sea.

When we got back onboard, Bert was his old self once again, the mate we knew. When we were alone in the foc'sle, getting ready to turn in, I asked Ted how he'd enjoyed his outing. Ted stood by his bunk in his long johns. "Oh, alright," he grunted. Then he said quietly, in a flat voice, "I'll tell you one thing, Nip."

"What's that Ted?"

Ted's voice dropped even lower, "I've changed my bloody mind about getting married. . . . G'night!"

15

Tansy

I spent two summers and two winters onboard *Second Apprentice,* and still those two winters, of '38 and '39, strike me as the physically hardest times in my life. It was work, work, work. In the winters we mostly plied between the Solent and France. As soon as we entered port we set to unloading the cargo. We might get a couple of hour's spell waiting for the next cargo to arrive, during which we performed the ship's chores. After that it was back down the hold for hours on end, using Tilley oil lamps, carrying on into the dark hours so that we could catch an early-morning tide. When there was little or no wind, or when the wind was a "muzzler," that meant first working our way around the Isle of Wight, using the four tides a day to "dredge" the ship with the anchor. We might drift, or row, with Ted and me on the sweeps to maintain steerage-way over the tide stream, then drop the anchor and wait a while, hammering in the cargo-hatch covers securely, lashing down the jolly boat, or doing any of a thousand other tasks. When the anchor was weighed again there was more labor on the windlass and the sweeps until we were clear of the Nab, or the Needles if the wind was easterly, and out clear into the Channel. Sometimes the cross-Channel run was easy; 130-odd miles on the starboard tack with the wind steady at twenty knots; sometimes it was a plain, twenty-two-carat bastard, with shifting winds and calms before a hard blow, and sometimes it was an exquisite hell of icy-cold northeasterly wind, hail, rain, and sleet.

When the weather was fair, Tansy (unless he was on watch), usually stayed below in his cabin, but as soon as there was a promise of any liveliness he came on deck. There, in his oil-skins and bowler hat, he plodded up and down, always on the weather side, with his stumpy pipe upside-down between his teeth, eyeing the topmast truck at intervals. Sometimes, after he had gauged the weather, he sat just inside the galley door drinking a pint of hot tea, or, if it was well into Ted's or my helm-trick, he might take over the wheel from us, to give us a spell.

While the weather was fair or uncertain, Tansy was rarely talkative. It was only when the die was cast, and a rising wind and a lively sea showed a determined intent to give us a good dusting, that he opened up and warmed to us lads. Then it was obvious that, like all sailors of any experience, Tansy owed nothing to, and was owed nothing by, the sea. The wind was there to be used, and the sea was there to be sailed over, and there was little that he or anyone else could do about it, so he might as well accept it and get on with it. He seemed neither to enjoy the heavy weather nor to abhor it. It was all part of life to him. He accepted it. He got on with his job; we should get on with ours, and the weather should follow the course the Almighty had set for it, and get on with *its* job, too.

Often, in very heavy going, the helm watches for us lads were cut down to an hour at a time. It was almost as much as I could do to hold the kicking wheel, and every time a sea caught the rudder and battered it I nailed my soul to the helm, hung on like a stout centurion, and prayed to the seven gods of the sea. Tansy, when he saw this, reached his arm around and calmly took the wheel. There was no magical transformation. The wheel didn't stop kicking, and neither did the seas give up battering or the wind cease howling, but somehow something happened—the ship quieted.

It took some time before I realized the difference between the mate and the captain. In Bert's case, he was in love with the ship. In Tansy's case, the ship was in love with *him*. That was why, when Bert walked the deck during the night watches, his footsteps clomped and reverberated all through the ship; when Tansy walked forward there was hardly a sound. With Bert the ship flirted, teased, and worked; Tansy she loved and obeyed.

In time, I always knew when the weather was going to

deteriorate. There was a barometer onboard, down in the skipper's lobby, but there was never any need to look at it, to see
whether it was dropping. As the atmospheric pressure fell, so
did Bert's spirits, and so, correspondingly, did Tansy's rise.

In *Second Apprentice* we needed no graphs or barometers to tell
us that a blow was coming—all we needed to do was look at
Bert's face. It was so obvious, the effect of the atmosphere on
him, that even Ted noticed it. As he put it, "If you screwed a
bloody cuckoo clock into the top of his head you could mount
Bert on the bleeding wall."

"You're a lucky chap, Nipper," said Tansy. We were bowling along on a dead run up-Channel with cement for Newhaven from Southampton. It was a blustery October day of
clouds shoving up to Dover with the wind. We were running
free, with the mainsail handed, and the squaresail boomed out
on its yard and pulling like a hero. To our north, the coast of
England lay misty blue on the horizon while out to seaward all
was dark cloud and gray seas, with their white tops boisterously celebrating not having washed up on the shores of
France. I liked being at the helm when we were running free.
It demanded a lot of concentration, but there was an urgent feel
to the forward thrust of the sails, the rigging, and the hull that
I imagine would have pleased any youngster. The wheel, although it needed more attention than when we were on other
points of sail, was less demanding of brute strength, and so a
lot easier for me to handle.

"Why's that, Tansy?" As I queried him my eyes stayed on
the pennant aloft and the squaresail. "Why do you say I'm
lucky?"

"Well, you weren't grown up when you came to sea. . . ."
He spoke as if my five months onboard had been five years.
"That's the best time of life to start at sea, like you were, just
out of school. You know enough to be able to understand
what's being said, but you don't know much about other people's . . . the way they do things ashore. The worst learners at
sea are those who come to it late."

"Why's that, Tansy?" The stern slid off a sea, sideways. I
heaved the wheel over to steady the ship. I was chewing on a

licorice stick. It was a habit Ted had introduced me to—they were much cheaper than toffees.

"Because they're always comparing the way we do things and the way it's done ashore, and of course, there can't be much comparison, because the way we do things and the way they do them are as different, leastways most of the time, as chalk and cheese. I mean if a bloke who's worked in a factory, say, comes to work at sea, he's not used to taking the weather into account, whereas we have it always in mind, all the time, even when we're on the beds for a refit. . . . Why, I once had a West Londoner came to work as a deckhand; in his early twenties, he was. He'd been highly recommended to me by someone. We were at anchor off Whitstable, and I happened to tell Bert that we should clean and check the anchor cable soon. The chap overheard me, it seems. . . . A while later Bert and I went ashore to get a few oysters and have a couple of pints. We were sitting in the pub, nice and cozy, when someone from another boomie comes running in all hot and bothered, and yells to me that someone is weighing our anchor. Of course Bert and I knocked off our pints and dashed outside the pub, and there was the ship, drifting out with the tide! Our factory friend was still pumping away at the anchor windlass weighing the hook! By the time we pulled the jolly boat alongside she'd drifted about a couple of cables. Good job there was hardly any breeze. . . ."

"What about the other crewman? I mean, didn't he try to. . . ."

"We didn't have a nipper onboard at the time. That was before Ted came to us." Tansy gazed at Ted, who was splicing a line in the lee of the hatch-coamings, sitting on deck, still barefoot and with no shirt. "Good job, really," said Tansy. "Ted would have crowned him." Tansy was silent for a few seconds. Then he said: "No, to be good in the trade you have to start off in the trade. It's different on the big ships, because they have so many people milling around that the good ones can cover up for the dead-legs and idlers, and the officers are not often much the wiser."

"How did you start off, Tansy?" I gave the wheel another half-turn, all the time watching the sails, checking the strain on the running backstay now set up.

Tansy walked over to starboard, knocked the ash out of his pipe over the side of the bulwark, and then returned to my side, smiling. "Me? Oh, I first went to sea in my father's lugger. We lived in Deal, you see, Nipper. I was six when I first started out, because there weren't much schooling for fishermen's sons in those days. That was in 1872. . . ."

I whirled my head to look at Tansy. He was staring at a sailing vessel far on the southern horizon. His green eyes slitted, he murmured, "She's an east-coaster, probably out of Essex, I'd say." I was hardly hearing him. I was staggered. I blurted out, *"1872?"*

"That's right. There were lots of luggers working out of Deal then. We used to launch them from the beach, then drag them back up, when we took the catch in, with horses, up above the tide-mark."

As he reminisced about the Deal lugger fleet, I reckoned up in my head: 1872 . . . that was . . . "Why, that's sixty-six years ago!" I shouted.

"That's right," said Tansy, as he refilled his pipe. "And when I was ten I went to sea in my first Rye trawler, my first real deep-sea boat. We used to fish off the Diamond Bank, off Dungeness, and land our catches at Ramsgate, because we could always get in there no matter what the state of the tide." Tansy caught my eye. His green eyes shone. He grinned. "Do you know, Nipper, the cook on my first Rye lugger was a lot older than I am now . . . and he'd started off at sea in the navy, and he'd been a powder-monkey at the battle of Trafalgar. . . ."

I started. *"1805?"* It was incredible. At school it had been the best-remembered date in British history, along with 1066.

"That's right. His name was Fletcher . . . Bill Fletcher. He'd been born onboard one of the men o' war. They used to allow women onboard in those days, when they were in harbor. The 'matelots' didn't get any shore leave, you see. Do you know what a powder-monkey was?"

"Boys; they used to bring the gunpowder up to the gunners, didn't they?"

"That's right, Nipper. Well, Billy was onboard . . . *Royal Sovereign*. That was Collingwood's flagship," he added casually, as if he were recounting something of the day before.

"What was your next ship, Tansy?"

The captain laughed quietly, as if to himself. He left the helm-shelter for a moment to look astern. Satisfied that the weather was holding steady, he regained the shelter. He took out his pipe, already charged, and lit it with an England's Glory wooden match. Then he gave one or two puffs to get a good draw and said: "Now I don't want you to get the wrong ideas, Nipper. What's gone is gone. We were arrested for smuggling brandy into Gravesend. The luggers, some of them, used to meet ships out at sea, and get a few dozen bottles or so, and take it into port under a catch of fish. But the Excise people got wind of it, and they came onboard, and the game was up."

"What did they do?"

"The laws were stiff. The Excisemen made us saw the lugger in half and jailed the captain. He got two years' penal servitude. The crew—there were four of us—two of the older ones got six months' hard labor, and us other two lads got the choice of going to prison for six months along with two dozen strokes —they still used the cat o' nine tails in those days—or joining the navy. My pal Bob went to prison. I joined the *Andrew* [Royal Navy]. Mind you, I wasn't sorry. Rough as it was, especially at first, it was easy compared to the fishing. That was in 1886, and do you know, this is the biggest joke of all"— Tansy clapped my shoulder lightly—"the first regular ship I was put onboard was a blessed Revenue cutter in the Channel! It was funny. They still ran the navy like they had in Nelson's days, at least they did onboard the smaller ships. We used to wear tarred straw hats, and when we armed for a boarding party our sidearms were cutlasses. Only the officer had a pistol as well as his sword. Our ships were brigs, and they were sailed hard, I can tell you, and never a lanyard out of place. It was more than your life was worth to misplace the smallest thing." Tansy shook his head pensively. "The discipline was . . ."—he searched for a word—". . . *a bit much.* Still, I was lucky after all, because we did get regular home leave, even if it was only once every three months. We used to have big red kerchiefs, then, that we wrapped our things in when we went home; perhaps something we had made ourselves as a present for home, and a couple of gold sovereigns . . . if we had any pay due after stoppages. A lot of the men used to spend their wages on stuff like prick [Tansy pronounced it "perique"] tobacco. You know, it was rolled up, like a huge cigar. Then they soaked the tobacco in rum from their ration, and either chewed it or smoked it in their pipes. They used to cut small slices off the roll, so it was almost the same size as a penny [a British penny, about one inch in diameter]. That's where the name 'Navy Cut' for tobacco comes from, you see, Nipper?"

"Did you board any ships, Tansy? What were . . .?"

"Oh, yes, quite a few. There was some cases of smuggling, but mainly we were, in those days, in the late eighties, after what they called the 'copers.' They were mostly coasters that bought booze from ships out at sea—there were a lot of Hollanders and Germans who supplied booze—and the copers then sailed around the fishing fleets and sold the liquor, duty-free and cheap, to the fishermen. They, or at any rate most of them, because they couldn't legally take the booze ashore, simply drank it all at sea, so they were drunk half the time, a lot of them. There were many sinkings and bad accidents caused by booze from the copers. At last the Admiralty decided to put a stop to that trade. Of course, we couldn't arrest the copers—they were out of territorial waters, you see—but we scared them like billy-o. Our skipper used to sail straight at their bows or sterns, and us with every stitch of sail up. We used to rig ramming gaffs out on the bow, and when we smashed them into the copers' rigging . . . well, there was quite some damage, you can bet a fiver on it." (I'd never seen a five-pound note in my life.) "We used to rip the mizzenmasts and bowsprits right out of the copers' hulls. It scared them to death. We sank a couple. They didn't often return for a second dose, I can tell you. If they ever complained to their own governments, we accused them of dangerous navigation, and then they lost all means of livelihood, because their governments took their fishing licenses away from them. So you see, Nipper, we had them all ends up, but it took a couple of seasons to stop the coping trade. It still hadn't completely fizzled out when I was drafted to a barquentine, and we sailed out to the Ashanti war. . . ."

The Ashanti war! My mind boggled at the thought. It was as if Tansy were talking about Caesar's invasion of Britain.

"That was . . . let's see now. . . ." Tansy stared at another ship that had hove into view, a steamer heading down-Channel. The smoke from her stack was thick and black, and it streamed astern of her in the wind, fouling the whole southeastern horizon. Tansy wrinkled his nose as he turned again to me. "Yes . . . it was in eighteen-ninety that we shoved off for the Gold Coast. It was blessed awful out there, what with the heat and everything, and a lot of our blokes died from malaria and a lot more went home with it, too. Inshore, near the jungle, it was terrible with the mosquitoes. We used to look forward to going out to sea for some breeze and to get away from the damp heat. We sailed up and down the coast, all the way up to Freetown and down as far as São Tomé, because we were still doing antislavery patrols, see?"

"Antislavery?" The wind had shifted a point. I adjusted the wheel.

"Yes. You see, slavery had been abolished in Brazil only two years before, although the importation of slaves into Brazil had been illegal for a long time. The Portuguese and the West Africans—it was mostly the West Africans, though, from Fernando Po and São Tomé—were still trying to smuggle cargoes of Negroes over the South Atlantic, and it was our job to stop them. It was strange, in many ways. There we were, on the one hand, doing our best to defeat the Africans in the Gold Coast, and, on the other hand, trying to stop them being sold into slavery. The Portuguese were supplying arms to the Ashanti too, even though they were supposed to be our allies. But eventually the Ashanti gave up, and their king—we called him Pompey, though I don't know his real name—was exiled to some ocean island somewhere. I was out on the Gold Coast for six and a half years, and it's a wonder how I survived it. A good half of the men I went out there with didn't get home. The sickness rate was terrible. That's where I first found the Lord, out there. . . ."

Tansy was silent for a while, his face serious, his eyes slitted as they gazed at the coast to the north. The wind was backing a touch now. He said, "That there change of wind is very convenient—get us in nicely, that will." Then he fell silent again.

"Did you come home in the ship? Or were you sent home

. . . I mean, from the Gold Coast?" I asked. My licorice stick was almost chewed to a frazzle.

Tansy grinned. "Oh, we sailed her home all right, with our commissioning pennant streaming out from the maintruck as we were towed up the Medway to Chatham Dockyard, and they gave us two weeks' leave, too. It felt good, I can tell you, to be on the train heading for London with twenty gold sovereigns in my kerchief and a bolt of woven silk for Nancy . . . she was only a bit older than you, then, and it was some years before we got married—when I got back from the Boer War. In that one we used to sail out of Durban, patrolling the coast of Mozambique, because the Germans up in Tanganyika and the Portuguese were smuggling arms down to the Boers, and our job was to prevent it. I came home in a trooper from there, because my twelve years' man's time in the *Andrew* was up, see? I can't say I was sorry, either. It was quite some time before Nancy and I had enough money put by to get married properly and set ourselves up in a home. I worked on river craft, and then on schooners and boomies as mate for seven years. Then, when I had enough of my wages put by, we bought a little place in Sandwich . . . but I stayed on at sea, because by then I had my first captain's appointment."

"What about the Great War, Tansy?"

"Oh, we had some fun and games, I can tell you. The Germans were sinking our coasters like bowling over skittles. At first the submarines weren't too bad. Some of their skippers even let our captains take a few of their belongings with them when they were ordered into the jolly boat before the ship was sunk. They didn't waste torpedoes on a coaster; they usually sank them by placing charges onboard, or by shelling them. On a couple of occasions, at the start of the war, the U-boat commanders even let our captains dismount their compasses and take them into the jolly boat, too. But as the war went on it got worse and worse. By that time I was back in the navy, in the reserve on armed trawlers. We rescued quite a few coaster crews, and we knew all about what was happening. The worst of the younger U-boat captains were machine-gunning the crews as they took to the water. In a few cases they took the jerseys and oilskins from the crewmen, even in wintertime, and quite a few of our chaps died from exposure. But the worst of the enemy were the surface raiders. They opened fire without any warning at all and did not wait around to see if the survivors were all right or not. They just left them to drown. By that time the Jerries were using armed vessels disguised as peaceable craft—some of them were auxiliary sailing ships. Then the Admiralty decided to give Jerry a dose of his own medicine. They mounted four-inch guns on strengthened sailing coasters, but the guns were hidden behind raised bulwarks and hatch-coamings. 'Q-ships,' we called them."

"Yes, I've heard of them." I spat out the last strands of licorice over the leeward side.

"Well, I was on one of the first Q-ships. We had a merry old time, I can tell you, patrolling between Scotland and Norway. The weather was mostly blessed awful. We stayed out for weeks. We never challenged any craft. We always waited to be challenged or attacked ourselves. That was the tricky bit. If she was an enemy craft, as soon as she showed her colors or surfaced, our bulwarks dropped down, the hatch-coamings after them. The four-incher, with the gun crew already ranged and ready, opened up, and we sank or captured the blighter."

"Did you pick up the crews from the sunken craft?"

"Only the officers, and not all of them, either. By that time we'd lost too many chums. . . . That was the U-boats. There were never more than a couple of survivors from them, if any. But the crews of the surface ships, we did our best to collect them. Too often, though, the weather was too bad, and in many cases the surface raiders were shadowed by a U-boat, so we always had to be wary that any compassion didn't put us in jeopardy."

Tansy reflected for a moment or two. Then he said: "War is a terrible thing. No young people ought ever to be sent to war. It should be fought, if it has to be, by people over the age of sixty." He thought for a moment longer and added: "And the admirals and generals should all be under the age of eighteen; then, instead of the stupid directing the inexperienced, we'd have the inexperienced directing the stupid. No—but seriously, Nipper, there'd be much more humanity, I think, shown at sea or on the battlefields. When you're my age, you're too conscious of your own mortality not to respect that of other people, see? You know, when you're old, that once something irreplaceable is lost, it can never be brought back, and besides, when you are a lot older you realize that nothing that the average . . . landsman . . . believes is worth dying for really *is*. That would be the thing! Start them all off as admirals at sixteen and let them work their way down to ordinary seamen at sixty! Then you'd see all the nonsense about the honor and glory of war exactly where it should be—over the side!"

"Do you think there's going to be a war, Tansy?" The Munich Pact, which sold Czechoslovakia down the river to the Nazis, had been signed only the week before. Most of the bargees I had overheard discussing it thought that war had been avoided.

"Yes." Tansy's voice was quiet, but he sounded quite sure.

"What should I do—shall I join the navy?" I didn't realize what I was asking; few boys of fourteen know the depths of their questions.

"Not until you're a bit older." Tansy walked over to the starboard rail again. As he went he murmured, "And trust in the Lord." Then he turned and came to the wheel. Brightly he said: "All right, Nipper, I'll take the rest of your watch. We'll be off Newhaven in a half hour, and the tide's right. You nip off and make a nice cup of tea, eh?"

I surrendered the wheel to the captain. As I turned the corner he called to me. I stuck my head back to see him. He was gazing steadily ahead as the bowsprit rose and fell. Suddenly the wind dropped, and the ship slowed down. A rainy drizzle descended upon us from clouds as gray as gravestones. The sea was now as dismal as a copse of dripping willows. As the ship wallowed she cried; lurch, bang, lurch, bang, lurch. I steadied myself on deck.

Tansy slowly turned to me. "Make it nice and sweet, Nipper," he said, "and don't fill the mugs more than three-fifths tide up!"

As I waited in the tiny galley for the kettle to boil, I heard the sound of Bert mounting the ladder from his cabin. He greeted the captain.

"Evening, Bert," I heard Tansy say. "She's a bit sloppy; we just lost quite a fair drop of wind. Funny, that; I'd just taken over from the nipper, and the wind dropped just like that. . . ."

"He's got the touch, that nipper," I heard Bert say about me. "He's either got the Devil or the angels looking over his shoulder." There was silence for a minute or so, except for the hissing of the kettle, and the creaking of the timbers, and the slam, slam of the gaffs and booms. Then Bert added, as I listened with my ear cocked to the galley forward bulkhead, "that little blighter must have been born with a caul over his head!"

"And probably upside down," added Tansy.

Later, when we were turning in, I told Ted about what Bert and Tansy had said about me. "Well, you are a lucky bugger, Nipper," Ted said, "let's face it, you've got the luck of a pox-doctor's clerk. If you kicked over a pile of cow shit you'd find a bloody gold watch underneath!"

"But I wouldn't kick it over unless I was looking for a gold watch, Ted."

"Clever sod," replied Ted, as he turned over and went to sleep.

I dreamed that night a half-nightmare, half-romance. I was a small boy in a man o' war with her cannons booming and men dropping dead and wounded all around me, and blood running down the scuppers. Then I was in a train with a red kerchief full of gold sovereigns. I was mounted in the shrouds of a Revenue brig, waiting, cutlass in hand, to board a transgressor. I was off a shore of bright sand, with deep-green palm trees waving and gleaming in the sun. I was floundering in cold water. . . . I woke with a start. There were a thousand sacks of old rags and fifty tons of scrap metal to load in the morning. I went back to sleep.

16

Home for Christmas

The most unusual cargo we carried was live horses and ponies. We did this three times: once from Harwich and twice from Gravesend. The animals were all either too old to work or disabled in some way. We took them to Boulogne, in France, on their way to the knacker's yard, where they would be slaughtered as meat for human consumption. We rigged three heavy lengths of anchor chain fore and aft in the hold, very taut, and to these the livestock were tethered. I'm not sure, but I think they mostly came from Ireland. By the time they were driven out of the railway cattle trucks, the animals always looked exhausted, hungry, and dejected. It was as though they knew where they were going. When they arrived they were fed with fodder on the jetty. The animals stayed overnight, in the rain and cold, in a temporary paddock. After that they were not supposed to be fed until they were landed, because of the amount of dung and urine they might deposit in the hold. But Ted and I generally managed to sneak them a piece of sugar and a handful of hay in the morning, and a few gulps of water out of a bucket.

It was obvious that Tansy didn't like this kind of freight. He was edgy and short with us when the animals were loaded onboard, one at a time in a net, kicking and neighing and scared to death. Ted, too, was much affected when he received each struggling creature, desperate with fear, as the net landed with a bump on the hold bottom. I held its tether. Ted patted its nose, and he usually gave it a lump of sugar and a name, all the time murmuring into its twitching ears. "Come on, me old son, whoops. . . ." A pony had nipped Ted's hand as it nibbled away for the sugar he had offered. ". . . Steady on, me old cock. *'Sprucer,'* that's what we'll call you, mate, because you're too bloody eager. . . ." All the while I tended the animal's tether, keeping well clear of its hind legs. To me it was heartbreaking, and I often felt torn between doing the job I was supposed to do and sinking the ship. The agony of the animals as the ship worked in a seaway was painful to see. All the horses had worked for their living—harness marks about them told the tale—and some of them were very old as horses go. The thought of their having worked hard all their lives only to end up in a knacker's yard was too much for me.

The only times I ever wept onboard *Second Apprentice* were when animals were involved. Once, an old cart-horse collapsed in the hold while we were in mid-Channel and couldn't raise himself again. He lay there panting and moaning until he was lifted out of the hold by French stevedores, who passed three ropes under and around him, heaved him up with their derrick, and dumped him onto the jetty, where he lay, whinnying and kicking for a couple of hours. All the while many of the French laughed at him and prodded him with their boots and with sticks until Ted threatened to fight any of them. Then the French police arrived and a gendarme shot the old horse. Because his body would have taken up too much room in a cattle wagon, they lowered him into the harbor with balks of timber lashed around him, and a fishing boat towed the dead horse off somewhere, probably to be hacked up on a beach.

That was the first time I cried in my first ship, and the only time I ever retched onboard. On the last occasion we were again freighting worn-out and "useless" animals. Some of them, when we went alongside, got into such a panic that their jerking and pulling, with their eyes bloodshot and crying, was so violent that the pelican-hook, which secured the anchor chain to the forward bulkhead in the hold, parted just as we moored alongside in Boulogne. The animals had been unsettled and frightened all the way across the Channel; it was quite a rough day. It must have been the bump as the ship ground up to the jetty that caused a sudden extra spasm of terror among the horses. A whole line of them—about fifteen animals— while still tethered to the parted chain, milled and frothed, kicked and whinnied, struggled and heaved. Topside, as we stared horrified at the pandemonium below, we could do nothing. The racket was excruciating, and the dumb terror of the beasts was tangible. Then someone—I think it was Bert—got the bright idea of capturing the eye of the pelican-hook with the derrick hook and hauling it up, so that the chain could once more be tightened. This took a few minutes. It is not easy to fish down into a hold full of fear-stricken animals, a third of them loose and stampeding. Eventually the pelican eye was hooked and the derrick whip was hauled up taut, bringing the loose end of the chain with it. Then the whip was transferred to a big capstan on the quay. The French dockers heaved away at the capstan bars until they could heave no more. The chain below rose up at an angle of about forty-five degrees, which meant that the beasts at the high end of the chain were lifted off their front hooves by the pull of the chain. Below was a scene of utter terror as the horses struggled to free themselves. Three of them broke their necks, and one broke its hind leg. From then on, until French police rifle-marksmen arrived, nothing could be done, and the hold was like an inferno. The gendarmes, grinning and evidently joking among themselves and with the dockers, shot all twenty horses on the broken chain. Eventually, when the rest calmed down somewhat, the corpses were unloaded, dumped into a dumb barge alongside, and towed away. It took another couple of hours for the live beasts remaining to settle down sufficiently for us to able to gently unload them. All the while Ted cursed the French police in particular, and all police anywhere and everywhere. "Bloody frog-faced fuck-pigs! Bleeding rozzers!"

"But they were only doing the only thing they could do," I told him.

"Well, the bastards didn't have to *enjoy* it, did they?" was Ted's reply.

Later, when the stinking hold was empty and we were cleaning out excrement, urine, blood, and straw, we found several bullet holes in the ship's side and floors, but the ship was built so solidly that only one of them had passed right through the stout timbers. Bert made wooden trenails and plugged up eight or nine holes.

It was night by the time we crewmen had finished work. We all—the captain, the mate, Ted, and I—went about our business without a word. I prepared supper—I remember clearly what it was: shepherd's pie made from salt beef and potatoes. Down in the lobby, when I served the meal, everyone was glum. Only Ted ate anything, and even he left more than half his meal on his plate. That was the only time I can recall that Ted didn't lick his plate clean. As I cleared up the plates and the men drank their pints of tea, Tansy shook his head. All three of us looked at him silently. Again he shook his head. Then he said quietly, "We don't carry any more livestock."

There was a silence pregnant with eager agreement for a moment. Then Ted said, "Thank God for that."

Tansy glared at Ted. The captain's beard bristled, his green eyes were afire. His fist hit the table, "Watch your blasphemy," he said very quietly.

"Sorry, Tansy," muttered Ted.

"All right," replied the skipper. "Too much risk involved, what with bullets flying around the hold. They could have scuttled the ship. . . . I'll write to the agents tomorrow. Only dead stock from now on. It paid well, but the damage risk is too much. . . ."

"What's the cargo from here?" asked Ted.

Bert broke in. "Ballast."

"Pity it ain't a few of those bloo . . . blooming froggie coppers. We could have landed them in Chatham. Them navy blokes would give them a run for their money. . . ." Ted saw Tansy's warning look and piped down.

For my first year onboard *Second Apprentice* Tansy never let me once go ashore in France, Belgium, or Germany unless I was either with him or with Bert on some errand or other. In England, on rare occasions, I was allowed to wander off alone. In Holland, on even rarer occasions, I was allowed to go ashore either alone or with Bert, but not in those other countries. Tansy had a very strict, typically Victorian idea of what was right and wrong. "It's for your own good, Nipper," he once said to me in Cherbourg, after I had asked him if I could go ashore. He shook his head. I struggled to hold back tears of disappointment. He repeated: "It's for your own good, Nipper. Some of these here foreigners are . . ."—he searched for a word

he might use to a fourteen-year-old . . ."—*a bit much.* Can't trust
. . . never know where you are with some of them . . ."

"How do you mean, Tansy?" It was a fine winter's day. The
sun was shining on the gray dock walls, and my voice was
choking.

"Well . . . some of the blokes . . ." Tansy furrowed his brow
and wrinkled his nose. He puffed at his pipe quickly. The
smoke curled up into the windless blue sky over his bowler
hat. The sunlight caught the edges of his suit so that it shone
a paler shade of green than his eyes. He frowned and looked
me straight in the eye. "Some of their blokes *wear scent and play
football on Sundays!*"

Tansy said this as if the miscreants were doomed to certain
hell. For a moment I imagined the whole of Western Europe,
except for Holland, crowded with millions of fancy-Dans all
kicking soccer balls over each other's frontiers. Then the captain added, "and as for some of the fairer sex . . . they're
. . . *a bit much* . . . but the less said about them . . . the
better. . . ."

Just before Christmas of 1938 *Second Apprentice* settled down,
as the tide left her, on barge-beds. These were long rows of old
ship's spars, some two feet thick, that had been pegged to the
river bottom years before; some of them were said to have been
there for over a hundred years, and the timber was still sound.
The barges sat on them so that their bottoms could be scraped
and cleaned, and painted with two coats of black varnish. This
was a hard, wet, messy job, and cold in winter. That first winter
I was lucky. *Second Apprentice* took to the beds up the River
Medway, near Rochester. Tansy hired another lad to take my
place while the hull was cleaned and painted, while I went
home to Wales for Christmas.

Ted was to spend Christmas with Bert, though since his
encounter with Mrs. Bert he was not too cheerful about it.
"Might as well spend bloody Christmas in Battersea Dog's
Home," was Ted's opinion on the prospect.

When the great day of my departure for Wales came along,
I packed my sea bag with enough clothes to see me through the
week ahead. I also packed a cheap celluloid doll, but dressed
up in fancy rig, for Angharad; some toffees for Caradoc; a
carved model of *Second Apprentice*—not very expertly done—for

Mam; and pictures of the ship that I had painstakingly drawn and framed for Dad and Cei Powell. For Branwen Powell, I took some pressed flowers from Holland. I had just my rail fare home and a shilling or so over, but I felt very grand as I stepped on deck in my shore-clothes all pressed under my mattress and clean, and my sea bag on my shoulder. Tansy was waiting at the gangway as I went to march over it onto the muddy bank, through the green meadow beyond, and so onto the road to the town and the railway station. He, too, wore his best suit. I had shined his shoregoing boots like mirrors that very morning. As I walked aft he gestured me over to him. His beard had been neatly trimmed. As I reached his side he held out an envelope. "Here's a Christmas box, Nipper."

I took the envelope. It was sealed. I thanked him and stood there feeling somewhat embarrassed. I hadn't been able to give him or any of the others, except for Ted, a present. To Ted I had given a packet of five Woodbine cigarettes and a few of my spare cigarette cards.

"Merry Christmas," Tansy murmured. "You can open it up."

I tore open the envelope. Inside was a whole, crisp ten-shilling (two-dollar) note!

"Gosh!" (I'd read quite a few of Ted's comics by now.) "Thanks, Tansy!"

"Watch how you go, Nipper. Don't miss the train in London. A lot of people there . . . well . . . they're sometimes . . . *a bit much. . . .*"

"Don't worry; I'll go straight across and catch the first train to Shrewsbury."

"That's right, Nipper. Now off you go, and don't forget to be back here on New Year's Eve!"

After shouted farewells and season's greetings to Bert and Ted as they scraped away, filthy and black, on the hull-bottom below, up to their ankles in soft, slimy mud, I made my way across the bouncy plank, bound for Wales and Christmas.

I had excitedly sent a postcard to Mam two days before I went home, telling her that I was coming. For some reason or other it didn't arrive at Llangareth until after I did, so my turning up was a complete surprise to everyone at home. I gave Mam six red roses I had bought at Shrewsbury station with two of my eleven shillings. Mam made a great fuss of me. Angharad was agog at the present I had brought her but would not show her until Christmas day, and Mam was pleased that I had grown an inch or so and filled out, but not too happy that my shore clothes were a little too small for me, and my boots pinched. I was even more pleased, not only to be with them again, but also because Dad was coming home on Christmas Eve, the next day.

The only sad aspect was that Caradoc was sick and dying. But he knew me all right, and he cheered up when I fed him the toffee.

On the night of my arrival all the neighbors came to see me, and their change in attitude, when I recounted all the places I had seen, and the wonders in foreign lands, made me feel important and very grown up. I liked it when the old sailors came round and I told them of Voorne and Rotterdam, Gravesend and Cherbourg. Their eyes lit up as they listened to me. They laughed and smiled, and sometimes frowned, as they remembered their own youth.

The moment that Dad showed up and turned to me after embracing Mam, it was clear that our relationship had changed drastically. He was more like a shipmate or a brother to me now, and instead of showing or explaining things to me, most of the time he asked me questions—about the ship, the voyages, and the crew.

On Christmas Day Angharad went into a transport of delight over her doll for a few minutes, and then sat quietly with it in a corner of the kitchen for most of the day, nursing it and murmuring as if it were a real baby. Mam, when I presented her with the ship model, at first laughed as she hugged me. Then her eyes watered as she gently placed it in a place of pride among all her other little ornaments—in the very center of the mantelpiece in the drawing room. Dad thanked me gravely for the picture of *Second Apprentice,* and said that he would keep it in his kit and show it to his shipmates onboard his tug. Cei gave me a new jackknife. His sister Branwen was very shy and quiet when I gave her the pressed flowers from Holland, but she promised to go to the pictures with me on Boxing Day. For my Christmas gift, Mam gave me a long, thick jersey she had knitted for me, and a bobble-cap. Dad gave me a real leather sailor's sheath, with an open seaman's knife and a marlinspike in it.

When Branwen turned up the next day, it was with her young sister, Lisbeth, but in the cinema I managed to wangle it so that I sat between them and could grope for Branwen's hand when the lights turned off. (Only the brave deserve the fair.) At first she seemed very nervous, and I don't think she said more than a dozen words all during the outing, but after a while she relaxed, and there was an unspoken bond between us. When we returned to her home it was evening. She sent Lisbeth into the house first and let me kiss her on her cheek. She and her sister went off to visit relatives in Rhyl the next day, and I didn't see her again on that holiday. The only time that I was glad that Ted was not with me was when I was with Branwen.

It was good to be back in Llangareth, and when I wasn't nursing Caradoc I walked out, sometimes with Dad, sometimes with Cei, but mostly I walked alone. I turned my back to the sea's knowing and walked out into the hills. The heather was blown flat in the wind, as if in angry sorrow at the impending death of Caradoc. As I stood on the heights, leaning against the wind, gazing at the black peak of Cader Idris away in the distance, I reflected that I was as was our land and our air; I was as low or high as the sky about me, as was the breeze in my ears. They made me and they made what I did, the way I was and the way I learned about things, and they shaped everything about me. Up on the heights I was sad and aching, happy and glorious, all at the same time. Caradoc was lying in his stable, slowly breathing his life away, and I was home in Wales, and bound again for sea, with all the world and my life ahead. I had no wish to escape the land, no longing to leave my people, no desire to abjure the blood and the spirit that Wales had given me. The hills whispered to me that I could never do that, no matter how I might try, no matter how far I might voyage. The mountains thundered that I might try to do it, but only at the peril of my spiritual impoverishment; and that even so, in the end, the light, the fire of Wales within me, would triumph. But I must do what I must do.

Sometimes, when Cei was out walking with me in the wind, I looked at him. He showed little expression. I was gradually aware that he accepted everything about him. His conception of himself did not extend to the wild and beautiful Welsh landscape about us. It was as if, to him, Wales was asleep and he wished to live his life without waking it; as if the hills, the gorse, the heather, the sky, and the wind were things not to be changed or antagonized. Cei unconsciously loved Wales, but he would never try to change it. He would never desecrate the land, and so it would be, for him too, in his soul forever.

When I walked in the hills alone with the wind and rain, I shook off my family, my home, my friends, the neighbors, the memories of my boyhood, and a young, violent spirit took over. I belonged then to no one but myself. I communed with no one but my own soul. I owned nothing, I wanted nothing but to be myself; I had no irreplaceable friends or deadly enemies; I had no road but my own, and that was the road to the sea and the lands beyond the sea. Yet there is nothing, I thought, this side of heaven, to compare with walking the hills of Gwynned on a blustery winter's day. Nothing ashore, that is, I reminded myself. It brought hope to my heart and glory to my feet, despite the pinch of my boots.

It was good walking with Cei, but I enjoyed it far more with Dad. At heart he was a poet, and we should walk the hills only with poets. When I was walking with Dad, I knew that he was a part of everything about him, even when he shivered on the ridges and puffed and scowled at the birds, which made so light of rising high.

As we tramped along, Dad said that even on a cold morning, if you greeted everyone you met with "Fine day today!" then it would slowly become so (and it did). He said that when a person is content inside himself, there is no such thing as bad weather, even at sea, even when the wind is howling its head off and the sky is as black as a widow's veil. He said that the prospect is enough to stir the blood in a healthy body. He said that anyone can enjoy a sunny day; it takes a poet to be uplifted in a storm. He also said that he was suspicious of people who talked too much about the weather. It made him wonder what they were really thinking and why they didn't come right out with it.

Dad wasn't impressed by most "modern" British writers—he didn't think that they appreciated the romance of reality. "They don't seem to know that the romance of reality is unparalleled. Reality has an ineffable beauty all its own. No one can write a novel that is more kaleidescopic than real life itself. But you have to draw the line somewhere, when you look at things as they really are, otherwise you might go insane; when you're older, that is. Now, you're lucky. Only children and young people see things as they really are. If you can keep that ability, your life will be far richer. Most adults waste a terrible amount of time trying to see how things really are, when all the time they *aren't,* you see. Reality has the brute force of truth, and sometimes it can be ugly or filthy, but all the same, it's glorious. Tristan." Dad stopped walking and looked at me. "You'll never find much pleasure in reality, but you'll find a lot of joy. That's why many sailors seem, at least to landsmen or people who don't know us well, to be somewhat childish or innocent in our outlook; it's because, by the very nature of our profession, we are *forced* to see things as they really are. That's supposed to be only a childish attribute. It's what makes children sanctified, no matter if they are little devils at times. That's why some of the best writers have been seamen in their time; Homer, Defoe, Cervantes, Melville, Conrad, London (though he was one of God's innocents anyway, even if he'd never gone to sea), even W. H. Davies; because they'd preserved the ability to see the nexus of everything that was about them." Dad sat on a rock, his back turned from the wind, and gazed into the hilly distance, all green-tinged, blue, and gray.

As I sat beside him, he said: "But the only way to see true reality is in solitude. One of the tragedies of human existence is that reality cannot be shared. What's real to you may not be to someone else, you see? The writer's job is to try to break through the veil that exists between us all . . . and if he can do that once or twice in his lifetime, he has justified his existence."

"What about bad realities, like cruelty or callousness?" I asked. I was thinking of the horses dying in the hold at Boulogne.

"They're still realities. The thing is not to rebel against them, or be complacent or comply with them. What you must do is figure out which bad realities are unalterable and which can be changed, and then try to change the alterable ones, no matter how unyielding they might seem."

"What about realities like death, Dad?" A vision of Caradoc in his stall passed through my mind.

"Those realities that are unalterable you must learn to accept. That makes the difference between a wise man and a fool; knowing what is acceptable and what is not . . . and why." Dad rose and started off back down the hill. I sat for a moment, thinking about what he had said; then I caught up with him, and I stayed at his side until we were home again.

Now that I was grown up and yet seeing most things still as they actually were, the love that Mam and Dad had for each other was real. They had no fear of it, and no fear of showing it to each other. They were no longer young; they did not gaze at each other very much, yet somehow they always seemed to be looking together in the same direction. There was an air more of freedom about their feelings toward each other than of domination on either side. They were united and yet they were separate, unified unto themselves. All the years of difficulties and hardship, separation, and struggle had created a bond between them that not even death would break. They never were out of tune; even when they argued about some small domestic matter it was always with humor. What might start as a violent disagreement generally finished with everyone in fits of laughter. Whenever Dad did Mam some small courtesy, such as opening a door for her or drawing back a chair, it was more for his own satisfaction than to express any kind of superiority over her, and if she seemed pleased at these little actions, it was because Dad's face showed his pleasure.

It wasn't that Dad was more virtuous than other men, except to Mam. She had a great imagination. To love Dad only for his virtues she would have needed one. It would have been perfectly obvious to anyone with two eyes in his head that she loved him; for an independent-minded woman like her to wait on him as she did, it couldn't have been otherwise. She must have had more good in her than Dad did. She had aged more, and that demands goodness, which is very wearing.

It took six months of absence from her for me to realize how much I loved my mother. Not in a sentimental way, not simply because I had by chance emerged from her body, but because she was who and what she was, and also because I realized now how much she loved me. That Christmas at home I caught her watching me at odd moments, looking for signs of change, perhaps of improvement. She looked distressed when she noticed the calluses on my hands, but she said nothing.

I suppose that like all mother-love—as far as I have seen—hers had a reverse side to it, a mother-hate; but she was a wonder at hiding it. If it showed, I never recognized it. I accepted her criticism just as I would accept anyone else's; it was neither more just nor more cruel because it came from her. I must have loved her very much, because whenever she did anything for me I never wondered how I might return the favor, as I did with anyone else who helped me.

I realized now that Mam was a wit, but never hard-humored, as men often are. On my first day at home I stepped on our dog Cesar's tail when I went outside. He yelped and howled, and Mam stuck her head out of the kitchen door. Cesar, who was a great pet of hers, whined and moaned and gazed up at her pitifully. I stood, waiting to be chastised. Mam shook her finger at the dog and cried: "You silly thing, I told you not to idle around in front of the door!"

Like all women, Mam was an aristocrat at heart, and she always made me feel that I was much better than I actually was. If I made an error of some kind she generally dragged out the name of some long-gone ancestor from Dad's or her family closet and told me: "Grand Uncle So-and-So would never have made such a stupid blunder. Where do you get it from?" She was no Darwinian.

It was obvious that Dad's absences were taking their toll on Mam. She seemed much thinner, and somehow smaller, than when I had first left home, and she fussed over Angharad more than she had ever done. But she put up a brave front, remarking, as if in passing, how much more freedom and ease she would have when Angharad, too, left home. Her relationship with Dad must have been one of intense union for short periods of time, and abysmal loneliness for the rest. It was only her unconquerable love for him that kept her going while he was away. While I had been at home I had been a sort of surrogate father to Angharad and, for Mam, a reflection of Dad, which salved her pain, but now that I too was to be absent for months at a time, she dreaded my leaving. She fussed and coddled both Dad and me, and gave us practically every moment of her attention, as though she were saving every word, every look, every smile, every gesture to remember when we were away. By the time our short visits were about to end, she had darned every one of Dad's and my socks, washed and ironed every shirt—even those that didn't need it—and cleaned and brushed all our clothes.

When the morning of New Year's Eve rolled around (far too quickly), all the neighbors came around to see me off. Mam dashed around the house getting everything together she could think of for me, while Dad blunted the end of the jackknife that Cei had presented to me for Christmas ("much safer that way, my son"), and shortened one of his own belts so that I could wear it. Angharad cried and snuffled to her doll. Cei assured me that he would do all he could for Caradoc. Blind Sioni felt my arm muscles and said that I was stronger than he had been at eighteen, and he'd won a gong-hammering competition at a visting fair then—took home five shilling, he did, and five shilling was five shilling in those days. After I shook his hand and drew away, Blind Sioni felt for my hand and shook it again.

Before I took my leave, I went to the stable with Dad, but he must have known that I wanted to be alone with Caradoc. Dad waited at the door, and I went in to bid my old pony farewell. He lay on his straw panting, with his tongue hanging out and his eyes closed. I was so distressed that I could not stay for long fondling Caradoc's nose. When I left him, I was crying bitterly but silently.

"He's a goner," said Dad. "Do you want me to put him away?" I stared at Dad's eyes through my tears for a moment or two. I remembered what he'd said about facing up to bad realities and accepting those that couldn't be changed, but I shook my head; I'd seen enough of animal slaughter. But by Dad's silence I knew that I meant, "Yes, but when I've gone away."

Soon after, I made ready to leave Llangareth. Mam had made up a large parcel of food for me to take with me. Catrin Powell came up the lane in her apron despite the cold, bearing a meat pie in a brown clay dish with a blue-and-white handkerchief tied around it. Cei gave me his most accurate catapult as a parting gift. "Might see a rabbit on the North Sea," he joked.

For one of the few times that I can remember, Mam took hold of me and kissed me. Cei shook my hand manfully. Dad walked with me wordlessly in the light drizzle up the brew to the road. We waited for the bus to trundle along and take me to the railway station. As we stood on the side of the road, we talked about how I was to try to get home next Christmas; how I was to try to write home to Mam more often and regularly; how I was to always hold on to something when the weather was rough, and especially when I was aloft; how I was to listen carefully to what Tansy told me. Then the bus rumbled up.

"Hwyl fawr, fy mab!"
"Hwyl fawr, 'nhad!"

I boarded and grinned at him as I took my seat at the back of the bus and stared through the rear window. I left him standing alone on the side of the road, gazing after the bus. Then he turned and walked slowly back down the brew, a lone figure moving through the rain to a little white cottage down a slope, fuzzy through the rain on the rear window of the bus.

I knew Dad was going to put Caradoc out of his misery.

It was the last time I saw my father.

3

The Crucible

Ar y ffordd wrth fynd i Lundain,
Hob-y-Deri Dando!
Gwelais hen wraig yn llyncu bricsen,
Can y gân eto!
Dwedais wrthi am beidio tagu,
Siân, fwyn, Siân!
Fod y dwr yn agos ati,
Siân fwyn, llawn o swyn,
Clyw y deryn yn y llwyn,
Siân fwyn, Siân, llawn o swyn,
Clyw y deryn yn y llwyn!

(To London along the road I was going,
Hob-y-Deri Dando!
I met an old lady who a brick was swallowing,
Sing this song again, boys!
I said to her you'll soon be choking,
Jane, sweet Jane!
But if you do the water's near you,
Sweet Jane, full of charm,
The birds are singing merrily,
Jane, sweet Jane, full of charm,
The birds are singing merrily!)

—"Hob-y-Deri Dando"

From a Welsh sea chantey of the mid-nineteenth century. It originated in Nefyn, near Portmadoc, and it was often heard off Cape Horn. The final verse was sung always partly in English:

I'll sing bass and you'll sing solo,
Hob-y-Deri Dando!
All about the clipper *Marco Polo*
Can y gan eto!

See her rolling through the water,
Siân fwyn, Siân,
Wish I was in bed with the Old Man's daughter,
Siân fwyn, llawn o swyn,
The birds are singing merrily,
Siân fwyn, Siân, llawn o swyn,
The birds are singing merrily,
Hob-y-Deri Dando, boys!

17

The Last Spring

When I rejoined *Second Apprentice* she was lying to anchor at Hoo, farther downstream on the River Medway, just as Tansy had said she would be. All the way through mid-Wales and England, I had been depressed at the thought of Caradoc's suffering and of leaving home again. That lasted as far as London. Once I left the train from Shrewsbury and boarded the bus to cross the city, though, it was as if I had started a new journey. I was no longer leaving, I was arriving, and so I felt better. Charing Cross Station, on the south side of London, had been crowded with soldiers and Royal Navy seamen and Royal Marines making their way back from Christmas leave. On the train down from London to Chatham I had been one of the few civilians in a flood of navy blue. They all carried little brown cases, and I felt out of place with my sea bag. Quite a few of the sailors nodded or grinned at me. They must have thought I was a new recruit; some of them looked even younger than I did.

Tansy and Daisy were onboard when I clambered over the side from another barge's jolly boat. They had spent Christmas together, and Daisy had looked after the captain while Bert and Ted went to Gravesend. Daisy had decorated the skipper's lobby with colored paper streamers, and she told me that they'd had many visitors over the holiday. Tansy grinned as he inspected me, and we talked about Dad and my family and Llangareth for a while. All the time Tansy's expressions changed, just as the old sailors' back home had done, and I knew that he was thinking of his visits to his own home long ago. I told Tansy about going with Branwen to the pictures. Daisy gave me a sudden look of surprise.

Bert and Ted arrived alongside just as I was walking forward to stow my gear in the foc'sle. They both looked refreshed, merry, and raring to do something. Ted told me, a little later, when we were in the foc'sle, that he and Bert had drunk three pints each at the station at Gravesend.

"How was your Christmas, Ted?" I asked him.

"All-blooming-right. Bert's old woman ain't too bad, really, leastways not once she gets used to you. She made us a bloody great turkey and Christmas pud, and me and Bert went down to the local every flipping day. She even came to the pub with us on Boxing Day. They left the young 'un outside in her pram. She kept squawling her blooming head off, so I nipped out and slipped her a bottle of light ale." Ted grinned broadly, "That put her to sleep."

"Meet any girls?" I wondered at Ted's "cleaner" language.

"They got a pusher in to look after the kid while we went to the flicks. Real bit of all right, she was. That was on Boxing Day, too, and I took her to the Pally [dance-hall]. We didn't get back 'til flipping one o'clock. . . . She works in a blooming grocers—the Home and Colonial."

I shot a questioning look at Ted. He knew what I meant. He grinned even wider and stuck one thumb in the air. "She couldn't get enough." Ted's voice deepened. "She's going out with me whenever I get back, she said."

"You'll be getting tied up, Ted." I struggled into my new jersey.

"Wouldn't mind that," he replied. "Bert's right, you know; nothing like having someone to blinking go back to."

We were soon back in the old routine. Our first cargo was bricks from somewhere near Rainham up to Grays Thurrock. We loaded them in the morning, sailed right away, and unloaded them that evening. That meant we handled one hundred thousand house-bricks (fifty thousand each time) inside of thirty hours, because the passage took only about three hours. By the time those one-and-a-half days were over, our hands and backs had forgotten the ease they had known over Christmas.

Next we sailed round the north foreland, into the English Channel, to Cowes, in the Isle of Wight, with treated leather from Germany bound for Parkhurst prison, where, so Bert told me, the convicts made boots, belts, and harnesses for the government. It was a rough trip, one of the roughest we made while I was onboard *Second Apprentice.* Once we rounded the south foreland we got a southwester straight in the teeth, and it was slog, slog, slog all the way to Dungeness, beating this way and that. After a few hours' crawling to windward against very steep seas, foot by foot, the wind and sea had risen into such a frenzy against us that Tansy handed all sail except the mizzen, lashed the helm alee, and called it a day. Bert stayed on deck and Tansy, Ted, and I went down below for a spell of rest after I had prepared a meal of boiled codfish and strong tea. The contrast below when the ship hove to in the gale was a wonder. Topside the noise and clatter of the sea and wind howling and crashing was deafening, and the movement of the ship, as she yanked, pulled, tugged, lurched, toiled, moiled, drudged, and grinded, was enough to quell the boldest spirit. But when added on to that was the seemingly impossible task of bringing down and quelling a flogging jib, a mainsail weighing a couple of tons, and a dozen wildly flaying halyards and sheets, all the time with the sea crashing over the bulwarks and smashing along the decks, it was like a riot in hell. The only way for us lads to deal with it was to think of nothing else at all but the job in hand. For Bert and Tansy it was different. They had to keep alive to everything about the ship and be ready for any eventuality, while the bats of damnation flew about their ears.

Down below it was like another world. In the glow of the small stove (with the fire guard in place to prevent live ash from falling), the skipper's lobby was like a haven for tortured souls. Beside the stove I ate my codfish straight out of the cooking tray with salty, bleeding fingers and listened to Tansy talk of tropical adventures, his quiet voice contrasting with the storm over the deck-light. Ted tried to match Tansy's tales with wild, incredible stories of the shrimp bawley in wild, incredible seas. Above us the lobby lantern swung rapid shadows across their faces, Tansy's old and craggy, Ted's young and smooth, as I, the quiet listener, broke my silence only to urge them on. Then it was Tansy's turn to go on deck. Unhurried, he made his way up the companion ladder into the wet darkness above, as always murmuring a thanks to the Lord for the meal. Minutes later Bert wetly descended, his oilskin agleam in the lantern glow, and he and Ted reminisced about a darts match in Bert's "local" on Christmas day. It seemed that Ted had claimed too high a score while Bert was at the pub counter, getting in the beers. I rose and left them, to join Tansy on the heaving deck.

We stayed hove-to all that night, but in the morning the gods of the weather relented and let *Second Apprentice* pass and go about her lawful occasion. By midday the wind was back to a mild breeze, every stitch of canvas aloft, and the sea would have made a pea-sorter look like a sarcophagus-plinth. Dusk saw us east of Bembridge, in the lee of the Isle of Wight, sitting in an apologetic sea and with no more wind than would blow out a candle. We finished up sweeping the glassy sea with the hefty oars up through Spithead. It was a clear night. A new moon sailed a starry sky like a jubilant princess. As I pushed the heavy sweep back and forth, back and forth, I could see the low, black shores of Wight and Hampshire on either side, and streams of little twinkling lights and hazy glows in the sky above them. They were all I could know of the hopes and fears, the sadness and the joys, the births and deaths, and sufferings and betrayals that the shimmering lights and the incandescent glows suggested to me. The lights of Portsmouth, millions of them, seemed to outnumber the stars above and to quell their light. It is only when we look at a city at night from the sea after a storm that we can realize fully how far man has come along our road of destiny. The paradox is that upon arrival in port after a storm at sea we also realize how far man has to go to even start to catch up with the appalling forces, the immeasurable strength of nature.

We discharged the leather in heavy batches with the electric crane at Pickford's wharf in Cowes, and off it went in lorries, on its way to His Majesty's Prison, Parkhurst. The following day was a Sunday, and on the pretext of accompanying Tansy to chapel, Ted and I got ashore early. It was a foregone conclusion that when we emerged from the house of worship Tansy would let us stay ashore for a while. The captain returned to the ship, where Bert was preparing the midday meal, and Ted and I walked around the town. We had enough money to buy ourselves a decent meal in a little café, and then we strolled along the esplanade looking at the yachts moored in Cowes roads. Some of them were tiny and bobbed away at anchor yawing this way and that like wayward children tugging on their weary mothers' hands in the fresh breeze of the early afternoon. Many were about thirty to fifty feet long, and they all were obviously moored for the winter, with big tarpaulins stretched over their topsides. A few very big pleasure-sailing craft rode to anchor, and some had uniformed crewmen onboard, cleaning and scrubbing, even though it was a Sunday in midwinter. As we strolled in a drizzle past a big Yacht Club that seemed deserted, Ted waved at the crewmen of a big black schooner—I think she was called *Black Joke*—and one of the deckies waved back. Ted cupped his mouth in his hands and yelled, "Bloody flunkies!" I shushed him, but it was all right —the yacht was too far to windward for the crewmen to hear us. We carried on in the rain past the Yacht Club, along the otherwise deserted seafront promenade. Ted shouted out to the waving crewmen: "Bleeding Gin-Palace asshole creepers!" and "Get me some Angostura, Jeeves!" and, in an attempted refined voice, "Don't forget to polish the Rolls, James, Master Montague's off for a drive to Ascot this afternoon!" I kept telling him to shut up, that someone might hear us, but he was enjoying himself, even though he thought no one else but I could hear him.

As we passed the end of the Yacht Club grounds, a voice hailed us. "I say, you there!"

We looked around, startled. A man was coming from the back of a boatshed. He was beetle-browed, much bigger than either Ted or me, and dressed in expensive yellow oilskins and smart sea boots. He wore a black captain's cap with a gold badge, and he had a neatly trimmed goatee.

"Afternoon, mate," said Ted. His voice quavered.

The big man ignored the greeting. "Who're you bawling at?" he demanded. "Where are you from?"

Ted said, "We're . . . we're out for a walk . . . we're off *Secon*
. . . we're from a ship in Cowes port."

"What ship?" The man glowered down at Ted.

"Second . . . Apprentice, sir," replied Ted. "Dandy ketch. . . ."

"You too?" The man turned and glared at me. "Well, boy,
speak up!"

"Yes, sir."

"Right, well buzz off! We know your type round here. If you
want to make a racket like that go over to Portsmouth or
somewhere."

Ted and I turned and started walking back to the port. As
we left we heard someone else come from around the boatshed,
and the big man say to the newcomer, "Blasted barge-tykes
. . . idling all damned day . . . never wash . . . ought to be
bally-well locked up!"

We kept our backs to the yachtsmen and trudged on in the
rain, hardly able to stop ourselves from spluttering with laughter. After that I was no longer "Nipper" to Ted. He renamed
me "Tyke." The first time that Bert and Tansy heard Ted's new
name for me they mistook it. They thought he'd said "Tiger,"
and that was what they all called me from then on.

I was still the nipper of the ship, but I had a new name, and
that name bred an air about me, as a name will with a lad. By
the time they'd called me Tiger for a week or two I would (and
could) take on any other boy of my own size in the frequent
scraps that took place when we were in port, mostly with the
local lads, but sometimes with youngsters from other ships,
too. One time, in Poole, I came back onboard all torn and
bloody after a stand-up knock-down bout that had ended up
as a free-for-all (my adversary had made some remark, when
he learned I was Welsh, about "foreigners"—that was more
often than not the cause of my fights). Tansy caught sight of
me and my swollen eye as I sneaked over the side forward of
the mainshrouds. He called me over, looked me up and down,
and shook his head. Then he said: "You know, Tiger, you're
a funny little bloke. You've got your nose into Byron and
Shakespeare one minute, then you're ashore getting seven bells
knocked out of you the next . . . I can't . . ."

"He called me a foreigner, Tansy, and anyway, I beat *him.*"

"Oh . . . I see. Well, that's all right then. Now go forward and get cleaned up." I started forward. I heard Tansy call me. "Tiger!" I looked over my shoulder. "Next time, keep your guard up more!"

Ted was a holy terror in a fight, and by the time winter had passed and spring was on us, we had quite a reputation all around the southeast coast of England and were more or less left alone. We even made good friends with some of our former taunters, swapped cigarette cards with them, played them at soccer, and got to know their sisters.

During the wintertime we made quite a few passages, mainly up and down the English Channel. In late April 1939 we made our last cross-Channel voyage before the spring and summer passages, with timber and foodstuffs up to the North country and coal back, or mineral water and scrap iron to Germany, or cheese from Holland. We took on a cargo of house bricks from a lighter in Sheerness, bound for St. Helier, Jersey, down in the Channel Islands. If a fit punishment were ever meted out for rapists or sadists or baby-beaters or traitors, I know of one that would suit them down on the ground: loading or unloading house bricks onto a barge continually for the space of six months. If that didn't make them truly repent and tauten up their backstays, nothing ever would.

We had a fair run around the Forelands and down-Channel, with first a northern and then an easterly breeze. That made up to some small extent for the brick-loading, and by the time we were alongside in the small port at St. Helier our hands were half healed up. This time there was a mobile steam crane on the jetty that could reach out over our hold and lower the brick pallets down to us. That meant that Bert did not have to work the gaff-derrick, so he could give Ted and me a hand with the bricks. Loading them onto the pallets, though, was still exquisite torture. What made it all the worse was that as the load of bricks diminished, we had to bend lower to pick them up. When the last brick was plonked onto the pallet, Bert crowed, "That's the bugger we've been looking for, lads!" Ted and I were too exhausted even to agree. We merely crouched, hardly able to straighten our backs, covered in pink brick dust, and panted. The brick dust got everywhere, in our mouths, in our noses, in our ears, in our throats, and we could taste it for a day after the last brick had gone ashore.

By the time we started loading the next cargo, barrels of offal in brine and cowhides to take to Greenwich, we thought we were well off. There were perhaps fifty barrels of offal, which stank so horribly that we had to wear rags over our noses and mouths. There weren't too many hides—about a hundred or so. Everything was heavy, greasy, and very smelly, but compared to the bricks the new cargo was a real pleasure to handle, and we all knew that it was better than returning the two-hundred-odd miles back to the Thames in ballast. Tansy said, as we warped out of St. Helier to catch the swiftly running north-going tide, with the offal and hides below stinking to high heaven: "Beggars can't be choosers. We're lucky to find this little lot."

Running before the wind back up-Channel we were all happy; Ted and I sang (we weren't ever allowed to whistle— it was supposed to bring calms and other bad luck), but because of the appalling smell rising and blowing forward from the hold we stayed abaft the hatches, to windward, whenever we could. Ted and I took turns sleeping in the galley, with our knees under our chins in that tiny space, because the whiff of the offal and hides down in the foc'sle was too much to bear for more than a few minutes at a time. But we were happy because we all knew that this was the last of the hard winter channel passages, and that once the ship reached Hull and loaded scrap iron for Emden, the occasional summer cruises to Holland and up the Rhine would ease the monotony of the grinds up and down the east coast.

We departed from St. Helier in the early morning, and by dawn the following day *Second Apprentice,* with a good steady breeze right on her stern, was bowling up past Beachy Head. By dusk we were at anchor off Whitstable, having found a fair northeasterly wind off the north foreland. We weighed anchor the next dawn and were soon moored off Greenwich a day before the hides were due to arrive. Tansy was so pleased with the fast passage that, in consideration of the unholy reek from the hold, he gave permission for Ted and me to go ashore with Bert to his home to sleep.

I was surprised at the change in Mrs. Bert when she opened the front door before Bert could find his keys. She knew we were coming—he had hurried to the post office and sent her a telegram as soon as we stepped ashore. Her hair was tidied, she wore a clean frock, and she was all smiles.

"Oh thanks for the telegram I knew you were coming and I've got tea ready and . . ." she blurted out even before Bert pecked her on the cheek. As he did this her wide-open eyes beamed at Ted over Bert's shoulder, then they looked at me and glazed over. We all traipsed into the dark, boiled-cabbage-smelling hall. Mrs. Bert took the lead, Bert and Ted followed, and I took up the rearguard.

"Do make yourselves at home boys I've got some lovely ham sandwiches and a jam tart and I know that Teddie loves jam tarts how are they feeding you on that blooming old boat Teddie? Don't worry Bert dear throw your coat over a chair and what's that other one's name? Where is he oh here you are. . . ." Mrs. Bert stood on tiptoe and beamed at me over her husband's shoulder; then she flashed an even bigger smile at Ted. All the while we men said nothing. After I had been at sea for a while, the insides of houses seemed so small, and such a small house as Bert's seemed even smaller; and yet, on the other hand, there appeared to be so much more room for everything than there was in the living quarters of the ship. We passed through the passage to the kitchen, feeling bigger than we were, more awkward and lumbering.

"Now you sit yourselves down boys Teddie you sit the other side from Bert and the other one can use the corner by you what's his name?" She addressed Ted with a coquettish glance.

"Tiger," chimed in Bert; as he said it he winked at me.

"Tiger? Oh I'm sure he is poor little mite looks like he should still be in school and what was the trip like dear and did you bring those shirts? the telegram must have cost an awful lot Mum's ill again I'm sure I don't know what I shall do if she has to go to the hospital it's those damn varicose veins again I'm going to see her and get supper ready at six o'clock now no pushing off to the pub again I'm sure you're a bad example you and Teddie for poor little what's his name? oh I forgot the teaspoons. . . ."

"Tiger," said Bert in a weary tone. Then he added, "How's the babby?"

"Oh I wish you wouldn't call her that Hermione is two years old now she's already upstairs in her cot asleep and when do you think we can put the down payment on that wireless that blessed old gramophone I swear I spend hours every day winding it up and listening to those same old silly six records you bought when we went to Brighton for our honeymoon three days . . ."—she was smiling at Ted now—"we had in a real posh hotel but they didn't half look at Bert when he came back from the pub sloshed didn't they dear?"

Suddenly there was a shocking silence in the little kitchen. Bert was lifting another ham sandwich up to his face and studying the pattern on the linoleum tablecloth. Mrs. Bert stood waiting, looking down at her husband.

"Bert!" she yelled.

Bert gave a start and looked up at her. "Mmm?"

"Oh I never did he's always the same when he comes home never stops stuffing himself I'm sure Teddie won't get drunk on your honeymoon will you Teddie?"

Ted, surprised out of his concentration on the sandwich he was gobbling and his contemplation of the jam tart that took pride of place on the table, mumbled, "What's that, Mrs. Bert?"

"Oh Teddie I told you to call me Nora you know that this is your home from home oh I should have said ship silly old me whenever you want to come I said that you won't get drunk on your honeymoon Teddie will you?"

"No fear," muttered Ted thickly as he munched away on yet one more sandwich.

"Not our Teddie no fear he knows how to appreciate a good girl don't you Teddie? and Rosie thinks the world of you and said what a good time she had at the Pally and I'll go round and tell her that you're here when I go round to Mums. . . ." Mrs. Bert talked away as the gallant mate and crew of the dandy-ketch *Second Apprentice* swiftly and silently reconnoitered, approached, attacked, seized, and demolished the small mountain of ham sandwiches and the two-foot round jam tart that the good lady had prepared for us, along with about a gallon of hot, sweet, milky tea.

When there were nothing but empty plates, a few crumbs, and tea stains left on the table, which took about five minutes, Bert glanced up at the steamed kitchen window and murmured: "Come on, lads, it's stopped raining. Let's take a stroll in the garden." He spoke as though he were in Marlborough Palace.

"Not Teddie Teddie's got to wait here for Rosie haven't you Teddie? and don't come trailing in any dirt from the garden Bert last time what's his name?" Mrs. Bert glared at me.

"Tiger," repeated Bert.

"Was here you mucked up the kitchen floor something awful and it took me all the next day to clean it up and what about that new stair-carpet you promised Bert?"

"I. . . ."

As he stood up to go outside Bert stammered, but Mrs. Bert didn't wait for him to continue. "And that there outside gutterpipe has to be fixed too it just pours water down over the window every time it rains and this blooming weather I can't get any washing dry outside now you wait here Teddie and I'll go round and. . . ." Her voice trailed off as she went through the front passage, and Bert and I went out into the back garden. It was tiny, about sixty by forty feet square, surrounded by dirty brick walls except in one far corner, where stood a brick outhouse. "That's the kaasi, if you want it, Tiger," said Bert quietly. Rain still dripped from an arthritic-looking tree that had exhausted itself in trying to escape over the garden wall for too long. Along the other wall a small glass house with dirty windows, despite the rain, looked as though it contained a leprechaun-stoker's ashpit.

Bert and I stood on the narrow concrete path outside the back door in the damp, blessed, gray silence for a moment or two. Then he said: "Come on, Tiger, we'll nip back in. She's upstairs getting her coat on."

I wasn't too impressed with Rosie when she turned up. She reminded me of Lilly Lie-back, the saucy lass from Liverpool who worked in a café back in Barmouth and whose moonlit escapades with the lads were legendary from Dolgellau to Aberdovey and, probably, by this time, to Cardiff. Rosie should have been about two inches shorter than my five foot six, but at one end she wore lipstick and at the other end three-inch-high heels that made her tower above me. Her dialect was even more difficult for me to understand than was Ted's at times. When she spoke she chewed on her words, as if they were made of some sticky substance. She completely ignored me, but she flashed Bert an old-fashioned look every so often, when she wasn't melting at Ted. I guessed her age at around Ted's, nineteen, but perhaps she was a bit older than he was. She took delight in telling us how her parents had never told her "noffink" and how she'd forgotten even that.

Most of the time Rosie was in the house Ted stayed silent, flexing his arm muscles on the tabletop. Soon Rosie had nothing more to say, so Ted jerked his head at the door and the pair of them went out. That left Bert and me to inspect his war medals after we'd cleared the table and washed the dishes.

Later that night, when Ted came in all glowing and grinning, Mrs. Bert gave him little Hermione's room, while I slept on the kitchen floor. "I'd let you sleep in the front room what's your name? only I don't want you opening and shutting the door and letting air in and out it's very bad for the furniture you know but you'll be all right in here and don't be afraid if the cat jumps on you poor old Tibby's a bit nervous of strangers aren't you my pet and Teddie if you need anything don't be afraid to let us know, eh Bert? You'll be all right in Hermione's room nice and warm in there because it gets the heat from the kitchen chimney bet you'd like to have Rosie up there with you eh? You saucy Teddie you she thinks the world of you I know she told me. . . ." So it went on until Mrs. Bert, followed by Bert, and shepherding "Teddie," finally left the kitchen firelight trembling in anticipation of her return downstairs next morning, and me dozing off on the rug before the fire, with Tibbie the cat curled up by my side.

The next day we went back onboard early, and by midforenoon *Second Apprentice* lay alongside an otherwise empty wharf. There we discharged our smelly cargo, and loaded acetylene and oxygen cylinders for Hull. They were heavy, but at least they were reasonably clean. This took us all of that day. The next morning, when we shoved off downstream and round past Shoeburyness out into the North Sea, we found that our luck had changed. We were headed by an adamant northerly. After Orfordness was abeam we had to beat all the two-hundred-odd miles north around the coast of East Anglia and up to the River Humber. Two days later, when Spurn Head, at the mouth of the river, appeared low on the northern horizon, the fickle wind dropped. Once again we rowed the boat day and

night for a full twenty-four hours before we were alongside
near Goole. We felt cheerful about it, though. The weather was
warming up—it was now almost May and the sun came out
more between the clouds—and the North Sea is generally a bit
less rainy than the Channel.

I felt cheerful for more than that, however. It was almost my
fifteenth birthday. Tansy had promised that if I did well he
would raise my pay by a whole 50 percent on the great day.
That would give me one shilling and sixpence (thirty cents)
daily—just over ten bob ($2.05) a week. Then I could send
Mam seven shillings and sixpence ($1.50) a week instead of
only five shillings (one dollar), and I would still have three
shillings (fifty cents) a week to myself. If I saved a shilling
(twenty cents) a week toward my fare home at Christmas, that
meant two shillings (forty cents) a week in my pocket. Why,
I would soon be able to buy myself a pocket watch like
Tansy's!

We got infrequent and often inaccurate news of what was
going on ashore, outside our own little world. We knew, from
reading a few newspapers and from the garbled accounts of
other bargees or stevedores, that Hitler had marched into
Prague and seized Memel in Lithuania. Prague was a mysteri-
ous place far away in Central Europe, but to the sailors Memel
was as well known as Dover or Calais. Many good sailors
hailed from there. We knew that Franco had at last defeated
the government forces around Madrid and that the Spanish
Civil War was, to all intents and purposes, at an end. We also
knew, and thought it was about time, that the British government had at long, long last abandoned appeasement to Hitler
and had warned him that if he took one step further—which
meant against Poland—we would stand by that country and
fight him. But to most of the bargees and dockers it all meant
little. I can recall no one ever questioning our loading scrap iron
for Germany. It was all so far away, Poland and Prague, and
anyway, the French were our allies. "The French might be a
poncey lot, but they've a big army, navy, and air force, haven't
they, and they've been building those lines of blockhouses
(what's the name, the Maginot Line?) since the end of the last
war. . . . Hitler would be a bloody fool to go against the
Froggies, and our navy, too. . . ."

One quiet evening—it must have been at the beginning of May—I asked Tansy, "Do you think Hitler will try anything against the Poles?"

"Of course he will. It's Russia he wants to really have a go at, and he can't do that until he takes over Poland. Anyway, like all bullies, he doesn't know his own limits."

"When, Tansy?"

"Either this year or next." The captain grinned as he looked at me and said, "It had better be, otherwise I'll be too old to have a go, won't I?"

When, in the foc'sle, I later told Ted what Tansy had said, he snorted: "What's the bloody difference? German government or ours, they're all bastards anyway. In any case, from what I've seen in Germany, the kids all well-fed and singing and everything, and them uniforms the government gives them free, I'm not so sure we wouldn't be better off with that silly sod Hitler in charge . . . at least he couldn't make much worse of a fuck-up than some of the stupid old twits we've got at the top."

"But Ted, you don't want Jerry officers stamping around and ordering you about, do you?"

"Couldn't be worse than some of the masters in the bleeding kid's home I was in."

"But you don't want Germans taking over and forcing everyone to work for them like slaves, Ted?"

"How many gas cylinders you loaded today, Tiger? The bloody Germans could hardly make you work harder, could they?"

"But . . ." I was running out of arguments against Ted's logic. "But you wouldn't want them marching and goose-stepping down Bert's street and taking everything over and raping all the women . . . even Rosie . . . would you, Ted? You wouldn't want . . ."

Ted didn't let me go on. "Oh, for Christ's sake, Tiger, the old girls would just bloody well love a bit of the old rape—and so would young Rosie, too!" Ted thought for a moment as I stared at him in shocked silence. Then he added: "As for Bert's street, anytime the fucking German army wants it, or their poxy navy, or their bleeding air force, and that fat fucker Goering, they're bloody-well welcome to it. I'd even stow the whole sodding street onboard and sail the bastard over to bleeding Germany, and give it to them on a poxy plate if they want it so bad—bloody garden-railings and all!'' He stomped up the scuttle ladder.

I found out from Ted the next day that Rosie had sent him a letter saying that she'd taken up with a soldier from the Royal Artillery Barracks in Woolwich, and that she wouldn't be seeing him again. Behind every great statesman there stands a woman. . . .

18

A Cup of Tea

During the summer of 1939 *Second Apprentice* made several trips over the North Sea to Holland, from East London or Hull, with scrap iron bound for Germany. We generally carried it to Dordrecht, and there we transferred it into German or Swiss barges that took it up the Waal and the Rhine. One load we took up the Rhine ourselves into Germany, to Duisberg, a big industrial town. There were many more uniforms about, and we saw quite a few even onboard the local barges. The tally clerk who came out in the lighter that moored alongside to accept our load of old boiler plate wore a brown uniform with a Sam Brown belt and a Nazi armband on his left sleeve. His jackboots were so shiny they looked as though they were made of glass. After Ted had offered the clerk a Gold Flake cigarette, which that worthy had curtly refused, Ted said he looked like "a bloody dog-track attendant."

The last trip to Germany was in late August. That was to Brunsbuttel, near Hamburg, with scrap copper from a shipbreaking yard in Inverkeithing, up in Scotland. There again the official who checked our cargo ashore was fully booted and armbanded, but he was an older man and quite friendly. The local stevedores seemed to get on very well with him. In Brunsbuttel, Bert, Ted, and I went ashore to buy a few fresh provisions and to send a cable to Hull, where our next cargo, of leather drive-belting for mill machinery, was bound. As we walked through the clean streets, there were Nazi flags everywhere. They hung from practically every window and draped every shopfront. In many of the shop windows there were pictures of the Nazi leaders, with Hitler taking pride of place.

His picture was in every shop we called at, in the post office, and on the walls at the agent's and the harbormaster's office. On practically every wall was the legend "Ein Volk, Ein Reich, Ein Führer!" We called in at a stevedore's pub for beers. Most of the workers were friendly. Ted managed to talk to several dockers about soccer, while they told us where the brothels were, but with Bert a married man, and with the amount of cash Ted and I had between us, they might just as well have directed us back to the ship. The German dockers invariably called us "Tommy."

There were only about fifty of the big leather drive-belts, so when we sailed the ship was quite light in the water. There was very little wind. We thought we would to have to row out to sea with the sweeps to maintain steerageway out of the River Elbe. Tansy had wanted to push off just before dawn, so that we could take advantage of the full ebbtide as well as the river current, but the harbormaster forbade it. We had to wait an hour or two and leave with a flotilla of other non-German vessels—Dutch and Danish coasters, mainly—under the escort of a German navy patrol craft. When the gaggle of craft got underway Ted and I started pushing and pulling with the sweeps, but of course we had no chance at all of keeping up with the other vessels, all of which had engines. When the escort craft saw our painfully slow progress, she came over and, without so much as a word to Tansy, got right against our port side so fast that Ted was lucky she didn't smash his sweep. If the Kriegsmarine (German Navy) skipper said anything, or if anyone else did, we didn't—we couldn't—hear it over the racket of the escort's engines. From the German craft a big man, by the look of him a chief petty officer of some kind, gesticulated to Bert to throw him lines and make *Second Apprentice* fast to the escort. Bert had been rushing around placing fenders over the side, and for a moment he seemed astonished almost out of his wits. Tansy was still at the helm, quietly studying the intruder. Bert turned and shot an unspoken question to Tansy. Our captain nodded his head, and only then did Bert obey the German. By the time I'd stowed my sweep, Ted had thrown his down on deck, and we helped Bert tie up alongside the escort vessel.

We got underway, and the *Kriegsmarine* pushed *Second Appren-*

tice out to sea at about five knots with no effort at all from anyone onboard except Tansy, who was still at the wheel. Ted, as much a clown as ever, climbed onto the cargo-hatch covers, stretched himself out, placed one hand under his head and the other on his waist, and pretended he was smoking from a cigarette holder. Everyone laughed at his antic, the German sailors too. Even the *Kriegsmarine* skipper was smirking over his bridge windshield.

It was a new experience to be sliding over a calm sea with the wind of our headway blowing straight back from the bow and no sails up, and *Second Apprentice* actually keeping up with engined craft. The German boat shoved us all forenoon, for about twenty miles, until we were well clear of Scharhorn and Neuwork, the islands northwest of Cuxhaven. Then, without any kind of warning she slowed down and stopped, and the German sailors cast off our mooring lines and pulled away slowly from our ships' side. *Second Apprentice* kept way on for a minute or two and then she, too, stopped dead in the glassy water. As we collected in our mooring lines and stowed them away, there was a sudden roar from the German craft. I looked up. There were all her sailors lined up on her deck at attention, facing our almost black, tattered, drooping Red Ensign, with their chief at the salute. As the escort roared away her captain, too, turned and gave Tansy a brief salute. Our skipper, expressionless, touched one gnarled finger to his bowler hat. With a cataract of spray and a mighty roar, the gunboat settled her stern in the sea and shot off toward the clear, calm horizon, leaving *Second Apprentice* wallowing and shaking in her wake, jiggling and jolting, like a jilted bride on the church steps. Ted and I shipped the long, heavy sweeps once more into the irons. Ted said, "Blimey, that's the way to travel, eh?"

"They could have asked permission to come alongside," observed Tansy in a piqued voice. "Blessed . . . no manners . . . they could do with a year or two in the *Andrew*."

"They must have good engines," I commented to no one in particular, as I pulled away on my sweep.

"Yeah . . . they got fifty slaves down below, all peddling away like mad," said Ted. After that there was silence onboard, except for the groaning and swishing of the sweeps and the creaks of the rigging as we pushed *Second Apprentice* at a painfully slow rate westward over a sea as smooth and glassy as a fishmonger's slab.

That evening, as dusk fell and a slight northwesterly wind slowly roused itself, we could still see the low, gray island of Heligoland over our starboard quarter, almost in the same spot where it had been when the gunboat left us. Even before the first zephyrs, Tansy was sniffing the wind and pulling a face. Before I felt any moving air, he turned to Bert, who was on the wheel, and said, "Muzzler, Bert, wester."

We all knew what that meant. On our course direct to Hull the wind was just about directly against us, right slap-bang on the nose.

"Typical," was all Bert answered. Then he turned to me. "All right, Tiger, stow your sweep and get supper ready. We might as well have it before it starts to blow."

By the time supper was prepared, all working sail was hoisted and the ship was driving northwest into an ever-rising sea, close-hauled on the port tack, so as to get plenty of sea-room. By the time supper was cleared up, the wind had risen enough for us to hand the forejib and the staysail, and reef the main down a point. By midnight the wind hauled round to the northwest; we came about onto the starboard tack, and it was time to hand the main topsail. In the overcast darkness all we could see was the occasional, faintly stabbing light of Heligo-land on the port quarter and a liverish sea all around the ship. All night we ploughed into steep sea after steep sea, with the noise of the wind's howling out-screaming the racket of the sea's crashes over the bow. By the middle of my trick on the wheel I could no longer control the helm. Bert ordered Ted to back me up. At about 3:00 A.M., out of a night as black as the Earl of Hell's riding boots, lightning blazed out everywhere, zigzagging across the solid black vault of sky and sea above, below, and all around us, and seeming to stab through and through the ship. For about a quarter of an hour it was purgatory with the lid off. Then, with a mighty rumble, a hiss, and a roar, down came the rain, and soon hailstones (in late August!) rattled down onto our decks and oilskins like gravel pouring down a hold chute. In between surges of the sea over our bulwarks and topsides, the hail rolled along on the decks inches thick, until it was swept away by yet another roaring watery boarder. So it went all night; wind, rain, hail, and frenzied seas desperately boarding the ship. Bert, Ted, and I took turns on the bilge pump as the ship worked, pumping, pumping; up and down, up and down, slosh and creak, slosh and creak.

At 4:00 A.M. we lads handed the helm over to Bert and tried to get a few winks of sleep, but in the foc'sle it was impossible. The ship's head reared up and slammed down like an elevator gone wild. We sat by the bogey-stove for a few minutes, to warm ourselves up, and then we staggered our way over the roaring deck aft. I slept hunched up in the galley while Ted laid himself down in the skipper's lobby, under the table.

Just before dawn we were all back on deck. Bert had picked up the light on Bordum Island—the most westerly of the German Frisian Islands. He sent Ted below to let Tansy know. The captain took over the helm from Bert, after he had gazed into the storm ahead of us for a few minutes. Suddenly there was a blistering flash of lightning that showed me every wrinkle on Tansy's face, every hair in his beard. He was grinning to himself as he gave the wheel a turn and changed the course a point or so off the wind. There was another stab of blazing light from Hell's black forge. Every part of the sails and rigging stood out brilliantly for a second, despite the rain and spray. It was as though some celestial warlock had suddenly transformed the plunging, black, sky-sweeping rig and revealed to us a great three-dimensional display of water-streaming, silvery magic. Then it was gone, and we were left in darkness once again.

Dawn hid itself behind sheets of rain and spray as the ship repented the sins of all onboard, and again and again baptized us in unholy gray North Sea water. Above us the clouds, black-gray comrades of the gale, mocked our labors at the pump as the bows sheered and dived, scurried, slid, and smashed onto, through, and out from the unending seas ahead, always ahead. As the bows plunged into a trough, the force on the sails was eased momentarily. Then, as the forefoot rose, there was a great strain on the shaking, rain-dark canvas; a pause as short as a shocked breath; an almighty surge; a seething of boiling whiteness along the lee bulwark and over the deck; a slamming-over of more spray; curses from Ted and Bert; and silent prayers from me, and no doubt from Tansy, as we were drenched again and again and again.

At one time, as I took a short breather from working the pump, I glanced forward. A momentarily clear gap between the blankets of rain showed shoreline dead ahead of our hammering bowsprit! I wetly whipped around and shouted something to Tansy, but he merely held up one hand from the wheel and nodded his bowler hat in my direction. All the while the ship plunged on and on into solid, mocking rain and, I thought, to our certain doom.

Suddenly—as suddenly as walking out of a crowded, rowdy pub onto a night-quiet quayside—the ship was in calm water. The thick rain still sluiced down and the wind still screamed, but the sea was merely stippled, corrugated, and gray with a yellowish tinge to it. Now the ship still lay over to leeward, and plunged and soared, but not nearly as violently as before. I shook the water from my eyes and stared through the pouring rain. Bert and Ted, both holding on to the windward shrouds but with their backs to the gale, were grinning broadly. Tansy looked over at me, raised one eyebrow, then dropped it again.

Bert took over on the pump handle, saying cryptically as he did so: "We're in the lee of Rottermeroog now, in the Wadden Sea. We'll have a nice, smooth passage from here on, until we get to Den Helder—that's about forty miles. We'll drop the hook there and wait till this little tea party blows its blooming self out."

We must have made an average of more than eight knots down the Wadden Sea, in the lee of the Dutch Frisian Islands, because we went to anchor in the lee of Texel Island, north of Den Helder, just after noon. I remember, as I made dinner, wondering to myself how many British boys of my age had ever even heard of the Wadden Sea. As Ted lumbered into the galley to drink his mid-morning tea, rain streaming from his black oilies, he mumbled, "Wadden Sea—they ought to bleeding call it sodden sea!"

The gale blew itself out by dusk the next day. We weighed anchor right after supper and moved out into the North Sea again, still headed by a northwester, but gentler. We were able to hoist our topsails, and the breeze sang to us. We had a good, fast passage across to the English offing, and before dawn we sighted the welcome gleam of Orfordness light on the coast of Suffolk. We went about and beat northward on the port tack all forenoon and afternoon, until dusk, when we returned to the starboard tack.

Off the east coast of England the North Sea plays up stink when any kind of a wind blows, except a westerly close inshore. With all the tide rips and shallows offshore, navigation is anything but child's play. That evening our devilish old friend from three nights before decided we hadn't had enough. He came back for a return visit. We rucked again all but the main and stays'l. By midnight the rain and spray were slashing at us in a high wind, and the short, frenzied seas were crashing onboard. It was as though the Wadden Sea and our relatively smooth crossing to the English offing were but dreams. By 1:00 A.M. lightning was blasting like the cracks of doom, and visibility was down to the ends of our cold, water-streaming noses. Once again both Ted and I were heaving and grunting at the helm, with Bert standing by. Once again we were warmly wrapped in several layers of clothing under our oilies, and once again they were sodden with the water that had streamed up our sleeves and down our collars. It was as much as Ted and I could do to hold the ship on course against the kicking of the wheel, all the time watching the bucking compass in its dim binnacle light and trying to keep an eye on the mainsail, now reefed down to a quarter of its area and badly out of shape.

At about 5:00 A.M., all around the ship the obscurity was an unnatural and threatening light that showed up our slitted eyes and drawn faces. It was such an eerie light that to witness it only taxed our endurance even more. As the waves worked up, the horizon around us seemed to have closed itself into a narrow circle in which the seas raged at the ship, leaping onboard and leaping out again. The spray and rain were like a flaying mist. Now and again a bigger, foaming sea came out of the mist and made for the ship with all its strength. Then we hung on tight to the wheel or anything else that might be chained to the center of Earth, stopped our breaths, and held on in a welter of smashing coldness. The stern of the ship went down, down, and as the wave broke and scattered over the lee side the bows reared up, up, as if in supplication to the heavens; then down,

down went the ship's head in the general direction of Australia as the mate, the deckhand, and the ship's boy eased the helm all together, to meet the headlong pitch of the ship. Then another sea, a hill of gray glass topped with frothing foam, towered close by and the ship, her sails flapping, rose to it like a ghostly pterodactyl rising into the sky. Ghastly gusts, roaring rollers, and toppling lurches; down below, the leather machinery belts had broken loose and were flailing around the hold like so many serpents gone insane.

I remember being jammed by a wall of water between the wheel and the binnacle. I was dimly aware that Bert had been bowled over by the same appalling force and was smashed over to the lee bulwark, and that Ted had spluttered curses as he went down to the deck still grimly grasping the wheel. I remember shouting to Bert, as the water wall passed over the lee side, "Good job we're sailing light!" and I remember his reply, in between curses, as he struggled up onto his feet from a cataract of swirling foam: "She's much steadier when she's heavy!"

For the next few seconds it was all hazy. There was a sea that came onboard, not as big as the previous one but just as forceful, just as ruthless, just as careless. Ted somehow was back on his feet; Bert had crawled across the deck and was embracing the bottom of the binnacle as the ship's bows flew up and smashed down. As *Second Apprentice* recovered from that blow and shook the sea from herself yet again, there was an almighty CRASH! BANG! Then another . . . horrible CRASH!

To say that the shocks jarred every bone in my body would be an understatement—they shattered my soul. I am not aware of the next few moments. All I know is that I gripped the wheel with both hands and stared at the now darkened, now hardly shaking compass.

Tansy's voice was in my ear. He was shouting across me to Bert, who was struggling to his feet on the strangely solid deck as it *banged down, banged down* every few seconds onto something very hard indeed. "The Hailsborough!" Tansy yelled. "We've struck the Hailsborough Sands!"

One moment *Second Apprentice* had been plunging along, working and laboring as hard as a ship can against the sea; the next moment, with a *crash* that could, it seemed, have been heard in Llangareth, she had struck. In the mighty shock, the topmast had splintered; most of it had carried way, fallen onto the port bow, and knocked the forward windlass right off its bed. In the slashing rain and spray coming from the dark night all around the ship, it was a scene of utter chaos from the nethermost pit of hell. I was paralyzed. I was deathly afraid. *I could not move.*

As soon as the topmast crashed down, Bert clambered onto his feet, and Ted strove forward against the smashing walls of water to let go of the sheets. In a blizzard of spray I stared as Ted let go of the staysail and main halyards. Still shocked rigid, I was aware of the clatter of the staysail as it shook itself down its staywire in the wind. I was conscious that Bert was with Ted, grabbing the main leach and somehow hauling the giant sail, flogging away and sounding like a machine gun, down over the main boom; heaving away with all their weight, grabbing the parrel rings and forcing them down the mast.

When the mainsail was almost mastered, Bert made his way aft. As he passed me he shouted in a thin voice, "Give Ted a hand with the main, Nipper!" To me, still frozen to the helm, it was as if his voice were coming from somewhere far away, down the bottom of a deep, deep well. Then Bert was gone out of sight aft.

I still stared at Ted struggling away with the huge mainsail as it weaved across the deck like some crazy animal. Plainly I heard him yell, "Give us a bleeding hand, Tiger!"—but I was incapable of any movement. I wanted to help Ted, I knew I ought to, but my limbs simply refused to move. All the while the ship banged the sea bottom, very, very hard each time. The shocks almost knocked me off my feet, but still my hands were welded to the helm. Again I heard Ted yell, "If you can't give me a bloody hand then get on the fucking pump!"

All I could do was stare at the wreckage of the topmast forward through the rain; at the shambles that had been, only a minute or two before, a sturdy emblem of natural pride, power, and grace. Our topmast lay splintered and bouncing on the banging bow with frenzied, white seas crashing over it from an evil darkness. My mind wanted to command my fingers to let go of the wheel spokes, but the message was simply not passing from my brain. I was cold and wet. The only place I was warm was inside my trousers. The stinging spray was flaying my oilskins and face. I knew I could find shelter behind "Yarmouth Roads" (the big deck locker), but my body would not move. I was frigid with fright. I stared for an eternity at the broken rigging cable-wires flailing over the deck and threatening to take our heads off any second; I gawped at the cold, wet hell of flogging wet canvas and the death-dealing seas smashing over all, and I knew I was going to die.

"What are you doing, Nip . . . Tiger?" It was Tansy's voice, as low and steady as a naval pension behind my leeward ear. Something snapped inside my head. I was crying. I couldn't see for a blessed moment.

"Rwyn llawn ofn!" I remembered, somehow, to speak English. . . . "I'm afraid!"

"What are you doing, Tiger?" the captain repeated again, his voice still low.

"We . . . Tansy . . . we're going to sink . . . I know we are . . . she's going to be smashed to pieces . . . what . . . what . . . can we do?"

The low voice waited a moment. Then it rose and said: "Do? . . . *Do?"* As he shouted, I looked round at Tansy. He was braced against the deckhouse. In one hand he held a tree-felling ax, in the other the spare hull-pump handle. Each one of them weighed about as much as I did. His voice rose even higher, *"Do?* Well, Tiger, I'll tell you what you can do. . . . You can trust in the Lord and go and make a cup of tea! That's what you can do!"

"But . . . but we're sinking, Tansy . . . she's going to break up!"

"We'll cross that there bridge when we come to it! Now, you nip into the galley, like a good sailor, and make a cup of tea!"

"But she's . . ."

Tansy's voice rose to the level of a foghorn. He bawled in my ear: *"Then make two bloody cups! They might be your bloody last! And make 'em bloody strong!!!"* He turned away and clambered forward over the wreckage of his ship's rigging, somehow avoiding the flogging cable-wires. Then he started chopping away at the topmast stays so as to secure the spar safe on deck. All the while the ship's bottom *banged, banged.*

I watched him, dumbfounded, through the streaming rain and spray. It was the only time I had ever heard Tansy curse, and it shook me down to my toenails. I was still staring at Tansy's dim figure, though the beating rain, when Bert staggered from aft, carrying a sledgehammer and a big, cold chisel. He struggled forward past me, holding himself against the wind, the spray, and the driving rain.

I watched the two of them, and Ted, as they struggled to free our ship of the dangerous junk on her deck. Suddenly I knew we were going to be all right. "Tansy knows what he's doing, and so does Bert," I thought to myself as I freed my fingers from the wheel and was half-blown aft. As I clawed my way toward the galley I caught another glimpse of the captain, the mate, and the deckhand as they chopped and hammered and pumped away to ease the ship's appalling pain.

Inside the galley was a scene from the ninth circle of hell. The hull bottom was still banging on the hard sand below, but not as hard as at first (the tide was going down, although I didn't realize it). The breakers still crashed every second or two against the ship's side, and the wind was howling even harder in the rigging. What was left of the rig was not giving way before the murderous assault. In the galley there was no light, as the oil lamp had been shot off its gimbals. On the deck the black water was ankle-deep and violently sloshing around as the hull battered itself on the bottom. Most of the galley fittings had broken loose and were bouncing around.

As I set to making tea, my hands shook with my remaining fear and excitement. I was completely unaware that the galley stove fire had been doused by a sea breaking in through the door, even though the galley was on the semi-sheltered side of the ship. I groped for the big kettle in the darkness, placed it empty on the cold stove, and tried to collect my thoughts. Then I realized that the kettle was empty and the stove was dead, and I laughed at myself for having been so stupid. I groveled around and lit the small kerosine stove that was stowed in one of the upper cupboards.

Now my hands were steadier. I knew that the situation we were in was no one's fault but our own, and that it was up to ourselves to get ourselves out of it. No amount of fear or moaning, whining or complaining was going to alter anything for the better. Fate was trying to overcome us, and we had to resist it. By not resisting, by not struggling against fate, we would be going against nature itself—*our own nature.* Man's nature is to fight for survival. Man's will to survive is part of nature itself. It is as strong as any other natural force, but the scales are tipped to man's advantage because he has *intelligence* on his side. In the depths of my mind, in the pale, flickering light of the little stove, I somehow became aware that fear is merely nature trying to redress the balance against man, trying to tip the scales back again in its favor. The discarding of fear makes man invincible. The realization of this and the doing of it is *courage,* and I somehow knew that courage was what I'd learned from Tansy that night.

As soon as this realization became clear to me I turned off the little stove and said to myself aloud, "Bugger the tea!" I made for the deck and clambered and staggered, dodged and clawed my way forward, to where Tansy was busy lashing down splintered bits of the topmast and bundling up the now-tamed rigging-wires. Ted and Bert were taking frantic turns on the bilge pump, trying to keep down the level of the water in the hull. As I watched, in the streaming rain, Bert started to shift one cargo-hatch cover so that he could go below into the hold to secure the leather machinery belts.

Tansy suddenly glanced up at me. He looked much older. There was exhaustion in his eyes, but there was still a gleam of wild will to survive, to fight on. "What's up, Tiger? Tea ready?" he shouted.

"Give me . . . the ax, Tansy, let me have a go at the topsail halyards before they . . ." My voice trailed off.

Tansy broke in, "That's it, mate, you do that, and I'll give Bert a hand." The captain handed me his ax, which I could just about lift, and made his way over to where Bert was struggling in the now-easing wind.

It was the first time anyone had ever called me "mate." It was the first time I had ever met real courage and recognized it. I had become a man.

Of course we survived the night. *Second Apprentice* had been constructed for that very kind of thing; she was built like Windsor Castle. As the tide went down the storm abated, and we found ourselves, after four or five hours of sitting high and dry, stranded on the sand, with a clearing sky and even some sunshine. By that time we had re-rigged the running backstays and sorted out all the mess on deck. Then, as the tide rose again, we slept uneasily for a while until it changed. Bert had already been out in the jolly boat and dropped the bower anchor well out in deep water, and as soon as *Second Apprentice* was afloat we pulled her off, using the leeboard windlasses to do it. After she was clear, in a mild breeze, right on the nose again from the east, we worked our weary way for some hours into Lowestoft, where we dropped hook and turned in for the night.

The next day we warped alongside the quay. It was a Saturday. As we landed all the damaged wires and spars onto the jetty, Tansy came up to me. "Here you are, Tiger," he said. He held out a hoary, hard fist and dropped a coin into my hand. It was a sixpence (twelve cents). "An extra tanner for you today, my son," he said.

I was delighted. It was supposed to be my afternoon off. "Blimey, Tansy, thanks a lot. . . . What's that for—keeping cool the other night?"

Tansy looked at me sternly. "Keeping cool be jiggered," he exclaimed as Ted and Bert and several bystanders looked on. "That's for working right through today and tomorrow, helping Bert and Ted to get that blooming topmast replaced. We have to be up in Hull by next Thursday, or we'll lose our cargo for Emden. . . ." Tansy was starting to clamber back onboard when one of the bystanders, a docker by the look of him, hailed him: "Captain!"

Tansy turned and stared at him. "Yes?"

"I think you've lost your cargo for Emden already," said the docker.

"What do you mean? Why's that?" asked Tansy, as we all looked on curiously.

"Haven't you heard the news?" asked another bystander.

Tansy frowned. "No, why?"

The first docker said: "The Jerries invaded Poland last night. It was on the wireless early this morning. My missus heard it and told me."

"Thanks," said Tansy. Without another word he climbed onboard and went below.

"That's torn it," muttered Bert. "Now the balloon'll go up!"

There was silence for a moment or two as the small crowd all looked seriously at one another. Then Ted said, "Right, now *I* can join the bloody Royal Artillery!"

Everyone was quiet as Ted straightened himself up and, in an aside to me, added, "Rosie wants a fucking gunner, she'll *have* a fucking gunner!"

I clutched my sixpence for a minute. Then I stuck it in my pocket and carried on helping Bert to lash the pieces of shattered topmast onto a borrowed handcart.

19

Off to War

Early the next morning, after breakfast, Ted and I went ashore to a local boatyard to collect the new topmast. The previous day Tansy had gone to the yard and chosen a length of spruce for the job. The boat builders had worked far into the night to cut the timber to shape and plane it down. When we arrived at the yard with our borrowed handcart, the new topmast was already waiting for us. It looked exactly like the old one, except that it was not yet festooned with metal fittings, not yet varnished.

On the way back to the ship, as we maneuvered the forty-foot-long, eight-inch-to-eighteen-inch-thick pole along the quiet waterfront, we saw a small knot of people standing by a pub door. In the distance we saw a church clock, its hands near eleven. "The boozers are early today," observed Ted, but as we neared the group it was obvious that they were not all boozers—there were some women and a respectable-looking elderly gentleman with a prayer book under his arm. They were listening to a wireless turned up loud. A man was speaking sadly. Ted and I stopped our mast-pushing out of curiosity and listened. ". . . that a state of war now exists between Great Britain and Germany."

"Who's that, mate?" Ted asked the respectable-looking gentleman. "Who's that bloke talking?"

The respectable-looking gentleman turned watery eyes to Ted and said in a quavering voice, "That was the prime minister, Mr. Chamberlain." The gentleman walked slowly away, his head bent.

"Oh," replied Ted. He turned to me. "Well, Tiger, we'd

better get this lot onboard before Tansy gets back from church. He'll have our guts for garters if he sees us around this pub. It'll take all bleeding day for the fucking varnish to dry . . . let's hope to Christ it don't rain."

The next day it was quite tricky wangling the heel of the topmast into the gammon iron and the trestle as it swung around suspended from a crane hoist. We had spent all day Sunday and most of the evening fitting on the top masthead's iron band with lugs and eyes, to which running blocks and tackle and the standing rigging-wires were fixed; making the fid hole at the heel of the mast, as well as drilling tiny holes at different points of the mast and squirting linseed oil into them from a sewing machine oil can, plugging up the holes, and then applying two coats of varnish to the entire mast.

When the new topmast was rigged in place the ship no longer looked hurt and bald. Tansy brought a brand-new owner's pennant out from his cabin, and we rigged on the nine-foot-long headstick and sent it aloft. When the job was finished, we all four went onto the jetty to inspect the set of the topmast, to see that Bert had properly raked it forward. Tansy nodded silently.

Bert said, "Bristol fashion—couldn't have done better myself."

Ted exclaimed, "I've seen that there ship before somewhere!"

As we went back over the gangway, before pushing off for Hull, Tansy went down below again. This time he brought up a brand-new Red Ensign, folded up like a blood-soaked sail. He made his way aft and substituted the new flag for the old, tattered one, which was almost black. Then he turned and said, "Well, seeing as we've got a war on our hands, we might as well show our colors. . . ."

Our passage to Hull from Lowestoft was uneventful. The topmast performed as well as, if not better than, its predecessor. There were some raised eyebrows when the customs man came onboard to check the cargo and found that it was from Germany. He turned to Ted and said: "You were lucky. If you'd been over there a week later you'd have been interned for the duration of the war. . . ."

Ted replied, "I wouldn't mind a few weeks' bloody rest."

We landed the leather belting and took on a cargo of coal for London power stations, to be transferred into lighters at Greenwich. This cargo was what we called "all or nothing," because power station coal was either fine dust or great lumps up to three hundred pounds in weight. It was the coal that could not be sold for domestic, railway, or ships' use. Next to bricks and cattle hides, it was the worst kind of cargo to both load and unload. When it slid down into the hold on a chute, fine black dust flew everywhere, so thick that it was impossible to see until the dust started to settle, which it never did properly. One chute would send down a couple of tons of dust, and the next sent down five or six great rocks of coal as big as railway engines. Our job was to spread the cargo evenly, by shovel or by brute force, and by the time it was all stowed properly Bert, Ted, and I were like three black rats, wild-eyed and scurrying still, because the coal came down so fast there was hardly time to breathe. Discharging the "all or nothing" was even worse than loading it, because every particle of dust, every massive lump, had to be loaded with shovels, or manhandled, onto a skip. It was no picnic, handling over two hundred tons of that stuff, and we were never as glad to be back at sea as when we had been humping power station coal, no matter what the weather.

Ted and I were a bit disappointed as the ship traipsed up and down the east coast between Hull or Scarborough and the Thames during September. There was little sign that we were at war, except that there were a few more naval inshore vessels and destroyers sighted, and more planes passing overhead. The only other difference from peacetime was that the authorities forbade us to be underway at night and arranged that the coasters should, wherever it was possible, sail in company. But it was time-wasting and cost money to wait around for other ships to work out their cargoes, so usually *Second Apprentice* went on her way alone. For the whole of September we carried on the "all or nothing" trade, along with quite a number of other coasters. By the end of September the coaltips at half a dozen power stations in London must have been built up to small mountains. It was obvious to us that emergency stocks were being hoarded.

The only break we had from bashing up and down from the

north country to the Thames was when we sailed around into the Channel to pick up a cargo of "finished leather goods" at Cowes. When a hundred or so crates were loaded onboard they were all marked "Boots, left, infantry, sizes . . ." and were consigned from His Majesty's Prison, Parkhurst, to Kettering Infantry Basic Training Camp, Yorkshire. When Bert saw the markings on the crates, he burst out laughing. Ted joined him, and Tansy made a wry face. It took some minutes for Ted to explain to me that the boots were probably made from the German leather that *Second Apprentice* had delivered to Cowes the previous summer. I still couldn't see the joke, until Ted pointed one finger shaking with merriment at the markings. "Can you imagine, if we get sunk with about fifty thousand infantry left boots onboard, a whole bleeding regiment limping to the front with only one boot on?" I laughed too, but only until I thought of Ted's words, "if we get sunk."

We landed the boots, at Grimsby I think, after I had spent the whole voyage wondering where the right boots for the infantry were coming from.

Our voyages were taking twice as long now, as we had to go to anchor each dusk until dawn. Coastal cargo-hauling was much easier in wartime, from a sleeping point of view, than it had ever been in peacetime. The cargo rates were higher now, and this helped the owners to balance up the loss of time caused by not sailing at night.

As the first wartime weeks went by, it was obvious that sail-in-trade was being revitalized. Old sailing-coasters that had been laid up for several years suddenly reappeared in the boatyards to be refitted. Sail-makers and carpenters were almost instantly the kings of the coasts, and old men who had retired from the sea for years were eagerly sought out for their irreplaceable skills. Old captains and crewmen started to turn up, too, and by mid-November we saw some coasters that looked, at first glance, more like floating oldfolks' homes, until we looked more closely and saw how clean the decks were, how tidily patched were the sails, how smartly belayed were the lines, and how shipshape was everything on which the octogenarians had clapped their gnarled, hoary, experienced hands.

I don't recall hearing of any sinkings of sail-coasters in 1939.

The sprittie *Ailsa,* along with some others, was blown up by magnetic mines, but that might have been early in 1940. *Ailsa* was a steel vessel, and we were never so glad to be in a wooden ship as we were in the first months of the war. The magnetic mine was a devilish new device, and at first there was no answer for it. The Germans were dropping them by night at a steady rate in the North Sea, especially off the Thames. We had seen the smoke palls of blown-up ships many times by the end of November.

Another reason that sailing coasters were suddenly in such great demand, and cargo rates shot up, was that many motor-driven barges were being converted to barrage-balloon craft, to be moored in the Thames estuary. With her masts and spars, *Second Apprentice* would have been useless for that kind of duty. As the motor craft were filched from the trade (and rightly so), the sail craft were worked the more, and soon we were working every day. I don't think that from the beginning of December until I left her, *Second Apprentice* spent one day without cargo in her hold. Even Tansy cut down his Sunday church visits to one a month, and we worked cargo on Sundays, a thing never heard of onboard the ship before the war.

Early in December, Ted left the ship to join the Army. He had been to the recruiting office in Gravesend soon after war broke out. The recruiting petty officer did his utmost to persuade him to join the Royal Navy, but Ted would have none of it and volunteered for the Royal Artillery. In due course, his calling-up papers arrived at Bert's house, and Mrs. Bert tearfully handed them over when she and Hermione, the latter still in a baby carriage, visited us in the rain on the coal dock at Greenwich. Ted wasn't due to report to his training camp, at Aldershot I think it was, until two or three days later, but as soon as Mrs. Bert handed him his brown envelope he disappeared down into the foc'sle. After a few minutes, he showed up again wearing one of Bert's cast-off blue suits, which had been presented to him the previous Christmas. He'd worn it only once before, the day it was given to him. It was much too small, but as he said to me: "Fuck it, it'll do. It's only till I get my bleeding uniform." He did look strange in the suit, a bit like a ship's deck broom poked through an oil drum. Ted had no socks, so I gave him a pair of mine. They were much too small for him, but they did for the time being. When our ship left Greenwich we expected to be at sea for at least four days, on our way up to Newcastle for more coal, so Ted bade us all farewell.

Tansy presented Ted with a small Bible and told him to keep it in his breast pocket. Bert gave him a jar of Brylcreem hair lotion, and I gave him a packet of twenty cigarettes. Ted said he bet the army had only right boots in Aldershot. We all shook hands with our erstwhile deckhand before he took off in the rain with Mrs. Bert, pushing Hermione's baby carriage through the layer of sodden coal dust on the jetty. At the last minute Bert asked Tansy whether he could buy Ted a pint. Tansy nodded, and the mate hurried off after the sad procession out of the dock gates, into the gray town beyond.

As our eyes followed Mrs. Bert and Ted, with the mate running behind, Tansy said to me: "Well, that's that. Now there's only you forward until we get a new nipper. I'll go round to the Labor Exchange before we sail . . . see if there's any . . . then we can pick him up when we come back."

I turned to, somewhat downcast at Ted's departure, and started flaking out the wet sheets and halyards, ready for sailing. Our cargo on that trip was ammunition from Woolwich to Newcastle, although none of us could puzzle out why the shells and bullets were heading north, when the "fighting front" was south of us, in France.

Now that Ted was gone my work was almost doubled, though both the mate and the captain helped a lot more with the deck chores. The foc'sle was a much more lonely and gloomy place without Ted.

The first night's anchorage on our way north from Woolwich was off Southend. At about midnight the air-raid sirens sounded in the town. Bert and I stayed on deck, watching the play of searchlights in the sky, but we didn't hear the dull throb that German bombers were supposed to make. It was quite an experience, sitting on top of two-hundred-odd tons of nitroglycerine, waiting for a squadron of Nazi bombers to do their worst. An hour or two later the "all clear" sounded, and I went back to sleep, leaving Bert to his anchor watch just as Tansy appeared on deck for his wash.

As Tansy went aft in the moonlight, he called to Bert, "If

you see any mines floating around, give me a shake, Bert." As he said that, he was so poker-faced and his voice was so steady that I have never been able to figure out, to this day, whether or not he was serious; but he certainly gave me a sleepless night. I lay in my berth, eyes wide open, listening intently. About an hour after I had turned in, I heard something bumping the bow gently. I jumped out of my berth in a panic, in my shirttails only, and scampered up the scuttle ladder in a cold sweat. Bert was down aft, probably making himself a cup of cocoa in the galley. I rushed onto the foredeck and stared over into the darkness. As my eyes cleared, I almost died with relief. There was a small tree branch caught on the anchor chain tapping the bow. I was walking aft, still in my shirttails and bare feet, thanking God and looking for the long boathook to push the branch free, when Bert emerged from the galley. We were both so surprised that we stopped in our tracks. Bert stared at me in my shirttails and bare feet. My knees were shaking with cold. Then, with a laugh, Bert said quietly and slowly, as he shook his head, "Why should England tremble?"

I explained to him what had happened. He reached down for the boathook and, still laughing, sent me back to bed. "I thought it might be a mine, Bert," I chattered in the cold.

"Nonsense, Nipper," he murmured. "If it had been a mine you wouldn't even have heard it."

Later we learned that twenty-seven big merchant ships and a destroyer had been sunk by Nazi mines in the approaches to London during November 1939.

We reached Greenwich again after about a week with another hellish cargo of "all or nothing" coal. As Bert and I warped alongside the dumb-lighters that took the coal upstream on the Thames, we suddenly heard a thin, piping voice shouting at us from a landing stage. I saw a small boy in overalls standing on the stage in the rain. All the while we worked at mooring the ship and removing the heavy cargo-hatch covers, his voice hullooed us. When most of the covers were off I clambered up on top of the bulwarks by the starboard shrouds. The boy was still waiting, but silently. In one hand he clutched a small box. He looked very lost.

"You the new nipper?" I shouted. The boy nodded. "He's the new nipper!" I called to Bert.

"Good, now we'll be all right," Bert replied as he studied the tiny, thin figure through the drizzle. "That's just what we need, a good hefty chap that can make a back-splice with one hand and steer with the other; just what we've been looking for. All right, Tiger, let's unship the jolly boat, and you nip over and collect Charlie Atlas over there before the wind pipes up and blows him away."

The new nipper looked very nervous as he sat down in the jolly boat. The first thing he did was drop his cardboard box into the rainwater in the boat's bilge and stick out his hand. "Wot cheer, mate," he said. "My name's William, but everybody calls me . . ."

". . . calls me Billy," I finished off for him. I shook his hand and told him my name, ". . . but everybody calls me Tiger." We were silent as I rowed Billy to the ship and he collected his water-soaked bits of clothing from the bilge. He was about five feet six inches short and had shoulders like a wine bottle. His wet hair was dirty, damp, dark auburn. His face was covered in freckles, under a layer of coal-dust streaks. His eyes were a sad brown, and he reminded me of a half-drowned spaniel puppy Ted had once dragged out of the river at Hull. Billy's once-blue overalls were about two sizes too big for him, and one of his boots had its sole adrift and dangling down so that it looked as though his foot was laughing.

Bert helped Billy over the side, "That's Bert—he's the mate," I called up as the laughing foot preceded me over the bulwark. Billy stood in front of Bert, nervous, small, and damp.

"My . . . name's . . . Billy, pleased . . . to meet you . . . sir," Billy greeted the mate.

"Now we'll have none of that high falutin nonsense here, Nipper. Don't 'sir' me. My name's Bert, and I'm the mate onboard this here ship. Where's our working gear?"

I walked forward and untriced the bowsprit dolphin-striker, to get ready for sailing. Bert needed an audience of only one for such a well-rehearsed routine.

It must have been the thirteenth of December when Billy joined us, because I remember an excited bargee boarding his lighter and shouting up the news to us that the Nazi battleship *Graf Spee* had been sunk. This cheered us all a great deal. The news from sea had been depressing. The liner *Athenia*, bound for America with hundreds of children onboard, had been sunk by a U-boat on the second day of the war. The aircraft carrier *Courageous* was sunk soon after; the battleship *Royal Oak* had been sunk in October at anchor in Scapa Flow naval base, and magnetic mines were taking a toll of ships around the British coasts. Even the lonely, gallant fight of the auxiliary armed merchant ship *Rawalpindi,* which with her little pop-guns had tackled the heavy Nazi battleships *Scharnhorst* and *Gneisenau,* was little cause for celebration. (We were told she was up against *Deutschland*.) *Rawalpindi* had gone down quickly, and only a few survivors had been picked up. Farther out in the oceans the deadly U-boats had started to sink one victim after another, day in, day out.

Tansy called down to the stevedore, "Where was *Graf Spee* sunk?"

"Somewhere in South America, off the Falkland Islands. She scuttled herself. She was clobbered by the cruisers *Ajax, Achilles,* and *Exeter!*"

"How about the crews?"

"Nearly all all right. Even the Jerries. They've all been interned."

Tansy closed his eyes for a second and said, "Thank God for that." I didn't know whether he gave thanks for the sinking of the battleship or for the safety of the crews.

In mid-December some officials came onboard at Gravesend bearing two large boxes. "What's that?" demanded Tansy.

"Radio transmitter and receiver—orders." The official in charge showed Tansy some papers. Tansy frowned as he stared at the forms. He looked around him, first at Bert, then at me, then at Billy, but finding no expressions among us but blank stares at the boxes, his brow creased in a deep frown. He turned back to the official with a quizzical look.

"Where do you want it installed?" asked the official. "We usually put the set in the master's cabin and the batteries . . ."

"Not in my cabin you don't," broke in Tansy. He looked over at Bert. "How about you, Bert? How about your cabin? It'll be all right there, I suppose, so long as you don't play it too loud."

Eventually, after a muted argument between the chief official, the captain, and the mate, a compromise was reached. The wireless set was installed in the skipper's lobby, in brackets over the meal-table. From then on it was Bert's job to report any unusual sightings at sea. Tansy huffed at Bert as the men unshipped the wireless in its gray casing and started to fix it in place. He said in a sarcastic way, "Now you can report a Frenchman with his topsail still hoisted in anything more than a light breeze . . . that's an unusual sighting, if there ever was one!"

A poster showing the silhouettes of German and Allied planes was fixed on the lobby bulkhead so that we could learn to identify them.

That Christmas, with Ted gone to the army, I could not go home. Tansy asked around for someone to relieve me, but most experienced deckhands had either joined up, were badly needed on their own craft, or were in well-paid jobs ashore. Through Bert's address I received a letter from Mam at the beginning of November. Dad had already been home, on leave before going out to South Africa to take command of a merchant ship whose captain had been German-born. Mam did not know the name of the ship that was taking him out, nor from where she was sailing, nor when. By the time I received the letter, owing to Mrs. Bert's oversight in not delivering it to me as soon as she could, Dad was presumably already at sea. I would not, it seemed, hear from him until he reached South Africa. I wrote Mam saying that while I couldn't be home for Christmas, I hoped to be at Llangareth early in the spring, and not to worry, we were only sailing on the northeast coast most of the time, out of range of German aircraft. This was a lie, but it would prevent her worrying about any additional danger to me. From all accounts the news of the terrible depredations on shipping by the Nazi magnetic mines was being kept out of the newspapers and off the wireless. I comforted myself that that, too, would save Mam extra anxiety.

Taking on cargo and discharging was much more work for me now, as "Ginger," as we had nicknamed Billy, was not very strong. Like Ted, he had been brought up in a boys' home. He had been, at the start of his working career three months earlier, employed as tea boy and general dog's-body onboard a floating crane in London docks. Ginger was one of the shyest people I had ever met; it took weeks before he began a conversation, and then it was about food. Ginger simply could never eat enough. It seemed that he had been deprived of anything like a good square meal for all of his childhood. Onboard *Second Apprentice* he certainly made up for what he'd missed in the past. A few days after he joined us, on his first trip, I caught Ginger stealing from the galley. It was only some bread and jam. I knew that if I reported the matter to Bert there would be hell to pay, so instead I made Ginger sit on the coal box and stuff himself with two full loaves of bread and a whole pot of jam. By the time he had finished that lot he could hardly move, and he swore he would never steal food again. I reported the bread lost over the side through my own carelessness, and soon the whole thing was forgotten.

Bert, Ginger, and I spent Christmas 1939 under the dripping hull bottom of *Second Apprentice* as she lay on the beds at Queenborough, on the Isle of Sheppey, in the Thames estuary. It took us three days between tides to scrape off all the barnacles and grass from the bottom and then to paint her with black varnish twice, using two-foot-wide brushes with long handles. It was one of the most miserably cold, wet, dirty periods in my time with the ship. After three days of sloshing around in slippery mud, climbing over the slimy bed-timbers under the ship's dripping, filthy bottom in the darkness, I was ready to try anything else.

It may have been the memory of those Christmas days, the most truly miserable I was to spend for years, that propelled me to the recruiting office in Greenwich in February 1940, when *Second Apprentice* warped in with yet another cargo of "all or nothing" coal. Or it may have been that I felt that I could do more, perhaps advance more quickly, in the Royal Navy, perhaps see more of the world. It was probably an amalgam of both those motives. Perhaps also, more than anything else, it was the news of the action of the destroyer H.M.S. *Cossack* when she smashed alongside the Nazi armed merchant cruiser *Altmark,* boarded her, and freed three hundred British merchant-seamen prisoners who were being taken to Germany after having had their ships sunk from under them. *Cossack*'s exploit fired the imagination of all the boys in the trade. That was good old-fashioned "Stand by to board, boys, and at 'em!"

stuff, the kind of thing at which our lads are superb. There was also the prospect of sending Mam a few shillings a week more than the ten she was then receiving.

Tansy reluctantly gave me time off to go to the recruiting office. The petty officer seemed happy to see me, until I told him my age. At first his face dropped. Then he told me that he would, in any case, sign me in as a boy-seaman, regular, on a twelve-year engagement from the age of eighteen, and that I should report again to him, or to any recruiting office, as soon as I liked after my sixteenth birthday. He made out the recruitment form, and I signed it. (Twelve years plus two equals fourteen!).

Later that day, when I told Bert what had transpired at the recruiting office, he pointed up at some of the dozens of barrage balloons floating over the Thames estuary and said: "You might as well be in the navy, Tiger, because when old Hitler really starts we're going to cop it on the east coast, you know. They haven't got that little lot floating around up there for nothing."

In the Thames estuary, in mid-January, the destroyer H.M.S. *Grenville* passed us close by, only two hours before she hit a mine and sank with the loss of over one hundred lives.

In early March we headed round into the English Channel, with military textiles in crates that were offloaded in Southampton. The crates were then reloaded onboard, and *Second Apprentice* again ploughed with the "textiles" around the Straits of Dover back to Greenwich. The reason for this round trip with the same cargo was not clear to us, but when we yet again offloaded and reloaded the "textiles," then turned the ship round and headed once more back to Southampton, we had given up worrying about it. As Bert said, "Well, at least it's better than carrying live ammunition."

In the next few weeks we made several cross-Channel runs over to Le Havre, France, mostly with military stores. On two voyages across the Channel we were loaded by crane in Southampton with small khaki vans for the British Expeditionary Forces in France. When the cars had been secured in the hold, big drums of petrol (gasoline) were lashed on deck. Tansy and Bert looked a bit glum as the drums were loaded and lashed, but when we found that two Royal Navy motor patrol boats were to escort us across the Channel, they livened up. However, the weather was so contrary, with very slight breezes most of the way over, that the heavily armed escort got tired of waiting around and circling us like hunting dogs on leashes. After a discussion with Tansy, and an offer to take *Second Apprentice* in tow, the navy craft shoved on without us. Bert, Ginger, and I finished up rowing the ship into Le Havre.

As soon as the escort roared away over the horizon, Tansy rubbed his brow with a knuckle and muttered: "Thank goodness for that. I thought they'd never leave."

"Why's that, Tansy?" I asked him.

"Well, I was worried in case they got into a fight, and us with all that blessed petrol onboard. I was ready to order Bert to ditch it the moment anything happened!"

The activity in Le Havre was frenetic, with war vessels, French and British, and merchant ships of many nations arriving and departing day and night. Whenever *Second Apprentice* arrived there, Tansy was supposed to go ashore to the harbor master's office and report, but he always sent Bert round with an excuse. There was a fuss the first time this happened. The French harbormaster and his British naval countepart marched onboard, demanding to know where the captain was. When Bert showed them down to the captain's cabin, they found Tansy on his knees, praying before his open Bible. They fell silent then and left him alone on subsequent visits. It was strange for Tansy to have been found like that, because moments before he heard voices coming onboard, he had been sitting at the lobby table explaining to little Ginger how to make a crown-knot.

I never once, during many visits to France, ever saw Tansy step off the ship in that country. Once when I tackled him about this, he said: "I just don't want their company, Tiger. Any time we get mixed up with that lot we lose something; it's like we start sliding downhill. Some of them might be well-mannered on the surface, but I'm positive they're not down below. They're supposed to be so civilized, so artistic, but you watch them closely, Tiger, and you'll see a herd of farmyard animals all scared to jump any real fences. They're supposed to be so charming, lively, and witty, and everyone who doesn't know France seems to think of a beautiful lady when they talk about it, but you keep your eyes wide open, Tiger, and what you'll see is a painted old hag counting up her pennies. I never saw a Frenchman yet that could do anything without beating around the bush, and when a Frenchman does you down, he's not playing with you, Tiger. He's deadly serious, and when you really need him you'll never find him, or if you do he'll be making a deal with your competitor."

In April, Hitler invaded Denmark and Norway. To many landspeople this meant only that he had attacked yet two more almost defenseless little countries, but to the sailors it meant much more than that. If the Nazis controlled the coasts of Denmark and Norway, they also controlled the entrance to the Baltic, the arctic access to Finland and Russia (if we ever needed it), a good half of the North Sea, and all of the Norwegian Sea. From Norway their planes might even reach the north of England and Scotland. There was a good chance that soon the whole of Britain would be under air attack, and nowhere would it be safe to navigate. The Channel, the average sailor thought, was a lot safer than the North Sea: "The French would always see to that."

At first the news from Scandinavia was gloomy. The Germans seemed to be landing everywhere they wished with impunity. Then came cheering word of the sinking of the German cruiser *Königsberg* in Bergen harbor by Royal Navy dive-bombers. (We didn't realize it at the time, but this was the first occasion that a major warship had been sunk by planes—it completely changed naval surface warfare strategy.)

When Tansy heard the news about Norway he took it calmly. "They'll put our coast in range of *them*," he observed, "but they'll also put their navy in range of *us*." When he heard the news about the *Königsberg*, he was concerned about me. "Try not to join any big ships, Tiger," he advised me. "They're the ones the German air force will be after. Get in the smallest ships you can find. They'll hardly bother to waste bombs on *them*." How mistaken he was!

In mid-April we ourselves came under air attack, although afterward everyone agreed that it must have been more a matter of *Second Apprentice* accidentally finding herself in the enemy's line of fire. We still could not believe that the Luftwaffe would waste its firepower on a little old sailing barge.

· 255 ·

We knew that other coasters and some trawlers had been strafed by Nazi planes, and that some had been sunk, but they had been power-vessels, and we imagined that the German pilots might have mistaken them for armed patrol-vessels. Most of the other sinkings until then had been caused by mines, magnetic and otherwise.

We had taken a cargo of tomato baskets to Guernsey; then we had been in ballast to Poole. From there we took on a load of sawn timber for Greenwich. We had spent a night at anchor off Eastbourne and set sail very early in the morning to be in the Thames estuary that night. We had a fine northwesterly breeze and were soon under all sail, on a broad reach. It was a brilliant morning and a lovely forenoon. There were a few clouds, and the Channel seas played as boisterously as ever; the day was a happy-looking harbinger of a good, warm spring.

Off Dungeness we were very slowly overtaken by a convoy of six fair-sized merchant ships under the escort of an armed trawler that was slowly plodding its way up through the Straits of Dover. With our broad breeze we were almost able to keep up with them. On we all ploughed, past Folkestone, Dover, and Deal, with the ships to seaward of us, like protecting policemen. As *Second Apprentice* passed the south foreland we were no more than a mile from the coast. From the galley door I gazed at the cliffs and the green downs, and wondered what the very tall steel masts were (we knew nothing about radar, of course).

Bert was on watch at the helm. Tansy was asleep below, having kept the middle anchor-watch. Ginger and I were in the galley preparing the midday meal. Now and again, to clear my head of smoke and fumes, I stuck it out of the galley door and watched the coast of Kent slide by, all green and gray and white and pale yellow. By late forenoon it was obvious that the convoy was pulling slowly ahead of us, but Bert thought that we would be within sight of the naval escort at least until we reached the offing of the north foreland. Then, when we headed westward into the Thames estuary, we would come under the protection of the forts that had been built on platforms between the coasts of Kent and Essex, and of the balloon-barrage. We were right in the middle of what was a little while later to become known as "Hellfire Corner."

At first there was something unreal about the attack—it seemed to be more like a rehearsal than anything else. The first indication I had that anything untoward was happening was a loud screech from the direction of the naval trawler, then a dull thump-thump-thump as her anti-aircraft guns opened up. As soon as I heard the screeching of the siren and the thumping I rushed out on deck, still holding a soup spoon and a salt pot. I stared at the convoy ahead, straining to see past the fluttering luffs of our headsails. The naval trawler was firing her guns all right. At first I couldn't make out in which direction she was firing, but then, in the direction of Walmer, I saw tiny gun-puffs bursting in the blue sky. They weren't white, as I'd expected, but dirty brown and yellow. I turned to Bert, who was also staring at the shellbursts. "They might be practicing," I called.

"Practicing be blowed, Tiger." Bert turned the ship off the wind a little. "This is the real thing! If I was you I'd get under cover, but give Tansy a holler first!"

As I turned to go to the companionway and rouse our captain there was a loud banging noise from the direction of the shore-line. More gun-puffs, white this time, blossomed in the April sky, almost directly over the convoy. It was at that moment that I saw them: five tiny black specks flying from the north toward the ships. At first they hardly seemed to be moving. Suddenly there was an ugly-sounding rat-at-at-at-at . . . and all the while the trawler thump-thump-thumped away at the oncoming pests.

With my eyes fixed still on the far-off specks over the wind-ward side, I shouted down the companionway, "Tansy!" The specks very rapidly turned into the same shape as the sil-houettes of Dornier DO 217's on the recognition chart down in the skipper's lobby. I heard Tansy's muffled reply from what seemed a million miles away: "Be right up!"

I seemed to be two persons now—one watching the enemy planes as they strafed the ships, and one trying to rouse the captain below. "Tansy! Air attack! The Jerries are . . ." But my throat went dry. I didn't feel in the least bit heroic, standing at the top of the companionway with a soup spoon in one hand and a salt pot in the other.

"What's up, Tiger?" came Tansy's voice from his cabin. I

didn't reply. The Dorniers were streaking over the convoy, and I gazed stupefied as little black dots left the planes and splashed into the sea all around ships ahead. It took a second or two for me to realize that the black specks were bombs. The enemy formation split up as they left the convoy. Four of them turned east, but one headed directly for us. I was paralyzed, as I watched a line of machine-gun bullet-splashes hit the sea, quickly nearing *Second Apprentice.* It was not the same kind of feeling that I'd had in the storm, when we'd gone aground on the Hailsborough Sands. I don't think there was much fear in me at all, if any. It was more surprise and curiosity, astonishment and indignation: "How dare they do this to us! We're under sail, and that's *Britain* over there! How dare they have the gall, the presumption to do this within sight of the cliffs of England!" Very quickly the splashes in the sea got closer and closer, and I remember thinking that whoever was in that plane couldn't, simply *couldn't,* be firing at us. He must be mistaken. He must be attacking someone else . . . when suddenly, for no apparent reason at first, he sheered off, his guns still firing rat-at-at-at-at, and banked right around and took off toward where his comrades had disappeared into the clouds. There was a stunning silence for a moment or two. Then, from over the English shore, came a dull humming, a roar, and a sudden noise of thunder. It was two squadrons of fighters, one of which passed almost directly overhead of *Second Apprentice* as we gawped up at them. Then Bert shouted "Hurricanes!" and we both danced and waved at them. But they were gone, climbing as they shot off in the direction of the enemy.

Tansy came on deck just as the last of the fighters disappeared into a cloud. There was still an air of unreality about the whole episode, as though the attack had never taken place. The sky was clear; there was no noise of guns; England was bathed in warm sunlight; the seas frisked; and the ships ahead plodded on past the north foreland. It had all happened in the space of no more than three or four minutes, yet it had seemed, while naked violence rent the air, to be an eon. Now that all the planes were gone, excitement and indignation, curiosity and pride were all replaced with an intense feeling of relief.

"What happened?" asked Tansy, rubbing his neck.

"They was RAF Hurricanes! Cleared the blighters off!" shouted Bert, still excited.

Tansy turned to me. "Did you see them, Tiger?".

Bert broke in: "They shoved off quick. You should have seen them go when the Hurricanes came on. Them old Jerries must have been scared out of their wits. . . . They took off like a dose of blooming salts. Went east, they did, back to Germany, you can bet your life."

I was going to contradict Bert. The Royal Air Force fighters had been Boulton-Paul Defiants. I had plainly seen the mid-ships turrets on at least two of them. Instead I said, "The Jerries were Dorniers, because they had a bloody great . . ." Tansy glared at me. "Sorry, Tansy . . . they had a big sort of glass house all over their noses, and two engines, and six machine guns. I could see the gun-flashes on the wings as clear as I can see your hat."

"Any damage done?" asked Tansy. We all stared at the convoy, now wearing the north foreland and heading into the Thames estuary.

"Don't look like it," said Bert, "and they never even got anywhere near us, even though one of the . . . bas . . . baskets tried it; but he saw them there Hurricanes and he was off. Those Hurricanes, they're so fast you can hardly see them coming. Did you see that RAF pilot wave back at us, Tiger?"

"No. They were much too high, Bert, and they weren't . . ." I got no further.

Tansy broke in and said, "Well, even if old Jerry had put a few holes in us, we'd have been all right with that sawn timber . . . it floats."

By late April I was half looking forward to my sixteenth birthday, half dreading it. *Second Apprentice* took a cargo of house bricks to Guernsey and brought back sacks of ormer (a kind of oyster) shells to Poole. There Tansy found a young man of twenty to replace me. Sebastian was hale and hearty, but had flat feet. He had volunteered for the navy but was judged by the doctors to be unfit for sea. He sailed with us around to Greenwich with a cargo of Portland stone for transfer to lighters. On the voyage, which was rough, he showed himself to be a strong, healthy, and expert deck-seaman who knew almost as many strange knots as Ted had. He had been at sea in sail-coasters from the West Country since he was fourteen. He had fingers like marlinspikes, hair like caulking oakum, and he swore like a trooper, much more than even Ted had. Tansy, when he first heard the name Sebastian, called him "Sebastopol" by mistake, and so he remained. (The Sebastopol was a sailor's pub in Portland.)

When the ship was in Harwich in the second week in May, just after my birthday, I reported to the local recruiting office. When I told the army sergeant that I had first reported to Greenwich recruiting office he firmly but kindly told me that I should report back to Greenwich. I returned onboard and told Tansy what the sergeant had said. "Well, Tiger," he observed, "there's no hurry, is there? I expect the navy can wait for you for a few days. Come on up to Yarmouth with us. We're taking a load of fish boxes up there, then up to Tynemouth for coal, then back down to Greenwich, see?" I accepted Tansy's offer.

Before the ship arrived in Yarmouth we heard the news over the wireless that the Germans had invaded Holland and Belgium, and that their armies were driving into France. "That's it," observed Bert. "That's it. Now the balloon has *really* gone up!"

As the wireless in the skipper's lobby gave out grave reports of one city after another falling to the Germans or being pounded from the air, even Tansy listened expressionlessly.

I had sent Mam the money I had saved for my canceled Christmas-holiday rail fare, and I had only a shilling or two. I borrowed my rail fare from Yarmouth to Greenwich from Bert, and I promised to write to Mam and ask her to repay the money to his wife by mail. Bert agreed, and between them he and Tansy gathered together the ten shillings or so I needed for fare, and a couple of shillings more as a parting gift.

When I left *Second Apprentice* it was raining. Bert was working the dolly windlass, winching pallets of fish boxes out of the hold and onto the jetty. Ginger and Sebastopol were down in the hold piling up more smelly, scaly boxes, and Tansy was standing in his bowler hat and oilskin by the gangway, puffing at his upside-down clay pipe.

"Cheerio, Tiger," called Bert. "We'll call you on the wireless if we get any fun and games with old Adolf." As I went to shake his callused hand he added in a low tone: "Now, don't forget what I told you. You find yourself a nice little homebody like Nora and get yourself a nice home and a nice family to go home to. It's the best thing a man can do, believe me, I know."

"Good-bye, Bert. I'll see what I can do."

I shouted farewells down the hold and walked over to Tansy. The captain held out a gnarled hand. Rain dripped onto my wrist from the brim of his bowler. I was always short of farewell words. I muttered something about hoping that he would have good cargoes, and a lot of them.

Tansy replied: "Oh, we'll be fine. We've got a good crew together." His voice lowered. "Not as good as you and Ted, of course, but we'll manage, and we've got all the cargoes we can handle. It's a good steady trade now. . . ." He shook my hand again and pressed a small Bible into it. "Godspeed, Tiger, trust in the Lord . . . and give them blessed Jerries a few for me!"

"Good-bye, Tansy, I'll make the most . . ." I was going to say, "the most of what I can of it," but my voice failed. I turned and walked onto the slippery plank that served as a gangway. As I reached the other side, Tansy hailed me: "Tiger!"

I turned in the rain and saw both the captain and the mate grinning at me. I looked Tansy straight in his green eyes. He looked impish. He shouted, *And make 'em bloody strong!*

I laughed, waved, turned away, and walked toward the dockgates. Before I reached the gates I looked back over my shoulder for a last sight of *Second Apprentice.* The sun shone for a few moments, even though it was still raining. My ship's varnished masts caught the sun. The reflection of sunlight from her spars was so bright that my eyes watered. I turned and hitched my sea bag more firmly onto my oilskin shoulder and marched straight through the gate, toward the railway station, without once looking back. I was off to war.

20

Personal Effects

Blind Sioni was walking home in late 1939 and was knocked down by a motor bus. In her letter, Mam said thank God the doctor said he didn't suffer. He is buried in the shadow of Cader Idris. His only memorial is the mountain and the glory of the Mabinogion stories he told so vividly.

Toward the end of July 1940, at the end of my basic training course, I went home on leave for a week. There Mam handed me a letter from Mrs. Bert thanking her for the repayment of the twelve shillings I had owed her husband. She also wrote about Ted. When he joined the army he appointed Mrs. Bert as his "next of kin." When he completed his training, the army drafted him into an armored regiment as a tank-gunner. Young Rosie was so impressed with Ted when he came home on leave in March, in his new uniform, that she agreed to become engaged to him. They were to have been married when he returned home on his first leave from France. On June 21 his battalion was part of a small force that attacked the Nazi Panzer divisions south of Arras, to take pressure off the Allied armies fighting their way to the beaches of Dunkirk. Ted was killed. His commanding officer sent Mrs. Bert a "very nice letter" and Ted's personal effects: a small Bible, badly mangled; a leather sheath containing a seaman's knife and marlinspike; and a packet of cigarette cards, together with ten French francs and a British half-crown piece.

Would I like the cigarette cards? Mrs. Bert asked in her letter.

In late 1941 my destroyer, badly damaged and weather-worn, hove into Greenock, Scotland, for repairs. Among several letters from my family and friends was one scrawled on lined paper with a pencil. It was from Sebastopol, who had obtained Mam's address from Mrs. Bert. In March 1941, he wrote, *Second Apprentice* had departed from Tynemouth, with coal for the Thames, in the company of a sister ketch, *Martinet*. They had fair weather and a "good fancy" westerly wind (when bargemen said that, they meant it was rough). Suddenly, out of the clouds, five Heinkel bombers appeared. Three of them left formation and attacked the two sailing barges, first with machine-gun fire and then with bombs. Both *Martinet* and *Second Apprentice* were directly hit at almost the same time, and sank within a minute or two. Sebastopol, Tansy, and little Ginger had been blown over the side by the blast of the bomb that struck the foredeck. Bert, who had been taking refuge from the machine-gun bullets behind the fore hatch-coaming, must have been blown to bits. Little Ginger struck his head on a floating plank when he hit the water, but Sebastopol and Tansy managed to keep the nipper afloat for two hours by lashing him to the plank with Tansy's belt. They and two crewmen from *Martinet* were picked up by the crew of a steam trawler out of Grimsby who had heard the attack from afar. Ginger was alive, all right, but the doctors feared he would never be able to hear or talk again.

Tansy was so angry about Ginger and Bert that he went ashore in Grimsby, straight to the navy recruiting office, and tried to join up, but they turned him down for regular sea service. Somehow, however, he managed to get into a naval armed trawler as mate, under the "T124X" scheme, which allowed men otherwise considered "odds and ends" to serve for nonspecified periods of time. Now he was up on the coast of Scotland. Sebastopol supposed he was mine-sweeping. As for himself, Sebastopol was still looking for a coasting berth or, if he couldn't get that, a river job; but considering all the bombing going on around the Thames Estuary, he thought he'd be safer at sea. It was a pity he had his "foot trouble," or he would join the RAF and try to get on a bomber and "give the buggers a taste of their own medicine."

I wrote several letters to Mrs. Bert and called to see her twice on the rare occasions when I was ashore in the London area in 1941 and 1942. The first time she was taking Bert's loss badly, and it was as much as I could do to cheer her up. The second time I introduced her to a leading seaman close to her own age, whom she later married. Much later, in the late 1950s, when I asked Tansy's daughter, Daisy, about Mrs. Bert and Hermione, she wasn't sure where Mrs. Bert, her daughter, or her husband were, but she said that the house on the long street had been demolished by a buzz-bomb in late 1944 and had since been rebuilt.

It was almost forty years later that I discovered that the Apollinaris mineral water factory at Remagen was owned, in 1938, by the Reichführer of the S.S., Heinrich Himmler.

The last time I heard from Cei Powell he was a successful businessman in Australia. What happened to my own family is part of another story. . . .

Epilogue

And death shall have no dominion.
Dead men naked they shall be one
With the man in the wind and the west moon;
When their bones are picked clean and the clean bones gone,
They shall have stars at elbow and foot;
Though they go mad they shall be sane,
Though they sink through the sea they shall rise again;
Though lovers be lost love shall not;
And death shall have no dominion.

And death shall have no dominion.
Under the windings of the sea
They lying long shall not die windily;
Twisting on racks when sinews give way,
Strapped to a wheel yet they shall not break;
Faith in their hands shall snap in two
And the unicorn evils run them through;
Split all ends up they shan't crack;
And death shall have no dominion.

And death shall have no dominion.
No more may gulls cry at their ears
Or waves break loud on the seashores;
Where blew a flower may a flower no more
Lift its head to the blows of the rain;
Though they be mad and dead as nails,
Heads of the characters hammer through daisies;
Break in the sun till the sun breaks down,
And death shall have no dominion.

—DYLAN THOMAS
"And Death Shall Have No Dominion"